D0319708

Holding Court

Holding Court

Chris Gorringe

CENTURY · LONDON

Published by Century 2009

2 4 6 8 10 9 7 5 3 1

First published in Great Britain in 2009 by
Century
Random House, 20 Vauxhall Bridge Road,
London SW1V 2SA

www.randomhouse.co.uk

Addresses for companies within The Random House Group Limited can be found at:
www.randomhouse.co.uk

The Random House Group Limited Reg. No. 954009

A CIP catalogue record for this book
is available from the British Library

ISBN 9781846055089

The Random House Group Limited supports The Forest Stewardship
Council (FSC), the leading international forest certification organisation. All our titles
that are printed on Greenpeace approved FSC certified paper carry the FSC logo. Our
paper procurement policy can be found at www.rbooks.co.uk/environment

Mixed Sources
Product group from well-managed
forests and other controlled sources
www.fsc.org Cert no. TT-COC-2139
© 1996 Forest Stewardship Council
FSC

Set in Baskerville by Palimpsest Book Production Limited,
Grangemouth, Stirlingshire

Printed in the UK by CPI Mackays, Chatham, Kent ME5 8TD

We are grateful to the following copyright holders for permission to reproduce
photographs: Tommy Hindley/Professional Sport, Michael Cole, Arthur Cole, *The Times*,
The Photo Image Unit and Russ Adams

The author and publisher have made all reasonable efforts to contact copyright holders
for permission and apologise for any omissions or errors in the form of credits given.
Corrections may be made to future printings

To Jen, Kim and Anna and our wonderful family, who I love
more than they know and I show.

And to the All England Lawn Tennis and Croquet Club
and its members – my second home.

Acknowledgements

It was never my intention to write a book about my experiences at the All England Club. If it was, then I would have set about it as soon as I retired in December 2005. The idea of the book came about after repeated pressure from members of my family and from a number of members of the Club. Then I was introduced to a friend of my daughter, Kim, who particularly wanted to write on Wimbledon and my involvement with the Club over the past thirty-five years. So I met Jo Russell who lived, at that time, nearby and she soon found out that I was a hesitant collaborator. However, through her persistence and my weakening, Jo set about drafting the contents of such a book, which I then shared with Tim Phillips, the Club's chairman, and John Barrett, a former Committee member and much respected scribe.

The next stage was to find a publisher! So I approached my good friend Sarah Wooldridge at the International Management Group (IMG) who believed in the project from the start and Tim Andrews of Random House, who had the confidence to publish *Holding Court*. If the book is a success, I will then add my thanks to my family for pushing me into it!

I am most grateful to Ian Ritchie, my successor, for contributing a postscript to the book and to Tim Phillips for agreeing to write the Foreword. As you will read about later, Tim has been, in my view, an excellent chairman and, as importantly, a dear friend.

Moving away from the book itself, there are so many people in my life to whom I owe a great debt of gratitude. First and foremost would be my parents who gave me an education that I thoroughly enjoyed. Their love, support and example have meant so much to me. Indeed, my whole family has been so encouraging and loyal to me throughout my career, especially during times when I would spend, it seemed, my whole time at the Club and very little at home.

As for my career, I thank particularly those who engaged me and had confidence in my abilities. I thank Michael Bevan for my first job with the Guinness family and then Peter Jackson for introducing me to the All England Club. Without Peter I would never have worked there. Also, I would like to thank all five Chairmen of the Club who had confidence in me and, as importantly, to all my work colleagues for their support and loyalty. They were all, without exception, wonderful people to work with, in our aim of 'maintaining The Championships as the premier tennis tournament in the world – and on grass'.

Contents

Foreword

Tim Phillips, Chairman, The All England Lawn Tennis
and Croquet Club

I was delighted to be asked by Chris Gorringe to write this
foreword.

In *Holding Court*, Chris records in considerable detail his
own views and recollections from a period of immense change
at Wimbledon. During his twenty-six years as chief executive of
the All England Club, he was in a unique position to influence
and observe these changes.

The staging of The Championships is very much a team effort
involving such disparate groupings as broadcasters, umpires,
caterers, the police, ball boys/girls and some 7,000 temporary staff
and volunteers of various kinds – besides, most importantly, the
players. Chris conducted the proceedings with great charm and
integrity and did a wonderful job for the All England Club and
The Championships. 'Thank you for your patience,' became his
sign-off on his acclaimed, pre-Centre-Court-roof weather updates,
which caused John Inverdale to say on radio that if the world
was coming to an end, he would know everything would be all
right if Chris Gorringe made the announcement.

Chris has the smallest handwriting of anyone I know and he uses it to record information that interests him, in his diary or elsewhere. This has greatly increased his recall of what happened at Wimbledon during his time as chief executive, which ended on his retirement in 2005.

I very much hope you will find *Holding Court* to be a fascinating account of how Wimbledon has both markedly changed and yet, in important aspects, stayed the same over the past quarter of a century.

Chapter 1

A Day Like No Other

If you can meet with Triumph and Disaster
And treat those two impostors just the same

Rudyard Kipling's words are boldly displayed in the All England Clubhouse, there to inspire all players as they wend their way from the dressing rooms down to Centre Court. As I stood staring up at them in 1991, during the wettest Wimbledon in memory, they had a striking resonance. The weather conditions had just forced us into scheduling an extra day's play for the Middle Sunday of The Championships – but right now we had no tickets, no security, no catering, no umpires, no groundstaff, and no precedent to follow. Whether triumph or disaster lay ahead – who knew?

It had been an absolutely dreadful start to the tournament. We had no play on the first Monday, and intermittent rain throughout Tuesday. Wednesday was even worse with just eighteen matches played, and by the end of Thursday, things were dire. For the players, it was a terrible ordeal. It took Stefan Edberg, the defending champion, seventy-three hours to finish his first-round match. 'Thank God it's over,' he said, at the end of his personal marathon. 'I haven't even been able to eat a decent lunch for four days.' And he was one of the lucky ones – at least he had made it onto court. We were almost a third of the way through the tournament and yet had completed only fifty-two out of around 240 scheduled matches. It was no surprise then, to find myself, chairman John Curry, Michael Hann, chairman of the order of play sub-committee, referee Alan Mills and Richard Grier, Championships director, gathered together during yet another rain delay, looking at the feasibility of play on Sunday – something that had never been done before. Richard and I were fairly negative, because we were the only people who had a real grasp on what a logistical nightmare it would be. We were effectively talking about staging a one-day national event, for up to 30,000 spectators, from scratch. No conclusion was reached, with everyone perhaps hoping for some divine intervention, although the intervention from the heavens so far had been less than helpful.

Ironically, the weather on Friday was very good, but, despite achieving a full day's play, the men's singles still had not managed to complete the first round. That meant that we were still too far behind. At 6 p.m. I went off to a security meeting – a daily essential during the Championships – while the committee of management considered recommendations that we play on the Sunday. With my meeting over, I went back to my office and John Curry came in shortly afterwards. He at least had the good grace to apologise for all that was about to be unleashed. 'I'm sorry Chris. This will probably come as a surprise, and I'm sure a dis-appointment, but taking everything into consideration, I think we have to go for it.' The forecast for the weekend was better, particu-larly on Sunday, and it would give us a fighting chance of finishing on time.

John was a master of understatement. I could think of many words other than 'disappointed' to describe how I felt. However, it had been a pretty much inevitable decision, and now was a fait accompli. There was no point in wasting any more time discussing it. With just thirty-nine hours to go, there were myriad things to consider. Actually, it was hard to tell how many things there were to consider, as we had never done this before. We were in completely uncharted territory.

Would we be able to get the ball boys and girls back and provide catering for a full day's play? What about car parking and public transport, or security and medical staff? How many courts would we have open? How would we sell the tickets? At what price and how many? And where would they come from – it was not a scheduled day's play, so none had been printed. How long would it take to get x thousand people through the turnstiles and therefore what time could play start? And just how many was 'x' thousand?

The biggest fear was not knowing how many people would come. The bulk of our tickets are sold in advance. People know they have the tickets and they can come in, and we know how many we have sold. If you are selling tickets on the day, how do you know how many people are going to pitch up? I was very afraid that when people realised that anyone could get in on the day, we might have 100,000 coming. If we shut the gates after, say, 30,000 people had entered, that would leave 70,000 disgruntled fans, potentially scaling the walls or forcing the barriers to get in. Bear in mind that the Hillsborough tragedy, in which ninety-six football fans were killed, was just two years previously, and the findings from the Taylor report were fresh in everyone's minds. The idea of presiding over a repeat of such a disaster did not bear contemplating. It seemed to me that the key lay in the pricing. We needed to set the price at something that was friendly, enticing, but not so low that it would attract more people than we could cope with.

I brought in Richard Grier and Peter Lovewell, the ticket manager, as they were the two key players in all this. We went through all the different teams with whom we would need to liaise and check that they could deliver. Personally, I wanted to make contact with the chief executives of the London Boroughs of

Merton and Wandsworth, and the chief superintendent of the police. This was a time when very few people had mobile telephones, so we would have to try and either get hold of them at work (unlikely given the time) or at home. Luckily, given that it was a Friday evening, I had their home numbers and they were in to take the call.

In some ways it was an odd conversation – half asking permission, half not. I was in effect saying, 'We're doing this. Are there any major things that you would suggest would prevent us?' I do not know that they could have stopped us, but they could have raised big concerns about safety issues. They might have said, 'You can play provided you have 90 per cent stewarding,' or some other such stipulations. But they did not. Everyone I spoke to was very helpful, very positive and very understanding. I think, because people had seen what had been tracking out during the course of the week, there was an element of 'That doesn't surprise us'. It would have been more of a shock if it had happened prior to 1982 when we started playing the finals on the Sunday.

I also wanted to speak to Canon Gerald Parrott, the Vicar of St Mary's church. That might seem surprising, but I knew all the problems that we had had when we first made the decision to play on the second Sunday. I knew how much our decision was going to impinge on the neighbours and the churches around the area. I had a good relationship with the Canon and I thought he would be able to speak on behalf of the churches. Similarly, the borough chief executives should have been able to speak on behalf of the residents. I could hardly get on the phone and talk to each house in the area – or even a representative from each of the residents' associations – there are countless numbers around Wimbledon.

The other key person that evening was the head groundsman. We needed to confirm that the courts would withstand the extra play. We needed to use all the courts to make the day as worthwhile as possible.

Then I faced the media. There was not much to tell at that point, but I wanted to go out on air that evening to get the message to as many people as possible, and I knew I had to rush to catch the last live BBC broadcast at 8 p.m. There was a palpable air of excitement when I broke the news, not least because, after one of the worst starts to the tournament in living history, there was something else for the press to write about other than Andre Agassi's hair and kit. This year was Agassi's first back at Wimbledon since 1987, and his flamboyant reputation and playing style had caused quite a stir. Agassi himself was revelling in the experience. He came off court after his first match, saying, 'Wimbledon is something bigger than tennis. You walk out there and the classiness of the surroundings hits you. I have never enjoyed playing anywhere more.' I am not sure whether he was a shrewd operator or a genuine enthusiast, but his comments certainly endeared him to the crowd, and guaranteed cheering fans wherever he went.

It was also crucial to talk to the media as they had to re-organise their scheduling, although, thank goodness, play on the Sunday did not clash with any other major UK sporting event. Fortunately, it was a simple communication exercise. There was no financial discussion. All the broadcasting rights were based on The Championships as scheduled, and no TV company paid us any additional money for play on that Sunday. The same would have applied had we run on to the third Monday. In fairness, the broadcasters would have incurred additional costs themselves, with the extra staffing required. That was something that would be felt by all of us. The majority of people working at The Championships are temporary, not full-time staff. Most would already have made plans for what they were going to do on that Sunday. So, at that time, we had to make sure that the majority of people could cancel all those arrangements and help on the day. We had to rely on their goodwill because it was not in their contracts that they should be prepared to work should the need arise. Nor did we have time to negotiate with them what the rates of pay would be, whether double time, or whatever. We relied on mutual trust. In any event, we had to do it. The cost of staging the day, whether it would make or lose money, was something we had to worry about afterwards. Ultimately, it was the Lawn Tennis Association (LTA) who would suffer were we to make a loss, as the surplus funds they receive from the tournament would be diminished. However, the decision to go ahead was made at a committee meeting with the LTA present, and the consensus was that it was more important than any financial considerations that the tournament be seen as a success in terms of being completed on time.

Friday night and Saturday morning were a blur of phone calls and meetings, with endless decisions to be made and people to be contacted to try to get everything in place. It had been obvious from the outset that ticketing would be crucial. First, we had to make sure that we had something to give to spectators. We had a spare set of unmarked, undated Centre and No. 1 Court tickets, which we keep in the event that they will be needed for finals carried over onto a third Monday. We could press those into service and get ground tickets printed up. How many to print was the second question. We had to liaise with the local authority, and the safety officer in particular, as to what our ground capacity would be. Under the Safety of Sports Grounds Act, there were stringent requirements on the ratios between stewards and security staff, and the number of people that we could accommodate in the ground. We had to prove to the safety team, the local authority, police, ambulance and fire brigade that the grounds would be fit to accommodate the number of people that we allowed in, that we would have the right levels of staffing and that everything would work. The PA system, for example, has to be tested every day and the safety team must verify that it is working. If there is a glitch, you have to have experts on hand who can put it right immediately. The same goes for the fire alarm, which experts must test every morning, in every corner of the grounds. In the event, we agreed on a ground capacity of 25,000, a reduction of 5,000 on our normal capacity, to take into account reduced staffing and general levels of safety given the first come, first served entry policy.

Richard Grier and I had acknowledged that pricing would be crucial, and we settled on 11,000 Centre Court and 7,000 No. 1 Court tickets at £10, and 5,000 ground passes at £5. Normal Centre Court tickets were £25, so tickets for the Sunday were very good value. Still, there were some who bemoaned having to pay at all. Their view was that they should be free, as indeed they were the following year when the men's doubles was held over until the third Monday (a marathon event that finally saw McEnroe and Stich victorious, winning 19–17 in the fifth). However, that was the end of just one match that had started on the Sunday, so there really was no comparison. People also took the view that, because so many days had been washed out, we owed it to the public to let them come in free of charge on the Sunday. I could not see the logic of that, given that people were going to see a whole day of fantastic tennis – but in any event, these arguments were of little importance in the face of our main concern that if we made it free, we could get 100,000 people pitching up, and we absolutely did not want that. We wanted a manageable number, able to enter the ground as quickly as possible – another reason for the £10 and £5 numbers chosen, which would greatly negate any need for change at the turnstiles.

About the only thing that was not a worry was counterfeiting. With no advance ticket sales, and little warning, it would have been all but impossible for counterfeit tickets to come into circulation. Even the blackest clouds have a silver lining.

Saturday, midday. Twenty-two hours to go. My days during The Championships were generally spent fire-fighting, particularly in the first week. All the preparatory work had been done, and it was simply a question of being available to answer queries and respond to the unexpected. And so it was that day. Having made most of the decisions by mid-morning, the heads of each department were putting plans into action, and I devoted myself to the honing of my self-styled moniker, Gloomy Gorringe! Much to the amusement of my fellow tournament directors, I spent the time actively dissuading people from attending my own event. I went on the radio, on TV and in the papers as saying, 'Please don't bother turning up unless you live locally.' To the question 'How will you cope with the crowds?' I answered, 'With difficulty.' Asked, 'Why dissuade people from coming?' the upbeat answer was, 'I don't see why people need to come, with full TV coverage.' With genuine concerns as to how many would turn up, my role was to keep levels manageable, but even I had to take my hat off to the harbinger of doom masquerading as a police officer, who cheerily told reporters, 'Unless you have good reason, I would stay away from Wimbledon on Sunday – stay away from anywhere near the place.' I let the press write all the stuff about 'being a part of history'. Sadly, I suppose that you see all the potential problems rather than the joy of it all, sitting where I was.

By the end of Saturday, we had been through the checklist and ticked off everything that needed to be arranged. We had gone from sorting out car parking and additional public trans-port to ensuring that there would be freshly laundered towels in the dressing room. Everybody from the head groundsman to the youngest ball boy had been contacted, with a full catering corps in between. We had done as much as we could.

On Saturday night, my wife Jenny and I went to the Wimbledon Ball at Grosvenor House. This event is held on the middle Saturday, and is run by the LTA, really as a thank you to county associ-ations up and down the country, and to various overseas guests. I felt I ought to go, although I cannot believe I was very good company. I certainly did not stay to grace the floor with my dancing skills: the Ball did not start until 9.30 p.m., and all in all it had been a very long day.

When we got back to Wimbledon, there were already thousands of people camping out, ready for the next day, which did nothing to quell my fears. I apologise now to those who were already in the queue, but I confess that I wished for nothing but rain overnight, which would keep the numbers down. I had rewritten the customer relationship manual: the customer is king – unless there are too many of them queuing together at any one time.

Sunday dawned bright and sunny. I know, because I saw it. I generally never used to get sleepless nights during The Championships, as I was too tired, but this was one exception. The forecast had been right, and we were set for a full day's play, which was the first bit of good news. We opened the gates at ten, but had decided we could not start play until midday, because of the time it would take 25,000 people to get through the turnstiles. In an ideal world, we would have started at eleven to make the most of the day, but we did not want a raft of angry spectators who would have missed the first match while queuing to get in.

I positioned myself strategically to watch the first of the crowds coming through the turnstiles. The first people in took fifty-six seconds to get to their seats – just above the scoreboard, incidentally, where they were likely to be seen on TV. There was huge excitement as people raced through, vying for the best spots. John Parsons, the *Daily Telegraph*'s tennis correspondent, said, 'I remember the rush, particularly for the front-row seats of the first tier of Centre Court. I am sure if I hadn't guarded the press seats, they'd have gone as well.' Everyone was extremely good-natured, however. People queuing outside were in high spirits, cheering the golfers on the course opposite as they filed past, and their festive mood continued throughout the day. On Centre Court especially, the atmosphere was incredible. All the seats were full by twelve when play started, and I have never heard so much noise, so much singing. Even the royal box had a different feel to it, with past champions having been invited in place of the usual dignitaries. Mexican waves were rolling around the seats, and the crowds, enjoying the role of unseasonal pantomime audience, treated the players and ball girls and boys to a rapturous reception. Meanwhile the 'villains', the linespeople and umpire, were booed. It appeared to be a totally different crowd from the normal. Gabriela Sabatini and Andrea Strnadová opened the proceedings, and seemed bemused but thrilled by the reception. During the warm-up, the crowd imitated their strokes, which brought out huge smiles from the girls. Sabatini said afterwards, 'It was great fun. I couldn't stop laughing.' However, there was respect for the players during the match. When the points were played, people were quiet, while the carnival continued when they were not.

The best was reserved for Jimmy Connors who was playing against Derrick Rostagno. He came onto court accompanied by chants of 'Jimmee', and the showman rose to the occasion. During the warm-up, the crowd counted every stroke up to ten, before tiring of it. 'What's the matter?' retorted Connors. 'Can't you count past ten?' Although ultimately losing, he came off court with a massive grin, and said, 'Now that's my sort of crowd.'

It turned out to be one of the most enjoyable and successful days in the history of The Championships. It was splendid in every way. I did various circles round the ground, trying to find the people who had made the Sunday possible. Without their support it would never have worked. I also wanted to show my appreciation to the crowd, and, during a break in play, I took the opportunity to thank the audience, over the PA, for being 'the most enthusiastic Centre Court crowd that we've probably ever had'. I said at the time that it was like being at the last night of the Proms, and it was. I sat on Centre Court at various times during the afternoon, because it was such a wonderful place to be, and there was not much to do by that stage. There were other visitors too. Martina Navratilova sneaked in to savour the atmosphere, having finished her match on No. 2 Court. 'I told Gabby you are one lucky woman to get to play out there,' she commented wistfully.

By 4 o'clock the gates were closed and we had successfully let in 24,894 people, all paying at the gate. It would be interesting to know how many were there who had never been to Centre Court before. Certainly, once in, very few people left, which did not suit everyone. I remember bar takings were down. It was a huge sense of achievement, thinking that we might have introduced so many people to the game and to Wimbledon, and that players and audience alike had revelled in it. Our biggest gamble had paid off.

The follow-on from that Middle Sunday was how do you repeat the party? The honest answer is that, by its very nature, you cannot repeat an instantaneous event. However, the following year, we decided to create People's Saturday, as it was dubbed. Instead of having 500 Centre Court seats available on the day, we had 2,000 available at a reduced price, to try and recreate that atmosphere. This proved very popular, but unfortunately became a victim of its own success. As the years went by, we had too many people queuing from Friday onwards, with trails snaking around the residential roads that surround the Club. We carried on for a decade, but then had to stop on public safety grounds.

We have now played on Middle Sunday three times. Each successive time, the pressure coming from the media, players and spectators becomes greater. We have proved we can do it, and therefore raised the expectation that it become the norm. Whether we make the day an official Championships day has been, and remains, a hugely debated issue. Do we play fourteen days like all the other Grand Slams, or do we keep Sunday as a day of rest but build in flexibility and start, as the French do, on the Sunday before the Fortnight? It is now in everyone's contract that they must expect to participate for fifteen days, including the Middle Sunday and third Monday. Until such time as it is made a fixed scheduled day, broadcasters get the Middle Sunday as a bonus.

One of the advantages of keeping Middle Sunday free is to

give everyone a break. It provides staff with a chance to go home and recharge their batteries. Yet, in addition to scheduled play on fourteen days, the US Open and Australian Open also have evening sessions, which you would think would put a lot of strain on staff generally, but they seem to survive. The residents would definitely prefer to keep the day free, giving them a one-day respite from the crowds and parking restrictions that otherwise surround their homes for the rest of the Fortnight. On the other hand, I think the players would, on balance, prefer us to play right the way through, and financially we would be better off, because of the increased television income. So there are swings and roundabouts.

The fact is that, by and large, even with some very bad Championships weatherwise, our track record of getting the Fortnight through in thirteen days is pretty good. The proof of the pudding is really 2007. It was a dreadful first week, but everything still finished on schedule.

One thing is for sure – if there was to be play on the Middle Sunday as a scheduled day, it would have to be like any other day. It could not be done on an impromptu basis, with all ticket sales at the gate. The risks are too great and the police and local authorities would not accept a free-for-all. In 2004, the police closed Church Road to traffic because of heightened security problems, and they would not want to do that every year. Sadly, I fear the days of heightened security are here to stay.

All the scenarios have been contemplated, but no decision has been made. It may be sensible to delay any decisions until after 2009, when the impact of the retractable roof on Centre Court can be assessed. However, that would not have helped us in the face of a backlog of 188 matches, as we had in 1991. If we do have another disastrous year due to the weather, forcing Middle Sunday on us, my advice would be to make any permanent decision fresh on the back of that. If playing on that Sunday is the right way to go, which I now suspect it is, the decision should be made as soon as possible after being forced to play on that day. The problems faced would still be fresh in the minds of the residents who might be more sympathetic. If the decision is not taken until the following year, it will become more troublesome to achieve. It is over to the committee now. I am just grateful to have been a part of the day the Proms and the pantomime villains came to SW19.

Chapter 2

The Road to Wimbledon

Sport has always played a major role in my life. It even dictated my education, with my enlightened parents giving me the option of going to either a soccer-based or a rugby-based school. We were a sporting family in that we were all interested – my parents, my two elder brothers and I – even if some to a greater degree than others. My father, Maurice, founded the Blackheath Squash Club, although I never saw him in action as he had to retire prematurely with a shoulder injury. He was the chief accountant and then director of administration of the Blue Circle Cement Co., and was in charge of transportation of all the cement lorries. He passed away in 1981, having been a wonderfully supportive parent. My mother, Hilda, was a housewife who found time for social tennis twice a week right up until her retirement from the game in 2006, at the tender age of ninety-five. I would suggest that she must have been one of the oldest people in the country to have been playing, and even now has tremendous energy. She lives in her own house, still drives, and has only fairly recently stopped doing meals on wheels 'for the elderly'.

Slightly less fleet of foot was the sixth member of the Gorringe household, my grandmother. She lived with my parents until the day she died, which was also the day that I started working at the All England Club. In a sense it was symbolic, the drawing to a close of one era and the start of another, but as a 28-year old embarking on a new career, I think the symbolism passed me by that day.

I was born in December 1945 in Walton-on-Thames, Surrey, where we stayed until moving to Weybridge when I was five. My family became members of St George's Hill Lawn Tennis Club, and I started playing a year or two later. I could not have asked for a better introduction to the game. My two coaches there were Tony Mottram, a former Davis Cup player, and Paul Douglas who was excellent, a great enthusiast. We were walking distance from the club, which made it very easy to play regularly and get involved from an early age. We were also good friends with a family, the Hadfields, who had their own grass court. I remember many a happy afternoon spent running around there. My two elder brothers, Adrian and Robin, were interested, but not to the same degree. My father was chairman of the British Automobile Racing Club, having raced at Brooklands before the War, and my brothers both shared his interest in cars. Adrian had also developed a fascination with all things rural. We lived near the Burhill estate and he used to go down there to see the animals and hop on the back of tractors. He loved it. He went on to become a farmer in Herefordshire, and remained so until his retirement. He hardly ever took any holiday, because he said farming in Herefordshire was like being on holiday every day, which is a wonderful testament to a life well spent. I realised farming would take me away from my sport too much, so I was never particularly tempted to follow in his footsteps. Robin stayed more local, becoming a management consultant in London. I did play the odd junior tournament with him, and he and his wife Rosemary are still regular players.

My first step into the world of education was as a pupil at

Milbourne Lodge prep school, in Esher. My headmaster was Norman Hale, who became the longest serving and oldest prep school headmaster in the country. Much like my mother's, his energy was boundless. His enthusiasm both on the touchline and in the classroom was incredible. He was a great motivator, and teams would go from one season to the next without losing. On the academic side, we were all encouraged towards scholarships before common entrances. I became head boy and was very happy there.

In 1959, I went on to Bradfield College in Berkshire as a boarder. Both my brothers went to Cranbrook, but when I failed my 11-plus examination, that ruled out the Kentish school. I just failed to get a scholarship into Bradfield, which was my preferred choice, but passed my common entrance. My parents could see that I had a sporting tendency, and wanted me to be happy. They were very supportive of whatever I wanted to do, without pushing their own thoughts or aspirations forward. They were quiet people who left us to get on with it, but knowing that we had their full support was a huge comfort. I could not have had two better parents. They were very happy together, and would readily put each other first. Before they were married, my father was a keen bridge player and my mother was a keen dancer, but neither liked the other's hobby. They had an unofficial marriage pact that he would not play bridge and she would not dance, which I always felt was sad, particularly with hindsight, looking at the freedom I was given to develop my own hobbies.

Bradfield was excellent for me, and I would like to think that, had I had a son, he would have followed in my footsteps there. I enjoyed the academic side, although my performance was fairly average. One regret was that I failed French A level twice, both times in my oral exam. Having studied the subject for ten years, I still cannot speak the language. That is frankly pathetic.

The sporting facilities were outstanding. As I was a boarder, the option was there to play six days a week, which was heaven

for an athletic teenager. I threw myself into pretty much everything that was available, but football, squash and tennis were my
strengths. I captained the football first XI and the public schools
representative XI, and continued to play for the old boys' team
for ten years after I left. The master in charge of football was
Peter Jones, who went on to become probably one of BBC radio's
best football commentators. He was also called on to commen-
tate at state occasions such as the Opening of Parliament and
Prince Charles and Lady Diana's wedding, as he had a tremendous ability to capture and portray the excitement of an event
through the spoken word. He was also the master who tried to
teach me French without any degree of success. I was very heavily
influenced by him. It was nice that our paths were to cross again
when he became a radio presenter at Wimbledon. His son was
later to become a tennis correspondent for *The Times* and we
would frequently bump into each other. Peter died prematurely
while commentating on the Boat Race in 1990, and I was asked
by the BBC and his family to read a lesson at his funeral, which I
was honoured to do. Peter was a great fan of West Ham, which
at the time had legends like Geoff Hurst, Bobby Moore and
Martin Peters in the team. He tried to model our school team on
their style of play. We looked very good and were very pretty to
watch, but probably not as effective as we could have been. I am
a devoted fan of West Ham to this day, even if they clearly do
not play as prettily now as the Bradfield class of '64. My wife
Jenny knows only too well what a huge difference it can make to
my Saturday evening or Sunday, depending on how they do.

I played cricket up to Under 16 level, but when given the option
to switch to tennis, quickly did so. I was very fortunate to have
good friends at the school who played excellent tennis. I played
regularly with Tim and Tony Billington, who are Tim Henman's
uncles and whose father, Henry, played in the Davis Cup. Mike
Stotesbury was another keen player. I captained the team for two
years, played for the public schools' representative team in 1964,

and was a quarter-finalist at the Junior Championships of Great Britain, held at Wimbledon and consequently referred to as Junior Wimbledon. I probably peaked when I was fifteen, having won the Surrey Under 15 singles title two years running, and at the time playing much of my tennis at St George's Hill.

It was during one of those Surrey Championships matches that I first came across my future best man, Robert Dolman. His recollection of the event is of seeing a thirteen-year-old boy on the other side of the net, with overly large feet and an ungainly serve. He thought he would have the whole thing wrapped up in no time. Three hours later and we were still there, slogging it out. We both played from the back of the court and did not have a winning shot between us. Robert found the whole experience so dreadful he came over and said, 'Shall we play doubles together, because I'm not playing you at singles again.' We played a lot together, including Junior Wimbledon. We also played the Junior Covered Courts of Great Britain championship and once had to play the No 1 seeds, Stanley Matthews and Graham Stilwell, who were the best juniors by far. (Matthews was footballer Stanley Matthews' son. He won Junior Wimbledon three times.) We lost comfortably, and the headline on the back page of the *Daily Telegraph* the next day was not something like 'Matthews and Stilwell gain easy victory' but 'Dolman and Gorringe soon crumble to favourites', which I thought was a little unkind.

Particularly after Bradfield, I also managed to fit in a phenomenal amount of squash, at one point playing sixty matches a season. I played for Hertfordshire, and in the Amateur Championships of Great Britain.

Away from the sporting fields I was made head of house and head boy. With so much on my plate, I adopted the practice of keeping a little red notebook with me. Peter Jones got me started here. He was very efficient, with a keen eye for detail, and was a prolific list-maker. I would write lists of things to do on one side of the book, and on the other I would record every match

I played. It was partly out of necessity, as to get 'terms' in tennis, which entitled you to free kit and rackets, you needed to be able to prove your results. I have continued the practice out of interest, and it often amazes people. I will say to someone, 'I remember I played against you in 1983, and you beat me 9–7 in the fifth.' Their reaction is always a picture. I have a record of every squash match I have played since sixth form – that is 906 in total (won 684, lost 216 and drew 6). I have also kept a list of all the books I have read since 1963: a wide variety, but not too many classics.

So pleased was I with the success of the little red book, that the practice followed me to Wimbledon. When I started to work at the Club, I would write down lists, this time in a black book, of everything that I needed to do, or notes of what I saw when walking around. It was far more efficient than having lots of scraps of paper that get lost. I have everything in my notebooks, and each one can last a long time, with handwriting as small as mine. It was primarily for my benefit, but it also gave comfort to people, to see that I was recording something and therefore something might get done.

My 'rain list' is perhaps harder to explain. Since 1969, I have kept a record of whether it has rained or not on each day of the year. If I am away, I have sometimes asked my daughters to keep record, or I get slack and average it out. I also do not feel the need to stay awake at night to see if it rains, so it is not an exact science. I have no idea why I started doing it, but it is hard to stop now. Our IT director Jeff Lucas drew up the information into computer tables and graphs for me, so it has become an impressive document. I was also very gratified when my habit was given some legitimacy by discussions at Wimbledon as to whether we should move the date of the tournament. When we were contemplating whether to move Wimbledon to start a week later, I was able, from my comprehensive records, to show that we would get better weather if The Championships were moved further into the year. Let it be noted that over a ten-year period, we would have had forty-seven dry days as opposed to thirty-five dry days across the dates that The Championships was actually played on.

I left Bradfield in December 1964. I had stayed on an extra term to play football. I think I was probably retaking my French, and I was meant to be doing English too, but I could not get to grips with the set texts at all. I went to see the housemaster and expressed my concerns that the books were not making much sense to me. He told me not to worry, and that I should give it up and concentrate on something else. So I took him at his word and my football came on a treat. I really did not have a clue what I wanted to do on leaving school, so I was sent on a vocational training assessment. At the end of it, four things were suggested to me. Two were utterly unmemorable, one was estate manage-ment, and the other was the Hong Kong Police. My housemaster said he could help with the estate management side: he knew the person in charge of the Shropshire area of the National Trust. As contacts in Hong Kong seemed unforthcoming, I met with the National Trust man and asked him what it was all about. It sounded promising and I applied for a place at the Royal Agricultural College, Cirencester. In the meantime, I went to work on a farm in Buckinghamshire for nine months, for a farmer who was captain of our Old Bradfieldian soccer team.

Cirencester was great fun. I lived in a nearby cottage sharing with a good friend, Peter Cooper, and met some very interesting people. There were also some old friends, including Tim Billington, which added to the enjoyment. One of the areas covered on the course was forestry. I enjoyed that side a great deal, particularly the people involved. They had a very relaxed and calm way about them, mainly I suspect because of the nature of their work. In forestry, you do not expect quick results. If you plant a tree, you know it is going to take sixty years to mature. There are no targets or weekly deadlines – things that dictate so many lives. I was so taken by this area that at one stage I sent for papers with a view to emigrating to British Columbia, even though I had never been to Canada. In the end, I decided I would be giving up too much over here, and did not take the application any further.

I came back to London every Saturday to play football for the Old Bradfieldians, and remained very active until I started at Wimbledon and was no longer able to commit to playing every week. I switched to choosing a team to play against the Bradfield colts once a year. We called ourselves The Veterans All Stars, which you can get away with when you pick the team yourself. My tennis was also keeping me busy, as I had become match fixtures secretary for the Public Schools Old Boys LTA, commonly known as the PUBS.

It was around this time that I was put down for membership of the All England Club. I had been proposed by Peter Jackson, who was chairman of the PUBS, and a member of the Club. I think Peter did it as I was a keen tennis player and also involved in amateur tennis administration through the PUBS. He probably thought I would be a beneficial member, and might be prepared to give something back to the game in a voluntary capacity. The procedure was for a prospective member to be proposed and seconded, and further supported by two others. My name was on the candidates' list for six years before I became a temporary member in 1972.

The Club has different categories of membership. There are approximately 500 members, including honorary members who are mainly former singles champions. All singles champions become honorary members, with two exceptions. In 1931, Sidney Wood won on a walkover, and was not made a member at the time, although that error was corrected retrospectively. The other exception was one John McEnroe, in 1981. The Club had recommended that he be fined the maximum penalty the rules permitted for his behaviour that year. The committee therefore felt it would be hypocritical to make him an honorary member of the Club, despite the fact that he had won. Subsequently, the committee relented and he was duly elected an honorary member the following year.

In addition, there are around 110 temporary members who are made so for one year at a time, and junior temporary members who are the sons and daughters of members. It tends to be younger people who can play in the teams and make regular use of the Club who become temporary members. Generally, this is a step towards being made up to a full member. It is a way of checking a person's standard of tennis, and that they are the type of person who will fit in. It is also a logistical necessity. The full membership list is full and it is a question of 'filling dead men's shoes'. You are a member for life unless you resign, something that people occasionally do through ill-health. People tend to hang on to their membership even if they have moved out of the area, because of the allocation of tickets to The Championships that comes with membership. Sometimes, only seven full members are made up in a year, but usually it is twelve or so, taken from a very long waiting list. It is an oft-heard joke that the easiest way to become a member is to win The Championships. It would be very easy to fill the membership with good tennis players, but it is important to keep a mix of standards, and a mix of characters, to keep the Club a vibrant, interesting place. It is also important to think about the mix of qualities that might be important for the composition of future Club committees.

One of my favourite anecdotes concerning the membership is that when the All England Club had a match against the Fitzwilliam Club in Dublin, one of our team asked a Fitzwilliam Club player how many members they had and was told 3,000. When the Irishman asked the All England Club member the same question, he was told 375. Puzzled for a moment, he replied, 'Have you thought about advertising?'

Having finished three very enjoyable years at Cirencester, and having qualified as a chartered surveyor (in land management), I took a position as the assistant land agent to the Iveagh Trustees Ltd. The Iveagh Trustees run the Guinness estates, which are vast, covering huge tracts of Yorkshire and a lot of land in Scotland, as well as Ireland. I was based in Bishop's Stortford and we looked after agricultural property and forestry in a number of counties including Hertfordshire, Essex, Suffolk, Norfolk, Huntingdonshire, Berkshire, and Bedfordshire. I worked closely with my boss, Michael Bevan, who was a thoroughly pleasant man. We looked after forestry as well as tenanted farms and home farms. I was seconded up to Elvedon near Thetford, for two days a week for nine months, working on a home farm there of about 35,000 acres. We also looked after some of the family business, matters such as insurance of home contents and property. I lived in a cottage that went with the job, called Bakers Farm Cottage in Sawbridgeworth. It was in a beautiful spot, and the cornfields came right up to the back of it. In the summer, the combine harvester drove right past the window. The cottage was close to where the Beckhams now live, but I think that is as far as the similarity goes in terms of our respective accommodation. I did not spot too many paparazzi lurking between the ears of corn. It was a very pleasant way of life and one I settled into very comfortably. I was doing interesting and varied outdoor work, surrounded by nice people, and unencumbered by the pressures of office-based work. I was also close enough to London to continue my sport, which was good. It was a very polite way of living, particularly among the forestry people, and my five and a half years there were very happy. The job did not pay very well, but I was not overly ambitious and put a greater emphasis on quality of life.

And then I was shaken from my rural reverie. In September 1972, the All England Club had placed an advert in the *Daily Telegraph*, which I had not spotted. It read as follows:

> Applications are invited for the post of club assistant secretary. Male, preferred age 35–45. Probationary period to start beginning 1973, with view to appointment 1974.

That advert would have employment lawyers licking their lips now, but bear in mind that this was 1972, and attitudes, as well as employment legislation, have moved on a touch. The first I knew of it was a call out of the blue from Peter Jackson. He asked if I knew anyone who might be interested, which was a roundabout way of asking if I might be interested myself. Peter was an All England Club member, and later to serve on the committee.

I went and had a look at the advert at the Club and thought it sounded interesting. I duly sent in my application, despite the fact that I was only twenty-seven at the time of applying. I was put on the shortlist made from the seventy-three applications received, and went for an interview at the club on 12 January 1973 at 11 a.m.

I did not know the Club very well at that stage, and it was quite a daunting prospect. I imagined that I would be standing at one end of a long table with a host of dignitaries sitting at the other, in the manner of the 1878 William Yeames painting of King Charles, *When did you last see your father?*

I checked in with Enid Stopka, PA to Major David Mills, secretary of the Club, who was a wonderful lady, and who immediately made me feel welcome. She took me up the main staircase, past the trophy case and into the members' lounge, which was a lovely room. It has since been changed, and slightly enlarged with different furnishings. However, at the time, there were sumptuous deep leather armchairs, thick carpets, and a painting of Queen Mary owned by the Queen, but on loan to the Club. There was a small bar in the corner and the room had the atmosphere of a London gentlemens' club, welcoming but respectable. When I walked in, I was struck by the fact that everyone was sitting down in the armchairs rather than around a table, so I immediately felt more at ease. It was such a nice ambience. I was interviewed by Herman David, chairman of the Club, Rex Sterry, who was chairman of the staff sub-committee, Air Chief Marshal Sir Brian Burnett, who was to become the next chairman, Eric Peters, another committee member, and Major Mills, who was there for part of the proceedings. It was all very friendly and sociable, and even at times quite amusing. At one point the conversation switched to my private life.

'Are you married?'

'No,' I replied.

'Well, are you engaged?'

I said no again, but, not content to let the matter lie, they came back a third time.

'Do you have a regular girlfriend?'

At this point, one of the others chimed in with, 'Oh do shut up, or you'll be asking if he's sleeping with someone next, and we certainly don't want to know that.' My personal status obviously troubled them slightly, as the information that, 'It might be lonely in winter,' was also proffered at one point.

During the course of the interview I raised a question to do with weekend duties. 'You seem to indicate that I'll be required to be at the Club every other Saturday and Sunday throughout the year,' I ventured.

'Yes, why? Is that a problem?' came the response.

'Well, I have been accustomed to playing football every Saturday during the winter months,' I said, but before I could get any further, someone had interjected with, 'Are you still playing football? You can't be,' which started a debate all around me: 'He's only twenty-eight (having had a birthday since applying). Why can't he be playing?' said one; 'We want someone who's young and fit,' said another. I surveyed the scene, watching these men gently bickering around me, about me, but not including me, and it really was quite extraordinary, and comical.

There were no searching questions in terms of my capabilities.

It was very much a personality interview, which is why it was so informal and relaxed. The closest we came was a question as to how much I knew about grass management. I said, 'Quite a bit,' and they seemed satisfied with that. I was grateful that my grass management expertise, limited to how many cows were sustainable per acre, was not explored further. I think my age was the greatest cause for concern, which presumably prompted the question: 'If we gave you the job here, would you be prepared to stay for the rest of your life?' There was an expectation, an assumption, that whoever took the post would stay until they retired, and a concern, understandably, that that proposition would not appeal to a 28-year old. I wonder how many other jobs exist with that degree of expectation of loyalty. And how many in which it proves to be so apposite.

After my memorable interview, I went down to my car, an Austin A35. I was sitting in the driver's seat making notes of what had happened, when there was a tap on the window. It was Major Mills asking if I could possibly come back in. I followed him into the clubhouse and they offered me the job there and then. Well, that was fairly quick and painless, I thought. I could get to like this job.

The confirmation letter was sent out to me later that day. I gave in my notice to the Iveagh Trustees, which was six months reduced to three, and said goodbye to the many friends I had made within the farming and forestry community. I might have been sad to leave them, but I did not have any reservations, despite the fact that it was a total career change. I was going to work in the premier tennis club in the world. With hindsight I can say that I was also going to take up the world's best tennis job.

Not only did tennis bring me one of the best jobs I could ever have hoped for; it was also responsible for introducing me to my wife. While I was assistant secretary, we had an annual fixture against the Lugano Tennis Club in Switzerland. As I was in charge of co-ordinating fixtures, I would put the teams together, four men and four ladies, and in 1975 the Club had asked that I play in this particular away match. I had already picked the players when, fairly soon before we were due to leave, Nell Truman, Christine Truman's sister, told me that she would not be able to come as she was pregnant. I started looking through the members' list for a replacement, and had got as far as C when I found Jenny Chamberlain. At first, Jenny said No, as she was a teacher and did not think that she would be able to get the time off. I asked her to go and check with the headmaster, and whether the fact that he was also an old Bradfieldian helped, I do not know, but he let her go.

I picked her up in my car to take her to the airport and carried her suitcase and opened the car door for her, all of which she seemed quite impressed by. From those firm foundations, our relationship developed very quickly over the course of our long weekend away. We had a game of squash when we got back, followed by more tennis and squash – our own form of courting. Jenny is a very good sportswoman, although rather unchivalrously, I never let her win in our games together. She was a former Wimbledon player, in the ladies' and mixed doubles, and entered a lot of tournaments in the UK. She played for Wiltshire County and at County Week for twenty-five years, often with her sister Bridget. Although not twins (Bridget is younger), they look and sound incredibly similar, which must have made them a memorable pair to play against. The Hurlingham was her main club, but she later became a member of the All England Club and St George's Hill. Her talents were not restricted to the tennis court. She was also an England reserve at lacrosse, her favourite team sport, and played first-team squash at Richmond.

It did not take me long to realise that I was onto a very good thing with Jenny. Over the Christmas break that same year, I travelled up to see her in her home village of Ramsbury in Wiltshire, where her parents were farmers. I proposed to her while we were out on a walk, and, delighted with a positive response, I took her straight back to the family house. My intention was to ask Mr Chamberlain formally for his daughter's hand in marriage, and to do so as quickly as possible. However, it was not the most appropriate of times as the football results were coming in. Everything stopped until we could find out whether Swindon had won.

Once the important matters of the day had been established, I started again. Having said my piece, my future father-in-law fixed his gaze on me and said, 'Well, David . . .' David being Jenny's previous boyfriend of nine and a half years standing. He also asked me if being assistant secretary of the Club was a full-time job. The happy outcome of the tale is that I managed to persuade him of his future son-in-law's prospects, he did grant me permission . . . and we are still good friends with David.

Jenny and I have been lucky enough to have two wonderful daughters: Kim, who was born in 1978, and Anna in 1981, on the same day that Prince Charles got engaged to Lady Diana Spencer. Not that she is the only one in the family to share a momentous date in history. Kim married Pascal in December 2002 and gave birth to a son, Marcus Jonny, on 22 November 2003. Any discerning rugby fan will recognise that date as the final of the Rugby World Cup. While the rest of the country screamed at that drop goal, Marcus chose the moment to make his entrance to the world. In the circumstances, Jonny seemed the only appropriate middle name. Both girls share our love of tennis, which I suppose is not surprising, having been immersed in it all their lives. As if it was not enough for their father to come home discussing the day job, they could look down onto the Club courts from their bedroom window. A gate in our garden gave access to the practice courts, where Kim and Anna watched many Wimbledon legends going through their paces. Both played for Surrey county juniors, and, happily, both held their wedding receptions within the grounds of the Club, with Anna having married Greg in August 2008. Wimbledon has never been just a job. It has been a way of life, and the fact that the girls chose it as the backdrop to such a happy but private family occasion pays tribute to that.

Chapter 3

The Early Years

I walked through the main gates of the Club on my first day in office filled with nerves and trepidation, and a small dose of excitement. It was a new job and I was coming into the most famous tennis club in the world, not really knowing how the thing operated. There was slight apprehension as to how well my previous work experience in tending to acres of pasture for cows would equip me for the Club's manicured courts. I had been told that my title was to be assistant secretary designate. I was to shadow the existing assistant secretary from the day I joined, 1 May 1973, until after The Championships the following year. That is an extraordinary length of time to understudy someone, and I can only assume that there was a feeling that Gorringe, this relative youngster at twenty-eight, needed to have an eye kept on him – or that the committee shared my sentiments regarding the gaps in my CV. I have often said that it would have been impossible to have had such a long term of understudy had Tony Cooper not been such a wonderful person. He was great fun to be with and had a huge amount of genuine charm. There are not many men to whom I could give that compliment. Tony had joined as the assistant secretary in 1963, fairly late in life, although he had harboured ambitions of taking up the position earlier, after the

War. After retiring from his post, he went on to become the first curator of the museum, which opened in 1977.

I was given an office adjacent to Tony's, which was to the left of the Clubhouse entrance, and we were separated by a wooden partition. It gave us both a degree of privacy, but allowed me to hear what was going on and get to grips with his role. It also meant that I was privy to some of the choicer language reserved for the more exasperating members – always after the phone was safely back in the cradle.

When I first started at the Club, probably 60 per cent of my time was spent on Championships matters and 40 per cent on the Club. On the Championships side, the secretary (the title was later to change to chief executive) would deal with the major contracts and the assistant would take over from there. Each year we would use a large exercise book with the things to do listed in alphabetical order: A for advertising, B for ball boys, C for cushions and so on. That exercise book, which we called The Championships Diary, became our bible. We took the headings from the year before, and then wrote down a chronological list of the actions taken under each heading. Details of all meetings and subsequent actions were recorded in it. That system stood us in good stead for a good fifteen or twenty years, until technology took over from our handwritten notes.

The only additional staff we needed were ladies in the ticket office for the public ballot. Four or five would start work in January and stay until after The Championships, under the watchful eye of Joyce Combe, the ticket manager. She held an enormous amount in her head in terms of the system, but everything was also written out meticulously by hand. She had to have the patience of Job, to deal with some of the more testing queries and requests raised by members of the public. My favourite three were: 'I would like tickets for each of Björn Borg's matches', 'How long will the final next Saturday last?' and 'Does a ground admission ticket mean that I have to sit on the ground all day?'

The other key person was Enid Stopka, affectionately known as the queen of Wimbledon. She was PA to the chairman and Major Mills, Club secretary, but turned her hand to anything – what she did not know about Wimbledon was not worth knowing. She would run things in an utterly dependable fashion and never became flustered. She did everything, from the royal box to press and photographer's accreditation, to members' subscriptions. She and Joyce used to work very long hours for not a great deal of pay.

The Club has never been over-generous in paying. There was always a culture that it was an honour to work there, which it was, and a privilege. Therefore it was not essential to pay huge salaries. The proof of the pudding lies in the fact that we have never had a problem filling a position and very few people leave. A lot of that is to do with getting the right people in position at the outset.

The Club takes a lot of care in each of its appointments. When Paula McMillan was appointed as PA to the chairman and myself in 1979 for example, I remember her being interviewed by the two of us and four members of the staff sub-committee. It might have seemed quite intimidating at the time, but her predecessor had been in post for a good thirty years, so it was not a position to be filled lightly. Some people might complain that they are not getting enough pay each week, but the view has always been that if someone is not happy they can move on – and people do not. That applies right from the top to the bottom. Staff are loyal because they enjoy working here. There is a sort of paternal atmosphere, with the committee loyal to the staff and staff loyal to each other. Because of the seasonal nature of the work, people have to help out at different times and everyone is prepared to muck in where necessary. Inevitably, these things change when the number of people and staff gets bigger, and the Club perhaps has a different feel to it now compared to then. You lose the personal contact, however hard the personnel department tries.

I am a fastidious note-taker, and on that first day I know that I had a conducted tour of the grounds, and helped prepare a revised edition of facts and figures about The Championships. I met the Merton park superintendent to discuss which trees needed trimming in the car park, and helped organise preparations for the Club tournament in the middle of May, when we always have a day for the official opening of the grass courts. Then there were final arrangements for the Club dinner to be held up in London. Historically, this dinner was a male-only affair. One or two lady members put up a bit of an objection in the early eighties, and the committee said that they would help them organise a ladies' dinner if they so wished. That proved to be a none too popular option, and things continued as normal until eventually an autumn mixed dinner was introduced, in addition to the men-only dinner that is still held today.

Even on that first day, there was huge variety in terms of work to do with the Club, The Championships, the grounds and the public. It was that variety that made the job so satisfying and so interesting. I think that those earlier years were possibly the most enjoyable, as you had to turn your hand to a huge diversity of tasks. When I became secretary in 1979, Richard Grier came in as my assistant secretary, having previously been at the Birmingham Chamber of Commerce. We have often said that they were the fun times. We did not have anything like the same pressure as we do now, although we were doing this wide range of work. Now, of necessity, the roles have become much more compartmentalised, as there is a need for specialists in the appropriate areas. We used to do all the marketing until 1985 when we brought in Rob McCowen to specialise. IT was the same, with Richard floundering rather less than I was, until we brought in an IT director, Jeff Lucas; and similarly with our finance director (FD), Tony Hughes – I suspect that our accountants were absolutely delighted with that appointment, given the parlous state of affairs up to that point.

Prior to our FD's arrival, Tony Cooper and then I were responsible for a broad range of financial tasks. This included such things as doing all the wages and salaries. The wages went out on a weekly basis, and we had to work out the amounts, including tax, NICs and NI, then get the money from the bank, put it into small brown envelopes and hand it out on a Friday. The salaries were done once a month, but thankfully by cheque.

We did all the accounts for the Club and Championships which meant checking all the bills that came in, authorising them, writing out the cheques, and putting each item into the journals or ledgers, deciding which was a tournament expense, a Club expense or a members' fund expense. We would prepare the accounts up to the stage where the auditors could come in and review them.

Tony Cooper, however, was no lover of finance. He did not think it was really necessary to try and balance the bank statements each month, as I liked to do. He just used to say, 'Well, I'll leave that to the accountants at the end of the year. That's what we pay them for.' He had a habit, when writing a cheque, of not putting in any punctuation. So he would write one for £18000 and you had no idea if it was £18,000 or £180.00. I think the auditors spent longer with us then than they do now, even though the number of transactions is massively higher.

It was not just the auditors who were confused by Tony's numbering system. He once ordered the toilet rolls for The Championships, and when they arrived, there were enough for five Championships. They had to go back. There was nowhere to store them.

There were probably about fifty staff, but the vast majority of those were groundstaff. These were the days prior to mechanisation. We had mowers, sprayers and seeders and that was about it. It was very labour intensive and we needed more staff then even though we had fewer grass courts than now – just fifteen then, compared with nineteen Championships grass courts and twenty-two grass practice courts today. Up until the early eighties, the worn areas, the baseline, and middle T were all returfed after each Championships. It would take three men going at it for four or five days on each court. Now, the whole court is reseeded mechanically, with one man and his machine. I suppose the flip side was that we had a much smaller maintenance team, as the estate property was far smaller at that time, prior to the expansion of the grounds and the developments within.

The secretary at the time was Major David Mills and he and Tony had some established traditions which speak volumes as to the relaxed tempo of life back then. Every day at 12.45 they would disappear upstairs to have a good club measure or two of sherry before lunch, and then enjoy a nice leisurely hour break. I seldom joined them – thinking it was one practice I could do without, given that I would have been useless for work that afternoon, or, more importantly and more likely, for a squash match that evening – but it was a very civilised thing at the time and the way things were done. The pace of life was generally very sedate without today's pressures, and things were relatively quiet. In fact I remember David Mills once saying to me, 'I hope the committee never asks me what I get up to in November or December as it's so quiet.' Now those months are just as intense as any other.

Lunch for staff would be served at 1 p.m. sharp. All office-based, as opposed to ground staff and others, would sit together at one long table. We were served by Lottie the stewardess, who was married to Leo the dressing room attendant. Lottie was a short lady, not the finest of chefs, but a formidable character. She would always insist that everyone turned up on time and there was no messing with her. If you arrived five minutes late she would be bustling out of the kitchen, finger wagging, shouting, 'You're late, you're late.' I remember when Air Chief Marshal Sir Brian Burnett became chairman, there was a sugar shortage at the time. He was having coffee after lunch and Lottie spotted that he had put three good lumps of sugar into his cup. She bustled over immediately and poked him hard in the ribs, saying,

'Don't you know there's a sugar shortage?' Sir Brian became puce red with embarrassment, and almost started to spoon out the sugar from the coffee. We all loved her. Friday was always fish followed by sponge pudding and custard. Most other days it was tinned peaches. It was all very institutionalised, very school-dinnerish. There was no choice; it was whatever Lottie had created. Apparently, though, she was better than her predecessor, who it was said could murder a piece of meat better than anyone else. Thankfully, over the years the quality of the catering has improved significantly.

Lottie and Leo made an endearing couple and were stalwarts of the Club. Leo, as head dressing room attendant, would always walk onto court before the men's singles finals carrying the players' bags and rackets. He was so short that the bags were almost scraping on the ground and it seemed touch and go as to whether he was going to make it. He always got a huge cheer and a round of applause from the occupants of the members' stand as he walked off. He was a lovely man, always very efficient, conscientious and extremely courteous – he always called everyone Sir. After a game of tennis, you could leave your shoes in the dressing room to be whitened, and be sure that Leo would have them ready for the next day.

A lot of my time as assistant secretary was spent arranging teams for Club matches. I would have to pick the teams, send out the invites, and make the arrangements in terms of catering and car parking and whatever else might arise. We would pick, from our membership, the team that was similar in strength to the opposition, but might still win the match 5–4 or 6–3. A side that played the armed services, for example, would not need to be as strong as one playing the International Club of Great Britain. It meant that different members would have the chance to play, rather than always relying on the best. Inevitably, you were unlikely to be able to field your strongest team. In theory, the Club could select Roger

Federer, Rafael Nadal and Venus Williams, as they are all members by dint of having won The Championships. That would be quite something, even if fielding a team of former champions would not quite meet our 'close victory but good match' criteria.

One of our most prestigious events is the Gregory Cup, a triangular match held between the leading clubs of Stockholm and Copenhagen and us. When the match is played at Wimbledon, it involves not only organising the matches, but also includes a visit to the theatre and dinners over the weekend. We had about thirty other matches during the course of the year. Most were home as most people want to come to us, and our members are not so keen on travelling too far unless the match is abroad. There were also about thirteen outside events, such as the National Veterans Championships of GB, where we allowed outsiders to come and use our courts.

More often than not, all this tied in with weekend duties. I had to be at the Club one weekend in three, alternating with Major Mills and Tony Cooper, and then, once Tony had retired, every other weekend of the year (with a day off in lieu on Monday). You had to be there on site in case there were any problems, but more generally to be seen to be there for the members' benefit. In those days, more members came to play at the Club at weekends, rather than on weekday evenings as is now the case. Therefore it was felt right that a senior member of staff should be seen to be there and there should be some interactivity between secretary and members. For a club to be a club, it should not just be a case of opening the front gates and letting the members in. It should be more welcoming and more inclusive. In addition, there were often sub-committee meetings held on Saturday mornings.

If there was a match on at the weekend, I would liaise with my chosen captain with regard to team pairings and as to what courts they were on, check that the courts were prepared, and that the drinks were on there ready. I would co-ordinate with the duty groundsman as to which courts could be used if there was bad weather, and liaise with the kitchen as to when the teams would come in for lunch and tea. Generally, the matches would start at two, but if the opposition were coming from a long way, we would have lunch beforehand so that it was not such a rush for them. At the end of the match, I would be on hand to fraternise with the teams, organising drinks, until everyone started heading off at around eight. All in all, it was quite a long day. The weekend duty strangely was not a chore – it was a good time to catch up on other work when it was quiet, and you had the opportunity to watch or play some tennis. I took part in some of the matches, generally when someone had pulled out at the last minute and I could put myself in as substitute. Playing tennis while working was not something I chose to do. I felt uncomfortable playing in the daytime, unless I was occasionally called upon by the chairman to make up a four.

The downside of the weekend duty was that obviously you were giving up a weekend at home, and with a young family that was difficult, but I had known that that would be a requirement of the post when I took it on, and I carried on the role until around 1984. Nowadays, the requirement for members of staff to be available at weekends during the winter months has been dropped. To an extent, security is more intense now, and so one of the roles that we were fulfilling has been taken on elsewhere.

In those first years I really was living and breathing the Club. Not only was I on duty at weekends, but also I was living on site in the secretary's lodge, before I moved into the newly-built assistant secretary's house on Somerset Road, again on site. Yet despite this accessibility, people would only contact me during office hours (which used to be nine to five, but have steadily risen), for which I'was very grateful. In fact, it seemed that the only people who did bother me were a couple of burglars when I was in the house on Somerset Road. The first time they took my TV, which was about all I had of note in my bachelor pad. A second lot came shortly after, and did not take anything at all, with my only possession already having been pilfered.

I am not sure if it was the same group that came back years later, when I was, by then, living in the secretary's house on Church Road. Jenny and I had gone to see a Davis Cup tie at Crystal Palace and returned to find Iain MacPhail, a member of the Club, and a police car sitting outside. Iain had been playing with his daughter and had heard our alarm go off. He came round to investigate, and found a Rover parked in the driveway, with a very big lady in the front seat. He asked if he could help. She replied that she had just found a cat that had been hit by a car. Then he looked up and saw a hole in the glass to the study. Looking through he could see someone in the kitchen. Ever the quick thinker, Iain leant in to the car and took the ignition keys out, at which point the man from inside the house leapt out. He was armed with a carving knife. Iain had his tennis racket. The standoff was short-lived, thank goodness, and Iain laid down his arms. The man and woman then ran off but were eventually caught and prosecuted, although how they managed to make any sort of getaway, given the size of the lady, I am not sure.

Two burglaries aside, the only other disturbances came during The Championships, when certain members of the public clearly did not abide by the standard-office-hours policy. One year, a distraught lady rang late one night with a crisis on her hands. She had been in the standing area of Centre Court, when it had got so incredibly hot that she had been forced to take off her tights. She had inadvertently forgotten to take them with her when she left, and would someone be so kind as to go and check and fetch them for her? Tony Cooper was the lucky beneficiary of that call and he gave her short shrift: 'I'm here to tell you, madam, that I am *not* inclined to go out to Centre Court at 1 a.m. and look for your tights.' I took a similar call in my first year from someone who had left a camera in the restaurant areas on Centre Court, but being the new boy, I was very obliging and actually went and found it for him. At least it was still there, and it is nice when things work out well from time to time.

I was certainly not alone in living on site, and that probably helped strengthen the feeling of a close-knit group of individuals working together. It also helped promote a distinct village feel. The Club had cottages and houses of varying sizes within the grounds, and also flats in Southfields, housing quite a few ground-staff and maintenance staff. In those days, fewer people had cars and there were no bus routes close-by. It was an asset to be able to offer people the option of living on site, reducing their trans-port and financial worries, while providing the Club with a reliable and accessible workforce. The option was taken up by quite a few of the groundstaff, as well as some of the other staff like Lottie and Leo, Paula my PA, and Richard Grier who was to step into my shoes – and my house – as assistant secretary. I lived in the Club's tied accommodation throughout my Wimbledon career, moving up to the secretary's house on my promotion in 1979.

For many years the curtain raiser for The Championships has been the pre-Wimbledon garden party at the Hurlingham Club, preceded by a ball staged by the International Lawn Tennis Club of Great Britain on the Saturday night, currently at the Dorchester Hotel in London. There are thirty-four International Clubs around the world, the first having been founded by Great Britain in 1924, followed by the French and the US. Their collec-tive aim is to promote tennis nationally and internationally, and create goodwill through the playing of the game. Members have either played for their club or country overseas, or represented their university or the armed services. It is the highest level of amateur tennis, played by people of varying ages. I was a fairly mature captain in 2007, while at the other end, the LTA put forward youngsters who would benefit from the experience of membership.

The ball itself is a good-fun, well-organised event, attended by a lot of overseas guests, including former Davis Cup captains, one of whom normally says a few words.

The following day, a garden party takes place at the Hurlingham Club, and traditionally, players who were short of grass practice would go along and games would be arranged for them, either singles or doubles depending on preference. Members of the Hurlingham Club and the International Club could go along and happily amble around the Hurlingham grounds watching some of the world's finest players in action on a lazy Sunday afternoon. One or two International Clubs from overseas would be invited over each year, and, having played a couple of matches earlier in the week and attended the ball, would then play at Hurlingham on the Sunday. It is quite something to be playing alongside the professionals at close quarters. In the seventies, before we had extended our own practice facilities, players were grateful for any opportunity they could take to hone their skills on grass and the garden party attracted some of the top players. More recently, the calibre of players attending has changed. As we have so many more practice courts at our Club, the same necessity for players to come to this event does not exist. They would also rather practise with their coaches than whomever the organisers had drawn as their partner. It tends to be more veterans than players from the main draw who now go to the party, but the tradition remains, and it is a lovely way to ease into the tournament.

There have been so many changes since my early days at the Club. For instance, each year I would be ousted from my office during The Championships, as it was taken over by the two or three people co-ordinating transport for the players and VIPs. Now, however, the transport office has moved away from the Clubhouse, primarily because we did not want cars coming down the main concourse because of health and safety issues. Health and safety was certainly not something that troubled us so much back in those days. The whole heart of the transport system today is in a two-storey temporary building by the covered courts. There is also another base in the Millennium Building for players' cars, so the whole operation has mushroomed enormously from when it was directed from my little commandeered office.

The most memorable event by far of my first year was the players' revolt.

Looking at the reason for the 1973 strike in isolation, it would seem at first glance to have been a massive over-reaction to a *cause* not very *célebre*. However, the foundations were being laid a decade earlier, when the calls for 'open' tennis were reaching a climax. For some years, professional tennis had been gathering strength, with the amount of money to be made outside the official amateur circuit attracting more and more players. The pressure increased when Jack Kramer took over the running of the professional tour, and many top-class players chose to turn their backs on the amateur game, meaning that the Grand Slams were losing the talents of people such as Pancho Gonzales, Lew Hoad, Rod Laver and Ken Rosewall.

Meanwhile, the amateur game had entered a farcical stage, with players receiving bungs under the table from their national associations to ensure that they continued playing the official events, in a system that Wimbledon chairman Herman David referred to as 'shamateurism, a living lie . . . the quintessence of hypocrisy'.

A motion had been put to the International Lawn Tennis Federation (ILTF) in 1960 to merge the two circuits, and for tennis to go open. However, it failed to reach the two-thirds majority required – partly, history reports, because some key voters were either asleep, on the toilet, or booking that evening's entertainment, when the crucial vote was taken.

Eight years later, the impasse was broken, when Herman David announced that Wimbledon 1968 would be open to contract professionals, whether the ILTF sanctioned it or not. The US Lawn Tennis Association followed suit, and the ILTF was forced to back down. The first open event took place in Bournemouth in April 1968.

However, this was far from being an end to the matter, and the politics of tennis became ever more complex. The ILTF felt its position increasingly threatened, particularly by the recently formed World Championship Tennis Inc. (WCT), a US-based organisation that had eight star players under contract. WCT had started demanding corporation fees for its contracted players to appear at tournaments. When no WCT men appeared at the French Open in 1971, the ILTF retaliated by banning all contract professionals from official ILTF tournaments in 1972. A compromise was eventually reached, but too late for any WCT professionals to appear at the French Open or Wimbledon that year.

That same year, 1972, the players' union, the Association of Tennis Professionals was formed, another source of antagonism for the ILTF. It seemed only a matter of time before a show-down between the two bodies, and the precipitating agent came in the form of Nikki Pilic, a dark and brooding Yugoslavian player, whose actions in this instance have arguably since surpassed his sporting achievements.

Although he hotly denied the charge, Pilic was said to have refused to play Davis Cup tennis for Yugoslavia when asked, preferring instead to play a more lucrative match in Montreal. Probably sensing an opportunity to flex its muscles, and nip the power of the ATP in the bud, the ILTF suspended Pilic for his actions. The ATP, conversely, took this as the moment at which to demonstrate that its member players were no longer answerable to their national associations. It called on its members to boycott Wimbledon, something which, given the allure of the tournament, the ILTF believed would never happen.

It is one of life's great ironies that Wimbledon had played a huge part in bringing about the era of professional tennis, and was now to fall an innocent victim to its consequences. The Pilic saga could not have happened at a worse time. The ILTF suspension meant that Pilic would not be eligible to play at Wimbledon. The ATP response, a players' boycott, may have been a swipe at the ILTF but it was Wimbledon that was caught in the crossfire.

It was a close run thing as to whether the strike would actually take place. Communications had not broken down completely and talks were being held between Eldon Griffiths, Minister for Environment and Sport, Cliff Drysdale, chairman of the ATP, and Allan Heyman, president of the ILTF. However, they came to nothing as the showdown rumbled on. Meanwhile, Pilic, with the backing of the ATP, sought an interim injunction against Wimbledon for observing the ban, claiming that the suspension was unjust. A ruling in Pilic's favour would have seen an end to the matter, but after a three-day hearing, on 19 June, Mr Justice Forbes ruled that the suspension did not breach rules of natural justice.

The week before Wimbledon was due to start, members of the ATP council met at a hotel in London to take a vote on whether to boycott or not. Voting against were defending champion Stan Smith, and Britons John Barrett and Mark Cox. In favour were US players Arthur Ashe and Jim McManus, and Jack Kramer who had reappeared as ATP director. That left chairman Cliff Drysdale, with the deciding vote. Dramatically, he declared, 'I abstain,' possibly not wanting to be the man to wreak havoc on the forthcoming Championships, but probably knowing full well that, according to ATP rules, a level vote meant that a motion was carried.

And so the decision was made. As Herman David said, 'So that's that. Now it's settled once and for all.' The inconceivable had happened, the ILTF had lost their gamble powerplay, and on 21 June, sixty-eight ATP players pulled out of the tournament.

The official draw should have taken place the day before, but had obviously been postponed, waiting for further developments. On 22 June, we did a reseeding in the morning, and at 11 a.m. announced the redraw. Ultimately, seventy-nine players pulled out, including thirteen of the sixteen top seeds. Many players had agonising decisions to make, including Roger Taylor. He eventually came down in favour of Club (he was a member of the All England Club) and country, but was fined by the ATP for his troubles, and was given a lot of flak by his fellow players. Ilie Nastase also refused to pull out, stating that he was under orders from the Romanian president, and other non-ATP members, such as Jimmy Connors and a seventeen-year-old Borg were still to come.

It was a worry and a tricky time, and I certainly saw the referee's office – to where I had been moved – stretched to its limit. The referee was Captain Mike Gibson, and his assistant was Fred Hoyles, who was to become his successor. I suspect I would have been seconded over there in any event, but an extra pair of hands that summer certainly did no harm. Everything was in a state of flux as we did not know how many people were going to pull out, and where it would all stop. We could not be totally sure that there would be sufficient players even to stage the event. We were fire-fighting, picking up the pieces, and trying to make the best of what seemed a pretty bad job at the time. The norm was to have sixteen players come through from the qualifying event into the main draw, but this time, as the main numbers diminished, we had thirty-two. When we had redone the seedings and the draw, 'lucky losers' were put into the place of players who continued to pull out after the first announcements on 21 June.

There were also a few rumblings from the female players. The Women's Tennis Association had just been formed, and there were suggestions from their head, Billie Jean King, that if the level of women's prize money was not raised, they would pull out too. Billie Jean stated at the time that, 'If we can get the top twelve women to back us, I should be all for pulling out of Wimbledon.' Fortunately, the threat came to nothing, although the battle over equal prize money was to rage for over thirty years.

Quite aside from the logistical headaches was the fear that, if the top players pulled out, people would not come to watch. However, the bulk of our tickets are sold in advance, so you would assume that people will turn up to watch regardless of who is playing. People have arranged time off work, booked travel plans, and set the day aside to come, so it was probably unlikely that we would feel too much of a hit that year, although on-day sales were likely to be down.

In the end, we had an extraordinarily successful Championships, and recorded our second highest attendance figures. Some people were a bit surprised, while others said that if it is Wimbledon, you will always get people coming – even if it is the secretary's grandmother playing on Centre Court.

The ongoing fear was what the long-term implications might be. We felt that we could probably go through two, maybe three Championships of inferior quality before we would suffer. We had already endured the loss of the World Championship players in 1972, and now this the following year. The players themselves had nothing against Wimbledon, but were supporting a cause. They wanted to give credence to the newly formed ATP. They would not have had any intention of not wanting to play the following year, but in the political turmoil of the professional tennis arena, who could say what might arise? How much patience would they have had with the situation? As John Newcombe said the following year, 'If I'd been kept out of Wimbledon for the third year running by another of these damn silly bans, I'd never have come back.'

After two or three inferior Championships, people would start questioning whether to buy a ticket in advance, if there could be no guarantee of the world's top players attending. There would also be a knock-on effect for TV and commercial partners. They would be even more suspicious and hard-nosed when it came to renegotiating contracts if they were finding that the top players were not competing. There was little that we could do to protect ourselves against the vagaries of a Pilic-type debacle, but we could certainly shore up our corner by increasing prize money to an even more attractive level, which we did. Total prize money for 1974 was £97,100, almost double the sum for 1973. The men's title in that boycott year was won by Jan Kodeš, who received £5,000, while the ladies' champion, Billie Jean King, won £3,000.

Jan Kodeš was a worthy winner and had already beaten British hope Roger Taylor in the semi-finals in a five-set thriller, but another man – or youth – stealing the headlines back in 1973 was a seventeen-year old Swede called Björn Borg. It was Borg's first trip to Wimbledon in the Open singles, although the boycott had elevated his status to No. 6 seed. However, it was his good looks and long flowing blond locks that were causing a stir as much as his tennis. Wherever he went, he was besieged by hoards of female fans, to the extent that he had to have a police escort merely to get from Clubhouse to court. Wimbledon had never seen the like as 'Borgmania' took hold. He was a total contrast to the other players on the scene at the time. He barely spoke compared to the likes of Connors and Nastase, making him an enigmatic figure. He was also the new kid on the block at a time when the British public had precious little else in the way of icons. The extent of the furore was such that Major Mills wrote to the heads of sixty girls' schools the following year, asking that influence be brought to bear to keep their charges under better control. I am not sure that the move was a total success, given that in 1974, Borgmania was as intense as ever. In just one incident on Court 2, the Viking god was mobbed, and in the ensuing scuffle, a policeman's helmet was knocked off and an officer knocked to the ground. Throughout, Borg looked utterly bemused by the idea that he was a teenage icon and that hundreds of females were desperate just to touch him.

Despite the rampaging females, and the boycotting males, life carried on as normal once the 1973 tournament was up and running. As assistant secretary designate and with little responsibility, I had the opportunity to walk around looking at all aspects of The Championships, and seeing how everything worked together. I was able to familiarise myself with every nook and cranny, which was very helpful and would have been very hard to do in later years. Beyond my reconnaissance walkabouts, I threw myself wholeheartedly into the endless round of cocktail parties that sit alongside the tennis. This started on the first Monday at 12.15, with the umpires' and honorary stewards' cocktail party in the Lodge garden, adjacent to the old No. 1 Court. Umpires and officials were plied with G&Ts and sherry before going out to officiate over matches that afternoon. It perhaps was not the most sensible of planning decisions. Indeed, the tradition came to a halt some time after Mrs Dorothy Cavis-Brown fell asleep while acting as linesperson on one of the tramlines on Court 3. Abe Segal, playing at the time, could not understand why she had not called to signal the ball out until he looked around and found that she had nodded off on the job. So soundly was she asleep that the South African Segal was forced to go over and tap her on the shoulder to waken her. Now the umpires' cocktail party has been shifted to an evening slot, a far safer time for all concerned.

The following day, again at 12.15, was the press party. Thursday evening saw the Commercial Union cocktail party, while Saturday evening heralded the members' cocktail party. The second week kicked off with the Lawn Tennis Writers' party on Tuesday lunchtime, followed by the Veterans' Club of Great Britain cocktail party that evening. (The Veterans' Club is rather similar to the International Club of Great Britain. It is a nomadic club of people who are over a certain age, who play in matches both home and abroad. At Wimbledon, they entertain more-senior former players, including former Davis Cup and Wightman Cup players.) The following day was the secretary's cocktail party, while the second Friday was reserved for the Service Stewards' party. The second Saturday was marked by the LTA Ball at the Grosvenor House Hotel. I was rushed off my feet. The drinks parties are an integral part of The Championships, and continue to this day, mainly as a means of thanking the various groups of people that have been involved in whatever form at the tournament or in supporting British tennis. I think the only thing that has changed is that, as the years progressed, my diary filled with other events around those that involved me raising a glass or two. Sometimes, progress is not all it is cracked up to be. Now all of these cocktail parties are held in the evening after play.

One area that saw an incredible amount of action was the general office, the hub of The Championships. Across this one desk, players who had made it through to the second week would pick up their second-week passes, umpires and stewards would collect their daily ticket allowances, the WRVS (Women's Royal Voluntary Services) would check in for their paperwork, royal box and general public queries would be dealt with, press interviews would be organised. The ticket counter was whirring away in the background, checking the number of people coming through the gates, while documents were constantly being sent back and forth down the chute connecting the general office to the prize money office or the main gatehouse. Meanwhile, the telephone switchboard, which was in one corner of the room, was in full swing. It really was a case of breathe in but do not breathe out. To the untrained eye, it may even have seemed a little chaotic, but everyone knew what everyone else was doing, and I believe that in many ways it made for a seamless operation, as people could cover for each other.

Lest I was in any doubt as to my dispensability in those early years, another event served to act as a reminder. It concerned a very talented player whose mother came over to spectate and was allegedly caught shoplifting. I was asked by Major Mills to act as surety for her. I had to go to court and swear that she would present herself in court on the second Monday of The Championships. If she did not, I Christopher Gorringe would be liable for imprisonment for up to six months. I was very expendable. I just prayed to God she would actually appear, although why it did not occur to me to escort her there I am not sure. I'm thankful that she did appear, and the option of my being a jailbird never arose. I do not know the outcome of that particular little incident, and although I have seen her a number of times since, we have never referred to it.

One of my responsibilities in my first years was to oversee the ball boys and girls (ball girls were introduced in 1977). It is a popular misconception that they are chosen from local children's homes. In fact, Dr Barnado's and Shaftesbury Homes were last involved in 1966 and 1968 respectively, and since that time, the teams have come from local schools. Today, around 250 children are selected from 700 applicants, and then undergo some pretty stringent training, starting back in February. The training was directed by Commander Charles Lane, and then Wally Wonfor, an ex-RAF sergeant, and I think the regime can take some children by surprise. The BBC made a documentary on the training that the ball boys and girls undertake, and one of them grumbled, 'It's a lot more disciplined than school is. If you give any lip, they kick you out.' By the time I met them at The Championships, they had been thoroughly schooled, and my involvement was more in dealing with logistics such as transport and refreshments than in enforcing discipline.

There have been many memorable Championships during my time at Wimbledon, and the early years proved to be no exception. For instance, in 1975 the Connors v Ashe final was one of the finest tactical displays of tennis ever seen. Fuel had been added to what was set to be a fiery encounter by the fact that Connors was actually suing the ATP and Ashe at the time of the final. Ashe had called Connors 'unpatriotic' for refusing to play Davis Cup tennis, resulting in Connors taking out a libel suit against him. Almost as if to rub salt in the wound, Ashe walked onto court in his USA tracksuit. What is more, Connors had previously filed other suits totalling around $20m against the ATP, of which Ashe was president at the time. Connors was the overwhelming favourite to win, but found he could do nothing in the face of Ashe's revised game plan, and was taken apart in the first two sets. Ashe, who was normally a formidable hitter of the ball, instead slowed the ball right down, frustrating the normally big-hitting Connors. As Ashe said, 'He feeds on speed so I gave him junk.' He continually hit low, lifeless balls and also used an away-swinging slice serve to Connors's double-handed backhand which proved extremely effective. I remember watching him from the stands, and being in awe of his immense concentration. At each change of ends, Ashe would sit there, either with his towel over his head or just meditating, working out what his tactics should be. Nothing would distract him. Despite losing the third set and seemingly allowing Connors back into the match, Ashe stuck to his plan, and won 6–1, 6–1, 5–7, 6–4.

Ashe was a very popular winner, because he did so much for tennis both on and off court for the black community. He was the first black man to win a Grand Slam and used his status to do a lot of community relationship work. Ashe, who died far too early, at the age of forty-nine in 1993, would like to be remembered more for his part in helping under-privileged black children than for being a fine tennis player. In many ways, being a fine tennis player was just a means to an end.

The following summer, in 1976, was one of the hottest on record. On one day alone at the tournament, 500 people were treated for heatstroke. The doctor on duty was doing his best to cope, but the sight of casualties laid out on the floor, the grass and even the tarmac paths was not the image we were hoping to convey to the rest of the world. We had worked particularly hard that year to ensure that The Championships, and Centre Court in particular, would be up to our usual exacting standards. Back in January, some vandals had broken into the grounds and onto Centre Court. They dug up chunks of the grass near the net area and daubed paint over the surrounding walls. It was a terrible mess. I was living on site and was one of the first people to see it when I got up that morning. It was very sad and depressing to see such mindless damage. Fortunately, as it was January, we still had time to mend the court.

The odd thing was that no one ever claimed responsibility. It was the time of the 'George Davis is innocent' campaign, and we thought there might be a link there, given the damage done to Headingley cricket ground. George Davis was a cab driver who, in 1975, received a twenty-year prison sentence for armed robbery, despite having an alibi in a man called Peter Chappell, who had seen him at the time of the robbery.

When Davis was convicted, Chappell campaigned to secure his release. As well as painting 'George Davis is innocent' on railway bridges and other public places, Chappell also helped dig up the Headingley cricket ground during an Ashes series, for which he was sent to prison for eighteen months for criminal damage. Still, it appeared that whoever was responsible for our own act of vandalism had no cause to follow, worthy or otherwise, or an axe to grind. It was just sheer bloody-minded vandalism.

We subsequently invested in guard dogs in an attempt to ensure that incidents of this type could never happen again, but made sure not to repeat the disaster that had befallen our counterparts at the Australian Open. In an attempt to guard their grass show court from intruders, the tournament organisers at Kooyong had invested in a guard dog, but had stopped short of a dog handler. Left to its own devices, the dog had fancied that there might be a bone buried somewhere around the service line, and proceeded to dig up the court to investigate further.

After the heat of 1976 came Virginia Wade's win in 1977, one of the greatest highlights of my time at Wimbledon. She was certainly never one of the easiest people to support, always coming agonisingly close and yet always falling at the last hurdle. After sixteen years of trying, she herself was only too aware of her shortcomings, and had declared that she was 'the best player not to have won Wimbledon and only because my attitude had been wrong'.

In 1977, however, the stage could not have been set more perfectly for the final between Virginia and Betty Stove. It was the centenary of The Championships, and also the Queen's Silver Jubilee, with the Queen present in the royal box to watch the match. Immediately before the Queen sat down, 'Land of Hope and Glory' was played, and there was a carnival-like atmosphere. When she lost the first set 4–6, it seemed as if Virginia would fall to her normal demons, but she rallied to take the next two 6–3, 6–1. Prior to Wimbledon, Virginia had been playing for the New York Apples in an American inter-city tennis league, with the likes of Billie Jean King, Fred Stolle and Sandy Mayer. Possibly, close liaison with these other players had had a positive impact both mentally and physically – when the going got tough on Centre Court, this time Virginia rose to the challenge. When she won the final point, she yelped with joy, but the sound was lost under the noise of every man, woman and flag-waving child leaping up and cheering and clapping. The Duchess of Kent leapt up too and gave a clenched-fist victory salute as everyone was carried away on a sea of emotions – a mix of joy and relief that Virginia had finally done it. Billie Jean King was to comment to Marjorie Fraser, the locker room attendant that 'This script was written in heaven.' And it was. During the presentation, the Queen spoke to Virginia, but her words were drowned out by the noise. In a wonderful moment of tact and discretion, the Queen moved back to allow the victor to take centre stage. Virginia's own take on it was that 'It was like a fairytale, with everyone cheering for the Queen and for me.' The 31-year old daughter of an archdeacon from Durban had come a long way.

Those early years were some of the happiest I had at the Club. It was partly just the thrill of working at the premier tennis club in the world, and partly the fact that as assistant you were involved in so many different aspects, albeit mainly at a fairly mundane level. In my first six months, I was thrown straight into The Championships and the boycott, and then, at the end of the summer, I went to America for the first time to the US Open and pre-tournament events. That was not a bad variety of things to have experienced in a new job.

I knew, when they asked me to become secretary six years later, that the responsibilities would be greater, and there would be more accountability. The tournament was getting bigger in commercial terms; we could not have stayed a relatively small club championship and at the same time have retained our premier position. We knew it would expand, just not by how much or how fast. It was challenging, and I was young enough to help to accommodate those changes. I had a sense that I would already be reflecting on some of my best memories, but equally, was excited at the prospect of growing the place and the business, without really knowing what it was going to become. I could not have anticipated the power of television deals and other commercial benefits, and the changes that lay around the corner.

Chapter 4

Balancing A Unique Brand

The All England Club's first mission statement is that 'We maintain The Championships as the premier tennis tournament in the world – and on grass.' The second is 'To enhance the unique quality, character and image of the Club and The Championships', while the third is 'To foster the best interests of tennis, both nationally and internationally.' These values drive everything that is done at the Club, and every commercial decision that is made.

The first two are inextricably linked in my mind. The Championships is the premier tennis tournament in the world because it is played at the Club, on grass. If we went to an artificial surface, I do not think that we would be half the tournament that we are. Similarly, it is the Club, with its history, its royal connections, its traditions and protocols, and its location, that provides the tournament with its unique qualities. If we were to compromise on any of these values, we would be chipping away at the very essence of what has made The Championships all that it is. Wimbledon could be a wealthier tournament: commercial opportunities have presented themselves that in the short term might have seemed very enticing – but would they have made for a better tournament? There is no question that they would not.

The challenge has been to skirt the line between generating the maximum revenue that we can for the good of British tennis, while being true to our mission statements.

When I became secretary of the Club in 1979, I inherited a legacy that was rich with history and tradition, but that had not been exposed fully to the rigours of commerciality. In my first year, the surplus from The Championships handed over to the Lawn Tennis Association – in effect the profit – was £306,737. In my last, it was £27m. The intervening years bore witness to the onward march of professional tennis, television's coming of age, and the marketing of sports stars and events in a way that changed the face of sport and tennis forever.

In the early seventies, the Club made use of two promotional consultants. The first was Bagenal Harvey Consultants, headed by Bagenal himself, an Irishman. The other was Mark McCormack, the US founder of the International Management Group (IMG).

Bagenal was one of the first sports agents, having made his name with Denis Compton, the Brylcreem boy. His success in fixing Compton's smiling face and gleaming hair on billboards across the country soon meant that others, such as footballers Jimmy Hill and Johnny Haynes were clamouring at his door. The Club's first involvement with him was with onsite promotions, or what we call presence agreements. That meant contracts that related to things that happened within the grounds. He was involved in negotiating the Robinsons Barley Water, catering, transport, and Slazenger balls contracts, for example. In 1972, he introduced us to British Leyland to help with the courtesy car service. Until then, we had hired in a fleet of chauffeur driven limousines, such as Daimlers and Princesses. They were smart black cars, but cost us quite a lot of money. Bagenal got British Leyland involved as our transport provider. In what was a new departure, they would provide the cars and drivers by and large free of charge, but in return would have their name on the sides of the cars and in the programmes.

Bagenal also helped extricate us from a ludicrous catering contract that had been agreed earlier. Unlike a lot of sporting events, we have not divided up our catering. During The Championships one firm is responsible for all onsite catering, whether for public, hospitality, Club, or players. At the time, the Club had signed up to a 21-year agreement with Town & County, where the only way to get out of it would have been on performance, and how can that be judged objectively? The contract itself was too onerous, so, with goodwill on both sides, we were able to recontract to our mutual benefit. Caterers now pay the Club a percentage of their turnover from their catering activities, and are obliged, where an official supplier deal has been negotiated, to supply Nescafé, or Lanson champagne, or whatever it may be.

Our first hospitality marquee arrived in 1975, courtesy of Bagenal, and was placed on one of our hard courts. We may not have been the first venue to have had hospitality marquees, but we were certainly one of the leaders. The decision was not an easy one to arrive at – there were concerns about adding another commercial element to Wimbledon, and also worries about the effect that erecting marquees would have on our red shale courts, which was where they would have to go. Concerns over the former were allayed, or at least lessened, by the fact that the marquee would be taken by Commercial Union, who were the main sponsors of the men's grand prix circuit. As such, they were already in the 'tennis family', and a more palatable choice. They did not have any direct involvement with The Championships, but because they ran the series around the world, were keen to be able to entertain guests. The experiment proved to be a success, and the use of marquees grew quite rapidly after that. We had eight hard courts, which were soon pressed into action. In a demonstration of the complexity of the relationship between the two, Bagenal sublet some of those hard court marquees to Mark McCormack for him to fill, as he had a huge client base and a great number of contacts.

Hospitality marquees have definitely been a good thing for Wimbledon. They are a very good money earner, which at the end of the day is important, not just for the LTA but in order to be able to keep ticket prices at a reasonable level. Secondly, people tend to dress up well, which adds stature to the event. I also think that to have big companies like ICI, Barclays and BP present is good for the British business image. Whatever the cynics might say, it is important for companies to invite clients to venues such as Wimbledon. The attraction of Wimbledon is that it appeals to both males and females. Demand for hospitality has always been incredibly high. We had around 90 per cent repeat business, which I am confident would have put us at the top of the list on that count. Wimbledon has also not suffered the fate of some venues, where the event becomes merely the excuse for a very boozy day out. We made it clear to the hosts that we wanted people to move out of the marquees as soon as play had started on the show courts. You cannot make people, but you can encourage them. Our primary reason was that we did not like seeing empty seats, but I think it helped on all fronts. We also did not do evening meals, just a few drinks before people were encouraged to go, half to three-quarters of an hour after play had finished.

In the seventies and early eighties there was quite a lot of gentle rivalry between IMG and Bagenal Harvey Consultants. Mark was much bigger even in those days. For the Club, it was important to diversify, as we did not want to put all our eggs in one basket. In fact, in the late eighties, we introduced another promotional consultant, Advantage International. They spent a few years trying to help us with areas like cameras, film, and security, but there was not the commercial demand there. We purposefully created a bit of tension between the agents because we wanted competitiveness. There was also a sense of suspicion about IMG and Mark McCormack because he was all-powerful. He controlled most of the players and a lot of the tournaments. He had a reputation for being ruthless, which led to a degree of misgiving amongst some of the committee. It was only when those people actually got to work with him that they really appreciated his true value.

Bagenal was a deeply respected person who had great integrity. He was very thorough and trustworthy. He was also quite short, and had a very high office chair and desk, so that when you sat in front of him, you were two or three feet below him. He was able to look down on you, which helped lend him a position of authority. And then he would stand up and the reality set in. I suspect I did not see Bagenal at his best, as I only became more involved in the eighties when he was getting on in years. He was quite a dour man. Which Irishman doesn't have a twinkle in his eye and a sense of humour, but he rather kept it to himself. He died in October 1987, aged seventy-three, by which time Geoff Bluett and a fellow director Geoffrey Irvine were already running the business.

Irvine was looking after a number of personalities, people like Michael Aspel and Richard Baker, but Geoff Bluett primarily, if not exclusively, worked on the Wimbledon account. He did so for thirty years before retiring in 2002.

Geoff, like Bagenal, was also a person of great integrity. Championships director Richard Grier and I often said to ourselves that Geoff appeared to be more loyal to the Club's ethics than we were. Whereas we were prepared to push the barriers a little more, whether on advertising, or the use of companies' names outside the Club, he was always a little more reticent. We had a say in the advertising strategy of our contractors if their aim was to link their advertising with Wimbledon. We needed to avoid any messaging that would conflict with our own standards, particularly when it came to programme advertising, but it rarely happened because of the role that Geoff played in keeping contractors on side and in line. All of his deals lasted. He was good for both Club and supplier. He was not a particularly hard negotiator in terms of financial return to the Club, but he was hugely respected on both sides. He did not drill down to the last penny – with many of the agreements, it was not just the fee that was our concern but also a very reliable service that would last. We did not think it was good to change our suppliers every three or five years, and were more interested in continuity. We might have got better financial rewards, but we all felt that as long as the money was fair and reasonable, the service from official suppliers was more important. It all links into being the premier tennis tournament in the world rather than the most profitable.

Geoff was and is a good tennis player. He probably played in the qualifying tournament at Wimbledon more often than any other player, and is a member of the Club. He has tennis at heart, and understands the Club, which from our point of view is very important. His first priority was to do what was in the best long-term interests of The Championships, which is quite a rare commodity for a commission-based agent, especially as he was working exclusively on the Wimbledon account. It was not as if he could see it as a loss-leading account, the value of which lay in its prestige factor, with money to be recouped else-where. It was almost like having another member of staff, although we would always choose to keep him as an agent. It is often useful, when negotiating, to be able to use a third party who could say things on our behalf that we might find difficult to say ourselves.

Another real bonus was that Geoff was able to set up a technical information service, which ultimately led to IBM coming on board in 1990. This was a service available for the media, giving them access to all the information they needed, whether results, historical information, or general facts and figures. Geoff was not professionally IT trained, but was really an IT buff and far more qualified than any of us in that area. He would come to us with his suggestions and ended up creating the system in a fairly piecemeal fashion, before it grew so big that we got IBM involved.

Geoff would involve himself more with the hospitality and

suppliers side of the account, while Bagenal was responsible for
negotiating the BBC contract for the UK, and Eurovision, covering
the rest of Europe, and Mark McCormack covered the rest of
the world.

The conflict between the two agencies was bound to happen.
Mark really wanted to be the one and only agent as far as the
Club and Championships were concerned. And certainly he was
starting to prove himself in terms of TV rights fees. He could
negotiate better television deals than Bagenal. He had more clout,
and was a tougher negotiator. Over the course of the years, during
the nineties, the role of Bagenal (and Advantage) diminished and
IMG became the dominant partner. It was not just the negotiating element, but the fact that deals were becoming increasingly
more complex and interlinked. For example, Bagenal had initiated our transport provider deal with British Leyland and then
Rover. Mark was later to bring along Hertz, but the deal to provide
the courtesy cars and drivers included a media package, whereby
Hertz could advertise themselves on US television and elsewhere
during the breaks in the Wimbledon coverage, which they were
very keen to do, and at very preferential rates. As a result of our
linkage with NBC, which Mark had also negotiated, the TV
company would provide us with a number of slots, which we
could use either for our own suppliers or for merchandising, or
promoting the museum. Companies wanting to buy advertising
in the US without the tie-in would have to pay significantly more.
Because Mark was negotiating the TV deals, it would have been
difficult for Bagenal to go to the TV companies and say, 'We want
Hertz to have some media slots in your TV coverage' when he
was not negotiating the TV deals.

As more and more elements started to overlap, it inevitably led
to the point at which IMG became our sole agent, which I am
sure was Mark's intention from the outset. Fortunately, this
coincided with Geoff Bluett's retirement.

*   *   *

Mark's and therefore IMG's involvement with the Club had started in 1968. The introduction came through Buzzer Hadingham, who at that time was not on the committee, but was chairman of Slazenger and as such knew all the top sports people. There were clear synergies between the people that Buzzer knew and the people represented by Mark, and so Buzzer suggested to our then chairman, Herman David, that he set up a meeting.

The first agreement that he brokered was for worldwide television excluding the UK and Europe. He also arranged the official annual film of The Championships. He thought it was firstly a wonderful record for the Club to have, and secondly that it could be sold as a video to airlines as in-flight entertainment, and to TV broadcasters for their pre-Wimbledon build-up. It was not something that the TV companies would be able to do themselves, as their rights are restricted to airing The Championships. It is actually not a great source of revenue, but has been useful, when selling TV rights, as a bonus that can be included in the package.

Our merchandising programme started up in the late seventies, and Mark played a central role. We had decided to go down the merchandising route as an alternative – albeit a far less lucrative one – to sponsorship. There is no question that our agreeing to, say, the Barclays Men's Singles would make more money than a merchandising agreement in Japan, but both Mark and Bagenal advised the committee that it would be wrong for Wimbledon to have direct sponsorship, whether of the tournament or events. It was not in our best interests that it became The Barclays Championships, or the Barclays Men's Singles Championships. As agents, they would have made infinitely more money. There are also very few events – such as the Olympics, the Masters golf and the FIFA World Cup – that do not have direct sponsorship (although they do have 'exclusive partners'), so I do not think they would have been on a hiding to nothing at least suggesting it. There are certainly no other tennis events without direct sponsorship, so in one sense, it would hardly have been radical. However, they genuinely believed it was in the best long-term interests of Wimbledon not to have sponsorship, and I guess they knew that they would get their commission over a longer period of time. And to be fair, they knew what the committee wanted them to say. Had they recommended it, the weakness might have come with the LTA delegates on the committee, as they are, quite rightly, far more attuned to the bottom line, as the LTA is the beneficiary of the annual surplus. You cannot deny the fact that if Mark had come to us with a huge financial incentive, it might have been tempting for some, but with the majority of the committee, the interest is solely to run the best Championships, and quality comes before money. The question does still occasionally get asked. I remember that when advertising first appeared on cricket boards, people were shocked, but within a few years, they had become completely used to it. Very few people look at the boards at Lords and say, 'Doesn't that look dreadful?' Possibly, if Wimbledon did go for direct sponsorship, after four or five years people would say, 'What was all the fuss about?' But I hope they never have to go down that route.

With sponsorship as a no-go area, merchandising was seen as a means of supplementing income. It also helped on the television side. With a strong merchandising programme in Japan, there were more licensees pushing to advertise on TV. We were able to offer them advertising slots on Japanese TV at a reduced rate. That had the mutual advantage of keeping their product and the Wimbledon name in the mind's eye all year round, rather than for just the two weeks of the tournament.

I mention Japan, as that is where we kicked off our merchandising strategy. It all started there because they have a huge interest in golf, so Mark was already familiar with the market. His career had started with Arnold Palmer, famously over a handshake, following which he had quickly signed Gary Player and Jack Nicklaus. With the Big Three golf players in his bag, Mark had tapped into the Japanese market, playing to their love of the game and their love of branded goods. He would go to Japan two or three times a year, and already had an office in Tokyo. The Arnold Palmer brand was well established, and Mark's experience from the golfing world, together with Japanese enthusiasm, made this an obvious place to start. As far as we were concerned, it had the added advantage of being a long way from home. If it all went wrong, people in the UK would not know about it and it would not matter too much. In fact, nothing could have been further from the truth. To our surprise, given that this was uncharted territory, our merchandising programme flourished right from the outset, and success in Japan soon attracted other potential licensees to follow suit.

Our first range of merchandising in Japan was not just tennis apparel, but also fashion items. Tennis kit would have been very limiting and, in any event, we could have struggled against very tough competition from the likes of Nike and Prince. Nevertheless, people in the UK might have thought it was strange to have Wimbledon on jewellery and leather goods, which was another reason for testing the concept far away.

The foundation of our Japanese licensing programme was with Renown, a large and well-respected clothing company, and their reputation and experience were contributory factors to our initial success. We also used one of the biggest advertising companies in the world, Dentsu, which controlled around 30 per cent of all mass media advertising in Japan. Our contact there, Mr Toshio Mamiya, was very helpful to us in promoting our marketing campaign and introducing us to the right people.

My first trip was in October 1979 for two weeks. Anyone who has been to Tokyo will know that it is quite an amazing place in itself. The traffic was unbelievable. You always had to leave at least an hour to get anywhere. All the drivers were very courteous, and there were never any hooting horns, mainly because everyone would just let everyone in. They apparently have a high rate of suicide among their chauffeurs, which I understand a little more now, having been there. They are very placid on the outside but underneath, they are clearly very frustrated.

The point of the trip was to see both our existing and potential licensees and to negotiate with television companies. However, as all the meetings were done through interpreters, it made it difficult to know how any meeting had gone. Mark had planned the whole thing in great detail. As part of the trip, we hosted an event that was rather like a mini-tradefair. We had taken over a host of memorabilia from the Wimbledon museum, which we had on display for potential licensees. The centrepiece was the two singles trophies. This was the first time they had ever left the country, and it caused me more than enough angst. They never left my sight, even occupying the seat next to me on the plane. Together, they are incredibly heavy, packed in wooden boxes, so it was no mean feat even getting them out of the Club, let alone all the way over to Japan. Still, they had the desired effect and were met with awe and astonishment by our licensees.

I was not the best ambassador for either Club or country, I am afraid to say, as I do not like Japanese food. I had to suffer it bravely because as I do not drink beer, I could not just wash it down. Raw fish is not my favourite and I did not want to know what was on the menu. The dinners were pretty formal and my discomfort was not helped by the fact that I also cannot use chopsticks. Still, there were some better memories from my trips to the Far East. Having endured a hair-raising trip to see our racket manufacturer, Kunnan, just outside Taipei, we were more than ready for some light-hearted distraction that evening. Chairman John Curry and I were taken by our hosts to a nightclub, where therapeutic relief came in the form of an introduction to Miss Taiwan. A most engaging young lady, as I recall.

I went to Japan once or twice a year for about seven years. I never minded the travelling. One of the joys of the job is that one moment you are dealing with the local authority on barriers around

Centre Court and the next you are off to Japan to see the head of NHK television. The variety I always found fascinating.

In 1985, we took on Rob McCowen as our marketing director. Rob had previous marketing experience at Slazenger, and took on the role extremely efficiently, doing (and continuing to do) an excellent job for the Club over the years. Along the way, he has earned the respect of those around him, including Mark McCormack. Once Rob had joined us, it made more sense to leave him to do most of the trips unless we were on the point of renegotiating a TV agreement. It was good at those times to turn up with the chairman and the chief executive to meet our opposite numbers and lend a bit of weight. It was something that the Japanese appreciated, and that we were happy to do, as it was never the case that we would leave IMG to do everything and then just sign the bottom line.

The importance of presenting rank and seniority to the Japanese was one of the reasons for the change of my job title during this period. The Club has been run by a secretary since 1868. However, the committee felt that the title was a little dated, and misunderstood in some areas: people who had been hoping to meet the chief executive were not so impressed when presented to the secretary, even if they were one and the same person. The Club felt that updating the title to chief executive would overcome this problem and it would also sit better with the titles of our gradually expanding executive.

From a standing start, our merchandising took off exponentially and is now a solid revenue base. Following the success in Japan, we initially set up our own shop in the Royal Arcade off Bond Street in London, which O. H. Hewett ran for us. It just sold Wimbledon merchandise throughout the year, and did well, but not well enough to justify the prohibitively high rental. We are still on Bond Street in Ralph Lauren Polo, and are also in Harrods. We have outlets at London Heathrow and Gatwick around the time of The Championships, and we are online all the time.

The biggest growth now is the shops that are on site. There are three major ones and nine smaller kiosks, manned by 250 staff. They are a significant contributor to our revenue. Funnily enough, the smaller the size of an item, the greater the volume contribution. In 2007, three of the best-selling items in the shops were mini-tennis-ball keyrings (19,899), twin wristbands (7,512), and Slazenger mini-balls (6,577).

The growth of the merchandising range was helped by some good creative input. With each suggestion, it was a question of weighing up the appropriateness of the association of the product with Wimbledon. We would look first at tennis related items, but we would not exclude luxury goods from companies such as Waterford. Always, quality was the most important thing. Ideas included Wimbledon liqueur, which was strawberries and cream flavour, and lemon-flavoured sugar, which we thought would sit well with the Japanese market. Another suggestion was putting our flying W logo on wheelnuts for cars, but the link to us was not obvious and we turned that down. The Club has currently about twenty-five licensed companies worldwide in eight international markets.

Quality was the guiding theme behind our official suppliers too. They are linked to us by association, and must therefore be companies of good pedigree and reputation. This is particularly true of those that will appear on Centre Court. The only advertising that we allow in front of camera is that of official suppliers whose products are needed for the actual running of the event and are therefore primarily for the benefit of the players and spectators. So on Centre Court, for example, we have Slazenger on the stop-netting, the umpire's chair, and on the balls. We have Robinsons on the umpire's chair, IBM for the speed of serve technology, and Rolex on the scoreboard as they provide the time mechanism. We would never have, say, a Kellogg's or a Mercedes Benz logo, because they would not be serving a purpose on court. A premium is paid for being on Centre Court. In an ideal world, we would like to have British companies as our official suppliers both on and off court, but it is just not possible these days. We would like to have British cars, but what is a British car? In any event, the perception with the UK market is that we are a fully international event, so I suspect that it is not really such a big deal.

Rolex is a prime example of the type of supplier with whom we are delighted to be associated. We had never had a clock supplier, and the introduction came through Mark, who was also engaged by Rolex as their agent. We were very happy, given that Rolex is one of the most famous watch- and clockmakers in the world. Rolex does not have many ambassadors. They are as select-ive in their endorsements as we are in our suppliers. It was a good match. Clocks are on site, however, and therefore a presence agreement and thus in Bagenal's domain. Bagenal could see that it was a prestigious deal to get Rolex, so he was not a stumbling block in any way, but he felt that he should get a slice of the action, so we ended up paying commission to both parties (although the same sum as if it had been one agent). It marked a watershed in terms of Mark's involvement with us, as it gave him an entrée to our presence agreements.

There was and is conflict in IMG's involvement. We probably could have got more money if we had gone to another clock or watch manufacturer, but Rolex invested a lot of money, not just in clocks on court, but also in putting up over 150 in offices in and around the grounds. They were a brand leader, had the best product and we got very good service from them. Money was not the most important thing – and in any event, for each renewal agreement since 1979, when the agreement was first brokered, it has gone up. They appreciate the importance of their position – part of their agreement is that no other company is to appear on the scoreboard. Philips, who have been involved with the design of the scoreboard have made approaches but have not been permitted to put their name on it.

Rolex is not a straightforward business. It is practically run by one person, first Andre Heiniger, and then his son Patrick, who became managing director in 1992 when Andre became chairman. You do not deal with anyone else at senior level. They believe in absolute discretion and their top executives hardly ever give interviews, believing that the product can speak for itself.

We went to Geneva several times for the renewal agreements, and Andre Heiniger was keen to entertain us while we cemented the deal. We would look at the factory in the morning, and then in the evening go to a nice restaurant for dinner. One time we went to a place that had a private dining area upstairs. There were ten or twelve of us, and at the end of a very good evening, we were saying our goodbyes on the stairs when suddenly, Andre came hurtling past me. I was halfway down the stairs and he had obviously tripped at the top, and proceeded to fall down the entire flight. He lay motionless at the bottom, out cold, and everyone's first assumption was that he was dead. The only two people who reacted were John Curry's wife Anne, who was a nurse, and me. I always carry a diary that is packed full of useless bits of information, so, on appraising the situation, I sprang into action, pulling out the little black book and reading the following to Anne: 'If the face is pale raise the tail. If the face is red, raise the head. Only give mouth to mouth if the casualty is not breathing.' I am very pleased to report that, thanks to the proffering of these timely pearls of wisdom, he survived and was taken away in an ambulance.

Thanks to our merchandising, TV, hospitality and other commercial contracts, our surplus grew exponentially during my time as chief executive. Mark McCormack played a fundamental role in that growth and we owe him a great deal. He seemed to know all the right people, and was a wonderful networker, whether with the heads of multimillion-pound companies or sport stars. If you have Arnold Palmer as your first client, followed by Player and Nicklaus, that is a pretty good start to building up an influential circle. Going on to represent the Pope and Margaret Thatcher meant that he must have had something going for him. He was very loyal to the high quality team around him, many of whom returned that loyalty and were around for a long time. The connections that he had were very important and useful to us, and he was a great negotiator. We were always very glad to have him on our team rather than on the other side of the fence. I remember going to a Eurovision meeting in Paris, where he really tore strips off one person because they were offering what he thought was a derisory amount. It was not particularly nice to watch, but it was interesting to see him at work when confronting the other side in a negotiation. His face would puff up and he would snarl across the table; 'How can you offer such a paltry amount for Wimbledon when you're paying this for a vastly inferior event? Get real.' Whether he had actually lost his temper, or deliberately worked himself up to that state I do not know, but he seemed to take it as a personal affront.

His memory was amazing, helped by his ever-present 24-month diary, as was his attention to detail. It was quite extraordinary, given that he also always had his eyes on the bigger picture, and had a hugely creative bent. It took a good deal of ingenuity to put together the TV, merchandising and multimedia packages that he did. We asked him early on for his thoughts on how the Centre Court could be used for other purposes. His suggestions were Viennese horseriding, concerts, boxing and bicycle racing, which were pretty left field! We did actually get close to putting on the odd concert, notably Barbra Streisand. There are certain people who say they will not do concerts unless they are held in a very striking venue, and I think the Club fits that bill. In the end, however, we decided that the grass is so fundamental to us, that even if we had a structure whereby we had a temporary surface raised above the ground, we would still be too worried about what the effect would be on the court.

Mark was very straight with us, and there was never any question of any double-dealing, or playing one side off against the other. I think those who knew him and dealt with him believed him when he said that Wimbledon was his favourite client. We had a special relationship. We trusted him and treated him as a friend as well as a business partner. I think that was probably quite apparent when it came to discussing his commission fee. He would often say to us on some deals, 'I trust you, I just want you to be fair to us. You tell me what you think is a fair commission,' as he was so keen to keep in with the Club and to act for us on as many fronts as possible. Mark used to be known as the 30 per cent man. If he sold an ashtray for you he would expect 30 per cent. We never agreed with that principle across the board and that was not the basis of our relationship with him. If an agent has sold your rights for £100,000, then the next time you are interested in what they can get over and above the £100,000. So we were more interested in rewarding well for what could be achieved over the base rate – but it was hardly ever formalised, it was more of a private word and coming to an arrangement each time. Some of the more straightforward arrangements were straight percentages and there was no quibbling. That was true of the merchandising and official supplier agreements. But with Mark, everything was always done very amicably. It was the extension of the man who started his business on a handshake. Since he died in 2003, things have gone onto a more formal footing, and I would say have got a bit more competitive.

The personal attention that we received was remarkable, given the size of IMG and the extent of Mark's workload. No matter what the subject, we could always make contact with him. We also had structured formal meetings set in place twice a year. Invariably at these meetings, he would present me with an impressive cheque, which he knew would set the right tone for the meeting and any subsequent negotiations. The fact was that I should have said, but could never quite bring myself to say, 'You owed me that cheque four weeks ago!' You knew that you were being treated to some classic textbook behaviour taken straight from one of his own management books, probably *What They Don't Teach You at Harvard Business School.*

Mark was great on US television deals, which was probably where he served us best, and in areas such as Japan where not everyone has an expertise, especially in the formative years. He had huge respect from people like Dick Ebersol, NBC Sports & Olympics chairman, or Donald Dell, head of sports marketing agency ProServ. Donald was probably Mark's biggest competitor, yet he had nothing but respect for him. It was the same with Kerry Packer, who became a close friend, despite many tough negotiations with him over rights fees for Channel 9 in Australia.

On a personal level, Mark was good company, although perhaps happiest with the camaraderie of other men. He had a boyish sense of humour and would often laugh at his own jokes, which was quite endearing. He was very loyal and generous to his friends. He was always going around with a camera, taking pictures. Then he would let you have copies the following week of whatever he had taken.

Golf was his first love, but he enjoyed his tennis. Jenny and I used to play doubles with him when he was in London. He would want to play at 7.30 or 8 in the morning, when most people are still thinking about breakfast, and would line himself up with a very decent partner. He would quite often play with Sharon Walsh who was a former US Wightman Cup player. It was the same at the IMG retreats, held once a year for his staff. There was always a tennis tournament, and Mark, strangely, would always find himself partnered with one of the best employees. John Curry and I played with him while we were in Tokyo once, and he had Virginia Wade partner him (another of his clients), thinking he would see us off. He had not reckoned on my service, however. Years before, in 1979, I had watched the Wimbledon final between Borg and Tanner and realised that I would never be able to serve that well. I am not sure why it took me that long to come to the realisation, but my mind was made up, and from the following day onwards I have served underarm. I have honed the technique quite well, and I played someone recently who likened me to the

Shane Warne of the tennis court, which I was quite pleased with. I suspect our game might also have been helped by the fact that Virginia played very sensibly and did not try to dominate, which she could have done easily. In the event, we won and Mark was not best impressed. He tried to get a repeat match, but John managed to avoid it.

In latter years he mellowed as a person a great deal. He was married twice and his second wife, Betsy Nagelsen, is a lovely person and was very good for him. They had a child together, Maggie, born in 1997 (on a very auspicious date – my birthday). Mark sent me pictures together with a note saying, 'We'd like to request a wild card into the women's singles Championships 2015 for Maggie McCormack. Although she only weighs 7lb 7ozs and is only 19.5 inches tall, she is in perfect health, very athletic, and her mother is sure that she is the most beautiful baby that was ever born.' It was a recurring theme. I was sent another photo of her aged four, holding a racket, with the message, 'Maggie has only 12 more years before her wild card request. As you can see she has started practising.'

Maggie has in fact already been introduced to Wimbledon, although it was an inauspicious start. Mark had initiated the deal with Working Title for the film *Wimbledon* to be shot at the Club in 2003. He thought it would be nice if Maggie could have a part to play. Without ruining the plot, the film ends with a small child, and it was agreed that Maggie could play the part. She was flown over on Concorde, but when she arrived, she refused point-blank to do it. She threw a complete tantrum, and went back home, on Concorde, never having faced the camera. Maggie does in fact appear, alternative arrangements having been made for filming on a date to which she was better disposed!

Mark never wanted to deal with too many people at the Club, so it was generally only the chairman, myself, and marketing director Rob McCowen. I think that lack of exposure meant that a number of other people were suspicious of him being too powerful, or too commercial, or having too many conflicts of interests. That was true of the LTA, where he offered to help a number of times but was turned down, and I know that he did not have a particularly comfortable time at the Royal and Ancient Golf Club, where the then secretary Keith McKenzie either did not trust him or did not like him. I suspect that, again, it was probably because McKenzie thought him too commercial and that he would take the Open down a route that he, McKenzie, did not want to go. I never asked as it was not my business, but I know that there was conflict between the two. I could never see Mark taking us down the wrong route, as we managed the agent, rather than the agent managing the Club. It is healthy for a club, whether us or the R&A, to be wary of an organisation as big as IMG, but, with good control from the Club, Mark did so much for the prosperity of Wimbledon, especially in the early years. People who were suspicious of his empire have now come to realise that his contribution was immense. Even if they did not have direct contact with him, the numbers speak for themselves.

In January 2003, we were renegotiating our US television contracts, and Mark would call me on a regular basis to tell me about progress. He called me on the 9th and 13th, as he said he would. He was always meticulous about sticking to times and actions. He said he would call again on the 15th. When he did not ring, I thought it was strange and very out of character. It transpired that the day before, he had had a cardiac arrest and gone into a coma. He remained in a coma for four months until he died in May. Our last conversation was totally work-related. It was terribly sad and so unexpected. He had recently had a successful medical check-up and then had a blemish removed from his face, but something subsequently went horribly wrong.

John Curry, Tim Phillips and I went to New York for the funeral. It was a very special occasion with some lovely addresses from Arnold Palmer, Jean-Claude Killy, Betsy and his son Todd. Later in the year, during The Championships, IMG put on a service

at Hampton Court Palace. The company wanted to do something in Europe to mark his life, and used Wimbledon as a date at
which many people would be in town. Mark had been made an
honorary member of the Club in 1993, and his family wondered
if there was some way in which Mark's name could be remembered there. It was quite delicate, as he had not been known by
too many people, but I am happy to say that the new look Centre
Court has provided that opportunity. When Maggie comes to play
at her first Wimbledon, she will be able to pop into the Mark
McCormack hospitality suite and see her father's name embla-
zoned there.

Players have told me that Wimbledon is the tournament that they
want to win above all others. It is not necessarily the one that
they enjoy the most, as many of them are not used to playing on
grass, but it is the one that they would most like to have on their
CV. David Miller, the well-known sports writer, summed it up
beautifully when he wrote: 'What characterises Wimbledon's
enduring appeal and unique sporting status is that, like the
Olympic marathon or Everest, it remains greater than those who
conquer it.' It is for these very reasons that we strive so hard to
retain the traditions – the grass, the whites, the royal presentations, the lack of sponsorship, the notion that players and tennis
must come first – in a commercial era. And I believe our efforts
are appreciated by public and players alike. As Serena Williams
says: 'I love Wimbledon so much. Everybody in their lifetime
should go to Wimbledon. It's like seeing one of the seven wonders
of the world. I feel so honoured to be part of Wimbledon history
for the rest of my life. The atmosphere, the tradition, the crowd,
the village, everyone wearing white, the grass – so clean and crisp.'
On a slightly more embarrassing note, she went on to say: 'And
that announcer! I'm telling ya. I go really insane when I hear him
say, "Ladies and gentleman, welcome to the fifth day of The
Wimbledon Championships."' But more of him later.

Chapter 5

The Leading Player on
A Global Stage

Jimmy Connors once compared the US Open with Wimbledon by saying: 'New Yorkers love it when you spill your guts out there. You spill your guts out at Wimbledon, they make you stop and clean it up.' I am not sure that we would include that description in any promotional material, but the swaggering New Yorker has a point. It would harm the courts after all.

I never particularly looked forward to going to the US Open. The heat and humidity in late August made New York an uncomfortable place to be generally, and the location of Flushing Meadows just exacerbated things. Yet despite everything that I say, the Americans are very friendly, and very hospitable. In all honesty, I always enjoyed myself more than I thought I would, once I had arrived.

The US Open was moved to Flushing Meadows in 1978, as the tournament had outgrown its former home, the West Side Tennis Club (commonly known as Forest Hills), with no possibility for expansion. The new site had been the venue for a world tradefair back in 1964, but since then had been left to go to rack and ruin. The state highways converge there, and it is very close to La Guardia airport, so close in fact that when planes used to fly over the courts, you almost felt as if you could touch them. Every ninety seconds. As a player it was impossible to hear the ball on the racket, and incredibly taxing on the concentration. Despite the plane interference detracting considerably from the ambience of the event, Flushing Meadows remained on the flight path for a number of years. Then David Dinkins was elected Mayor of New York. He was a big tennis fan and managed to do a deal whereby, save for an emergency, flights were diverted for the fortnight. That improved things considerably.

Planes aside, the US Open is run on very different lines from Wimbledon. Each Grand Slam has changed and become more commercial, but none more so than the US Open. When it was played on grass at the West Side Tennis Club, it was an event not dissimilar to our own. West Side was host to the tournament from 1915 to 1977, although it was known as the US Nationals until 1968. I first went there in 1973, my first year at the Club, and was struck by the similarity to Wimbledon. That may have been because it was played at a members' lawn tennis club, or maybe it was just because, thirty-six years ago, everything was much more low key.

I had been invited over by our referee Fred Hoyles. Fred had been asked by Gene Scott (a former US Davis Cup player and, through his outspoken views in his own tennis magazine, the self-appointed conscience of US tennis) to referee one of the pre-US Open grass court tournaments in South Orange, New Jersey. Gene was director and co-owner of the tournament. Fred agreed on condition that he could take me as an assistant. I had to take the trip as holiday time, but did not begrudge that at all, given the experience I had.

Fred and I first went to the Merion Cricket Club in Philadelphia (they play tennis there too) and then after South Orange, we went on to the US Open in New York for the fortnight. I remember the draw being held in the United Nations building in New York, which was a pretty impressive backdrop. The whole thing was a wonderful experience, and memorable in that it was the last time that the US was played on grass at West Side. To be honest, the courts were not the best quality. Grass in the US is not rooted. It is very soft and breaks up very easily. I watched a match at Merion between, I believe, Buster Mottram and Vijay Amritraj. As one of them picked up a whole sod of turf from the middle of the court and carried it back to the stop netting, one spectator said to another, 'Gee Bob, it looks like South Vietnam out there.' It just peeled like an orange. One of the other things that amused me was watching officials running around with a fire-extinguisher-type device on finals day at Forest Hills, spraying green paint on the baselines to make it look better for TV. I would love to be there to watch the reaction from Wimbledon's head groundsman, were the same treatment suggested for Centre Court.

The moves away from grass and from Forest Hills were prompted by a fear of losing the US Open. West Side Tennis Club was inhibited by residential developments and train tracks all around. It was clear that there was not enough room for the expansion and development needed to keep pace with increasing commercial demands, and the grass surface was proving tricky to retain at world class standard. The first move was to American green clay, alternatively and less appealingly known as modsod. Then came the move in 1978 to Flushing Meadows, also in the district of Queens, and another change of surface to a hard court, Deco turf.

Flushing Meadows is the home of the US National Tennis Centre, renamed the Billie Jean King National Tennis Centre in 2006. When the tournament first moved there, the Louis Armstrong stadium was used as their main court, seating around 15,000 spectators. Subsequently, in 1997, they created the Arthur Ashe stadium, which had greater capacity. The top layers were then taken off the Louis Armstrong stadium, which became their equivalent No. 1 Court, seating around 10,000. The Arthur Ashe stadium now dominates the grounds, as the biggest purpose built tennis venue in the world. It is colossal. It seats around 23,000 people, with the stands rising to a phenomenal height. I took Jenny up there once. Granted, she does suffer from vertigo, but she had to climb up the steps on her hands and knees to the top because it is so high and so steep and totally exposed. There is no protection for spectators from either rain or sun. There are also no court covers, so if it does start raining, court staff get down on their hands and knees with towels to rub the surface dry. They used to have these contraptions that looked like hairdryers, but they now have slightly bigger machines, which are still very noisy. I have never understood why they do not use covers.

On the up side, so to speak, the views to be had from the top of the stadium are spectacular. Those that make it up the innumerable flights of steps are rewarded with a magnificent view over the Manhattan skyline, particularly in the early evening, when the skyscrapers that dominate the landscape are set against the fading hue of the setting sun. The stadium is an incredible place to be when it is full. The atmosphere created during some of the night matches, or the finals, takes some beating. When Connors was at his best, firing up the crowd, it was electric.

However, the stadium is seldom ever full. Invariably, even if all the seats have been sold, people will not stay there the whole time. Our belief was always that a stadium for more than 15,000 spectators is not suitable for watching tennis, given the speed of the game and the size of the ball. From the top of the Arthur Ashe stadium, it is impossible even to tell whether the players are male or female. We would also much rather see our courts nearly full as often as possible. It does not provide much sense of occasion when players are performing to rows of empty seats.

The other striking difference between the US Open and Wimbledon is that at the former scheduling is primarily geared towards television and the viewers' needs. At Wimbledon, first and foremost, the aim is to be fair to the players. Every effort is made to give players who have made it through to the second week rest days on alternate days. At the US, they play the semis of the men's singles on Saturday and the final on Sunday, so there is no respite. That is particularly hard for the person playing the second semi-final, especially if it has turned into a five-set marathon. Also, the timing of the singles finals can vary, depending on other sporting events being covered by TV. At Wimbledon, players *know* that the final will start at 2 p.m. In the US, they tell the players that they will not be playing before 4 p.m., but they cannot give them a precise time, as it has to fit in after other sporting events that may be running late. They are far more beholden to TV; they have a senior executive of CBS at their match scheduling meeting. We will not let TV executives into a committee room forum, although we will hear their views beforehand. Ironically, we believe the proportion of the total revenue generated by TV income is greater at Wimbledon than the other Grand Slams. Wimbledon does not have sponsorship income to the same degree as the other three, and there are no night sessions which would increase spectator revenue, but we still would not give TV companies that level of input.

Officials at the US Open describe the tournament as a sporting and entertainment spectacular. I would not deny that the Grand Slams are in the entertainment business, but we would always say that the integrity of the game must come first, before the entertainment factor. I think we have stood the test of time in that respect, and, importantly, I think it is what people expect of Wimbledon. The way that the US Open is run is right for Flushing Meadows and the hustle and bustle and vibrancy of New York, but it would not be right for Wimbledon. I am not even sure that it would be right for California. At the US Open they have had stars from music, stage and screen performing throughout the event, and sometimes music playing at the change of ends. They have live bands playing in the main piazza, which is very close to the outside courts. One year that I was there, the juniors' singles final was being played on one of those courts with a jazz band at full tilt right beside them. I asked an official, 'How come that band is performing when there is a final being played? What about respect for the junior players?' He just shrugged and said that they would stop when the men's singles final started in the main stadium, and in the meantime people were enjoying the music while eating their pizzas. We always maintained that a player's interest comes first in those situations. If a player cannot hear the umpire or the ball on the strings of his racket because of the music, that is just not good enough. We constantly monitor the sound system on Aorangi Terrace (better known as Henman Hill) to make sure that it does not disturb Courts 18 and 19.

I think the preference towards the spectacle rather than the player is what prompts comments such as the following from Boris Becker: 'Once you've finished playing your two weeks in New York, you feel happy . . . that you have survived.' No doubt Stan Smith echoed that sentiment, although his problem was a more physical challenge. At the US Open, ball boys are trained to fling the balls overarm, baseball style, which is the quickest way. They throw them incredibly fast and balls are flying across the court very efficiently. On this occasion Stan Smith was playing Onny Parun, it was the final game, and Smith was about to serve when a ball flew across the net and caught him right on the ear. It almost took him out, but he managed to shake off the effects and go on and win the match. I think 'a bit peeved' would have been a polite description at the time.

Nonetheless, players do enjoy playing there, not least because traditionally the tournament offers the greatest prize money. Everything is just generally bigger in the US – bigger prize money, bigger stadia, even bigger arrivals. I looked on in amazement when President Bill Clinton came to watch the women's singles final between Venus Williams and Lindsay Davenport, supported by a cavalcade of twenty-eight vehicles. Because the Arthur Ashe stadium is so big, they have much more room under the bowl than is available under Centre Court. They can fit in many more facilities. Certainly the players' lounge area is more extensive. I guess it is all bigger, but not necessarily better. We are often comparing facilities. Their press room was probably the best in the world until we built our Millennium Building. In a few years' time, I am sure they will upgrade and it will be better again. But that is progress and to be expected.

I would go every year to the US Open, as with each of the Grand Slams, to attend the Grand Slam Committee meeting. Before the committee was formed, the chairmen would just meet informally at the respective Grand Slams. At the time, men's professional tennis was governed by the Men's International Professional Tennis Council (MIPTC), formed in 1983. The council comprised three player reps, three tournament reps and three International Tennis Federation (ITF) reps. The first administrator was Marshall Happer III, a big man and a US lawyer. He was joined by Bill Babcock, again a lawyer, who played on the ATP circuit for a while.

In 1989, the Association of Tennis Professionals (ATP), the male players' union, was pretty dissatisfied with the way that the MIPTC was running professional tennis. They wanted to meet all their players during the US Open to gauge opinion and levels of discontent. The US Tennis Association president felt he wanted no part of it and barred the meeting from taking place on site. Sensing a fantastic publicity coup, the ATP instead held the meeting in the car park, thus portraying themselves as the aggrieved party. The man running the show at the ATP was the media-savvy Hamilton Jordan, who had previously run Jimmy Carter's successful US presidential election campaign.

As a result, the MIPTC was disbanded, and the ATP launched its own ATP Tour, and the Challenger Circuit. It sidelined the Grand Slams who did their own thing, while the ITF ran junior tennis and the development of the game, and small satellite tournaments with the ATP. That situation still exists today.

In order to present themselves as a more effective united front

to the ATP, the four Grand Slams formalised the existing arrangements with the chairmen and created the Grand Slam Committee
in 1989. Bill Babcock became the administrator, and still is. It was
set up at ITF headquarters in London. The Committee meets at
least five times a year, at the four Grand Slams and the year-end
Tennis Masters Cup (formerly the Grand Slam Cup). The host
Grand Slam chairman decides on the dates and sets the agenda.
We invite the head of the ATP and the female union, the Women's
Tennis Association (WTA) to make separate appearances, and
hear their comments and concerns. Generally, all is fairly amicable
but there have been exceptions.

In 2003, the ATP came to the conclusion that the Grand Slams
were making vastly increased amounts of money from their events
and that the players were not getting their fair share. They likened
themselves to American baseball and basketball players, and
demanded a 50 per cent rise in prize money. The focal point on
prize money issues is always the winner's pot, though it is fair to
say that the Wimbledon champion immediately becomes a million-
aire, irrespective of whether you pay him one dollar or a million.
The runner-up also receives a significant sum, but does not get
the same kudos or endorsements as the winner, and neither obviously does anyone else below that. In that sense, arguments about
prize money really concern the people lower down the rankings,
who are dependent on the sum itself, but it is the winner who is
the figurehead in the argument. That is the benchmark from
where these discussions start.

The 50 per cent demand was raised at the French Open, and
the threat was that if we failed to meet it, there would be a boycott
of a future Grand Slam, in all likelihood Wimbledon or the US
Open, given their greater resilience than the Australian Open.
However, in asking for its price hike, the ATP had ignored the fact
that at all the Grand Slams, all the money goes back into
the national associations for the furtherance of the game, and not
into promoters' hands. We showed what we did with the money

and how we improved things, not just at grass roots, but at a professional level. Secondly, they had to realise that if we agreed to a 50 per cent rise for the men, we would have to do the same for the women, and we certainly did not have the funds for both. Because it was such an outrageous request, it made it easier to say No, although we tried to be accommodating and ask if there was any way in which we could help if they felt undervalued. They had brought in consultants to put together some figures supporting their cause, but in the end they sensed that we would not give way and that they would have to take it to the wire and go ahead with the boycott. Good sense prevailed, although it took nine months.

The committee has brought the Grand Slams closer together than ever before. They are now much more similar. For most people, that is a good thing and has made the group stronger. On the negative side, twenty-five years ago, if Wimbledon had said we wanted to do something, we would have done it and there would have been no argument, but now no Grand Slam can act quite so unilaterally. Some differences remain – anti-trust laws, for example, prevent any discussions on prize money.

The people present are the four Grand Slam chairmen, four chief executives, the president of the ITF, and Bill Babcock. The US also brings its vice-president who will take over, as the USTA president's term of office is just two years. We would discuss things like ATP and WTA demands, the deduction of prize money into players' pension schemes, and changes to the rules. We would also keep an eye on combined events, where men and women play at the same tournament, which might therefore pose a threat to Grand Slams. The general agreement was that the ATP and WTA limit the number of combined events that they hold, in return for the Grand Slams honouring their ranking system.

Quite a lot of the debate would be on the agreements with the ATP and WTA, for example over rankings, or the year-end events, calendar issues, or the Grand Slam Development Fund, more of which later.

For me, there was also real value in the meetings held with the other chief executives, normally the day before the committee meeting. We were able to go through all the logistical things that a Grand Slam offers players, such as transport, or medical staff. This helped us prevent players, agents or the media trying to play us off one against the other. It was quite common for someone to claim, for example, that they had just agreed with Australia that there should be an increase in the food allowance, or the per diem allowance (which goes as a contribution towards their hotel rooms), and so would we do the same? Or for TV directors to compare notes on facilities provided. It was a great help to have the facts in front of you to make sure that you were keeping ahead of the game. It did not mean that you had to follow suit. On something like ticket allocation, it would be impossible for us to be as generous as the Australians with the number of tickets we can give to players or their families, as our demand is much greater. On the public ballot, only one in five or six is successful. But forewarned is forearmed in terms of negotiations. In crude terms, we were happy to share information on how much we were paying for things, but not how much we were getting.

One of the committee's greatest assets was putting a formal structure around cementing relationships. Even if weighty decisions were not made, we were more comfortable about comparing notes and ringing up counterparts throughout the year. In terms of post-war Grand Slam tennis, Wimbledon has historically been the leader politically, pushing the Open tennis era forward. It remained at the helm until the creation of the committee levelled the playing field. There now has to be a unanimous decision on voting and there have been tricky moments with differences of opinion. It was not even plain sailing over the 50 per cent pay hike demand, with some members holding out more than others. In that particular instance, our chairman Tim Phillips was very definite and very strong. He rightly pointed out how much prize money had already increased since Open tennis – far in excess of inflation.

Through it all, Bill Babcock did a tremendous job. He was employed by the ITF but seconded as Grand Slam administrator. He needed a lot of tact and was serving a lot of masters. He did it well and with good humour.

The tennis year, which follows the calendar year, starts with the Australian Open. I did not make it over there until 1990, when I had already been chief executive for seven years. The Grand Slam Committee was not established until 1989, and prior to that, it had only been the Club chairman that made the journey. The view was that Australia was a long haul and it was not worth the expenditure. In the eighties the Australian Open was going through a low period. It was the poor relation of the four Grand Slams. They paid much less prize money, and often did not attract all the best players to go down there, partly because of the time of year, being around Christmas and New Year, and partly because of the distance. The feeling was, 'What will we learn from it?' I think it was a slightly blinkered view. There are four Grand Slam tournaments and we need to keep a close eye on what each of them is doing: you can learn on either front – things that you would want to copy or things that you think are totally wrong that you would not want to bring back. It is also not just the formal meetings, but all the other official or unofficial meetings that take place. All the key people who run tennis tend to congregate at the Grand Slams, in much the same way that those involved in running golf will go to the four majors.

My first trip was with Jenny and we both discovered that to go to Australia in January in the middle of the English winter is really quite appealing. I always stayed at the Hilton Hotel in Melbourne. It is just a ten-minute walk from there through a park to the tennis centre. The walk in the morning sunshine was a very nice way to start the day. The hotel is also adjacent to the Melbourne Cricket Ground, which is a huge stadium in its own right. It is a good location, frequented by many of the junior players and officials. The seniors tended to head downtown into the centre of Melbourne. The manager of the hotel, an Austrian, was a very keen tennis fan who was always very hospitable to tennis visitors from abroad. The Australians always seem such wonderful, friendly people. I could not fathom that out at first, as I thought all Australians had a dislike of the British. But I have never found that to be true. The Australians love the English – as long as they know they are not going to stay.

The group of Australian tennis players who were in their prime in the fifties, sixties, and seventies, were wonderful personalities who never took themselves too seriously off court. Players such as Sedgman, Hoad, Cooper, Fraser, Emerson, Fletcher and Newcombe liked to have a good beer after their tennis, and certainly that has not diminished over the years. Just sitting and being with those great players is wonderful. The best is when you have two of them talking and reminiscing over their playing days, and you are a fly on the wall, listening in. It was interesting hearing them comparing their lives with the players of today. Their feeling is that they had more fun. It was not necessarily better. The travelling was much harder, going by ship, which took days, but it was less intense. The hospitality given to us is reciprocated at Wimbledon, when Neale Fraser and his wife Thea come to stay with Jenny and me during the tournament.

The Australian Open has changed enormously since their day. The principal reason is that, similar to the US Open, it has moved from a private members' lawn tennis club to the National Tennis Centre in Melbourne Park, at the same time moving from grass to rebound ace surface (now plexicushion).

Of the four Grand Slams, the Australian Open is the youngest, having started in 1905. It rotated around the states before settling in Melbourne in 1972. However, it was only at Kooyong tennis club for seventeen years before it outgrew the site. It had a railway track on one side and a road on the other, and there just was not the room for expansion. I suspect the move followed a degree of

The crowd and officials revel in the atmosphere on the first Middle Sunday in 1991.
For me, it was my worst and best day.

Bradfield College tennis team with front row left to right: myself, Tim and Tony Billington, uncles of Tim Henman.

The Club's permanent and temporary office staff in the 1970s, still small enough to fit around one desk: myself with Enid Stopka (front left), Major David Mills (centre), and Joyce Combe (extreme right).

The Queen presenting the Ladies' Singles salvers to Virginia Wade in 1977. This was one of my favourite memories.

One of the Club's earlier licensing receptions in Japan in the 1980s. Left to right: John Feaver, Alan and Jill Mills, Virginia Wade and Mark McCormack.

The Lawn Tennis Association's official sponsors' marquee in the 1980s. Wimbledon was one of the first venues to accept corporate hospitality.

Rolex, our official supplier since 1979.

Philippe Chatrier with himself.

The Millennium
Building.

(*Below*) The Centre
Court with the old
roof and (*below right*)
part of the new
sliding roof in place.

The new No.1 Court.

Pete Sampras savours victory with John Curry and myself.

Dino Martin, Ali MacGraw and Pancho Gonzales add some Hollywood glamour to Wimbledon while filming *Players* in 1978 in front of the Centre Court.

The 75th Anniversary of the Diocese of Southwark in July 1980.
One of the more unusual events on Centre Court.

Björn Borg.
A Wimbledon legend.

(*Above right*) John McEnroe.
Another of the all-time greats.

Mirka Varinec and Roger
Federer – not only one of the
best ever players, but also a
great ambassador for tennis.

Martina Navratilova with Alan Mills and myself.

tension between the National Tennis Association and the club, with the former feeling that revenue was being limited by the restraints on ground space. Kooyong was a beautiful setting, but in truth it was not a venue on a par with the other Grand Slam sites in terms of size and facilities.

The tournament changed very significantly with the move. Moving from grass was abhorrent to many Australians, and there was a lot of negative reaction. However, there could be no going back, as the National Tennis Association did a deal with the city of Melbourne and State of Victoria to build the National Tennis Centre. In order to fund the venue, it had to be capable of being used throughout the year, and not just for tennis events, but for concerts or other major events. Hence the stadium has a sliding roof and an artificial surface better able to withstand heavy usage. It was a brave decision, but a good one. They realised they could not retain their Grand Slam status unless they moved on. It is a very tough market in Australia in any event. They are tucked away in the south-east corner of the world and it is quite diffi-cult for them to attract major sponsors and visitors. When they moved to Melbourne Park, Ford was the main sponsor. Their name was everywhere so it was very much the Ford Australian Open. Without their support they would have floundered, and in that respect they were a tremendous boon.

For the players, the timing is tough. If they want to be properly prepared for a Grand Slam, they need to play a few tournaments beforehand. In Australia, that means playing immediately after Christmas. At one point it was clear that the tournament was being better supported by the women players, and it was a key factor in the Australians' decision to give equal prize money to the women. Their support deserved reward and recognition, even if the sums involved were smaller than elsewhere.

They are still the smallest of the four Grand Slams in terms of prize money, and I guess income stream. However, they have no lesser status. There was a distinct period when the tournament

went into a bit of a trough in terms of player attendance, profile
and revenue. One of the reasons that it was able to pull itself back
out was because the other Grand Slams (led by All England Club
chairman John Curry) rallied together and agreed that, irrespective of prize money, the winners of the tournament should receive
the same number of rankings points as any other Grand Slam.
This was particularly important, as the Grand Slams, by agreement with the ATP and WTA, carry more rankings points than
any other professional tournament, and their status as the premier
events in the tennis calendar is assured.

The Australian Open always has good attendance figures,
primarily because they have a daytime and night-time session, as
does the US. The night-time session starts around 7 or 7.30, but
is usually just on their centre court. Play is held at night up until
around the second Thursday, with just one session for the last few
days. It generates extra seat revenue, but its primary purpose is
for television. It is certainly not necessary in terms of scheduling.
Having a day and night session means that either one or the other
will suit the US or European TV market. If you are a US player
being covered by a US network, the organisers would take that
into account when scheduling events. It is just one of the considerations, but probably quite high. Doing an order of play is not
straightforward. There are twenty-eight different factors that our
referee needs to consider when compiling the order of play. In a
nutshell, he or she needs to consider the interests of players,
spectators and the media while at the same time aiming to
complete the tournament on time.

One advantage of the night session is that it is cooler, but some
players never take to it. Borg hardly ever won a night match. I
am not sure whether he did not like the lights, or it might have
been that he always came up against someone like Connors who
whipped the crowd up. It tends to be more raucous at night, and
there is generally more of an atmosphere. If there are only two
matches scheduled, you can expect everyone to be there all the

time. If you buy a centre court ticket for the day, you might wander off and go and watch something else for a bit.

It is interesting, and rewarding, to watch a major sporting event in a country that is sport crazy. Australians will watch TV coverage of Wimbledon through the night, which helps explain why Todd Woodbridge said that, right from the first moment he hit a tennis ball, his dream was to win Wimbledon. The Australians see their sports stars as sporting heroes rather than celebrities. There have been notable female champions such as Evonne Goolagong/Cawley and Margaret Smith/Court, but in their time, the likes of Laver, Fraser, Newcombe, et al dominated the sport, and have been incredibly successful in the Davis Cup. The Davis Cup means more in Australia than probably any other nation. You would not get any Australian players finding excuses not to play. They had a wonderful, visionary captain, Harry Hopman, who trained them and commanded huge respect, which would be hard to recreate these days. Back in the fifties, he appreciated the importance of supreme fitness and insisted on new levels of physical condition, achieved through hours of training with medicine balls and on-court drills. This was decades before the advent of physical trainers and fitness experts, and there were few men who could tell players to knuckle down in such a way. The results spoke for themselves – an incredible fifteen Davis Cup victories. That basis of tradition has moved forward into the current generation of Australian thinking. It makes it all the more surprising that, over the past few years, they have been through a dearth of good players. There was Pat Rafter and Lleyton Hewitt who won Wimbledon in 2002, but prior to that, there had not been any great success, other than the Woodies (Todd Woodbridge and Mark Woodforde – the most successful men's doubles team ever) or Pat Cash back in 1987. It is strange as everything is in place: they have a wonderful tennis facility as a result of the Sydney Olympics, now the home of New South Wales tennis; they are a prosperous tennis nation as they have the

Grand Slam; and the climate is an asset. They have the enthusiasm and interest, but even so, they are struggling to keep pace with the competition that has opened up all over the world. Sadly, they are not alone, as we are discovering.

After the Australian, the French Open follows, and then, in very quick succession, Wimbledon. The dates of the four Grand Slams, particularly the proximity of the French and Wimbledon, has been a source of debate for many years, and I am sure, will continue to run. The question as to why they are so close, and why one cannot be moved back or forward so that there is better spacing of events is a good one, often asked. The simple answer is that it is actually a very complicated area.

Save for two years in the seventies, when there was only one week, there has always been a two-week gap between the two tournaments. For as long as I can remember, Wimbledon has started on the sixth Monday before the first Monday in August, although most people would think of it as the last week in June. The Club has felt for a number of years that it is to our disadvantage that there is only a two-week gap. It makes the grass court season a very short one indeed. Many of us feel that ideally, the four Grand Slams should be evenly spread throughout the year. Australia should start later, and there should be four to six weeks between Wimbledon and the French, and then end with the US. It is very difficult for anyone to win at Roland Garros, with all the build-up tournaments and the longer rallies that clay produces, and then succeed at Wimbledon. Players have to adapt from playing on the slowest surface in France, to the quickest on grass, in no time at all. It is a measure of how hard that adjustment is that, since Open tennis, only three players have succeeded – Rod Laver, Björn Borg and Rafael Nadal.

The problem is compounded by the fact that nowadays, the depth of talent is so much greater. It used to be that the best players would get fairly easy matches in the first few rounds. Not any more. There are some fantastic players at 75–100 on the rankings list, meaning that there is little room for error in the earlier rounds, when the leading players may still be finding their 'grass legs'. Those top players may also be playing against lower-ranked players who did not make it beyond the first week at Roland Garros, and therefore have had an additional week in which to practise on grass.

Were we to decide unilaterally to move Wimbledon by just one week further into the year, surely that would be better for grass court tennis and not that tricky to implement? Not so. The first of the problems comes in deciding how to fill the gap that the extra week creates. At present, for the men, we have Queen's followed by Nottingham or the qualifying tournament, and for the women, there is Edgbaston and then Eastbourne or the qualifying tournament. If you have a three-week gap, you would expect Queen's, the most prestigious, to be in the middle. However, that would then clash with Royal Ascot, which would hurt Queen's a great deal, both in terms of corporate hospitality and television revenue. It is almost certain that the date of Ascot would not move as it is a fixture in the Royal diary. It also means there would be only one week between the end of Wimbledon and the Open Golf. The BBC currently cover both so it would be tight for them to move all their equipment up there, particularly in the days pre-roof when we could run a day late. The BBC also televises the Scottish Open at Loch Lomond, which would then fall into the second week of Wimbledon. Some have justifiably thought that it would be good for the pre-Wimbledon grass court season if the Queen's week became a tennis Masters Series event. However, the Queen's main stadium court has limited capacity and would need to be extended, and they would also have to raise significant increases in prize money. Given its success in its current format, the organisers have little need or inclination to go down that route.

Another issue is that if the Club went for the three-week gap, and had another tournament to fill the additional week, where would the finance come from? The LTA so far remain unconvinced that it is a viable financial proposition.

If the gap went up to four or six weeks, it would mess up the calendar even more, primarily in the US. If Wimbledon moves further into the year, it then moves closer to the US Open, and their own Championship build-up, which is made even harder in Olympic years. You could say that is not Wimbledon's problem, but you have to weigh these things up. If the gap extended to six weeks, there is also the risk that the top players would not stay in the UK. The US players may well want to go home after Roland Garros, having already been away for a long period in Europe. It would also push Wimbledon firmly into the summer-holiday period, which brings its own problems in terms of staffing and UK attendance. The French will not bring their event forward as the weather is not so good, and the earlier European tournaments then become more susceptible to frost.

It looks quite simple to resolve at first and I was never surprised when people asked me why do we not just get on with it and do it, but when you uncover all the factors, it is not an easy decision to make.

Yet still my view remains that it would be in the long-term interests of British tennis to extend the grass court season, if a way through can be found. Looking at the broader long-term picture, having an extended season in which to showcase the game on grass, rather than have it as a feature for just four weeks of the year, would be hugely beneficial both for the game, and for tennis in the UK. Others counter that Wimbledon has been hugely successful as it is. The tournament has not declined in popularity. Why bother to change it?

We started considering this question in 1991. I had a written agreement from Philippe Chatrier, the French Tennis Federation president that if we moved Wimbledon, they would not follow us. Without that, there would have been no point in taking our internal discussions further. It would be too galling to go through the logistical headache of changing our dates, only to discover that we were still two weeks apart. Discussions so far have proved inconclusive, although the point continues to come up from time to time, usually when new committee members join. We asked IMG and the BBC to look at it, as well as the heads of the players' associations. We were particularly looking for positive suggestions as to how we could make a profitable event slot into a three-week gap, but, so far, there is no golden solution. We also spoke to the television companies with whom we have contracts, looking at the implications were we to clash with another major sporting event. We would almost certainly have lost out in Europe, for example, if we hit the final stages of the Tour de France. The Club committee remained in favour, the LTA less so. They were concerned by the cost of staging further events and the risk that their investment may not be recouped, despite the argument that more exposure for more British players at more pre-Wimbledon events would be a good thing.

It will be interesting to see if and when it does change. When I left, I suggested that we should not contemplate doing this until after the London Olympics in 2012 at the earliest. If we made this monumental decision to go for a three/four-week gap, there would be no way that we would be able to get the courts back in shape for the Olympics. That would mean that, having just changed it, for one year we would have to revert to a two-week gap, which would be odd. However, it is a good debating point, and one that I will be following closely.

The French Open has had a chequered career. It started in 1891, and up until 1924 it was called the French National Championships, and was restricted to French players only. In 1925 it became the French Open, and since that date has been played at Roland Garros in Paris, on clay. The stadium is named after a French aviator and fighter pilot, who died five weeks before the end of the First World War.

Roland Garros was built at a time when French tennis was

enjoying unprecedented success. Female star Suzanne Lenglen had excited many with her balletic elegance yet formidable talent in the early part of the century. Then in the twenties and thirties came a new band of heroes, four Frenchmen known together as the Four Musketeers. René Lacoste, Jean Borotra, Jacques Brugnon and Henri Cochet were outstanding players who reigned supreme, winning most of the major titles and bringing the Davis Cup to France. It was on the back of that success that Roland Garros was built. Having beaten the US on their own soil, the French needed a stadium that would be big enough to accommodate the anticipated large audience for the Davis Cup Challenge Round the following year. However, this 'high' was not sustained. Following the golden age came the darkest days of the Second World War, when the stadium was used by the Nazis as a holding station for Jews before their transportation east.

After the War and by the seventies, the French was probably the weakest of the four Grand Slams. Players were starting to turn away from it, for a variety of reasons. The stadium had become unloved and had not had money spent on it in years. A lot of players around that time were starting to question whether they wanted to play Roland Garros *and* Wimbledon or whether they would just play one. I guess Americans and Australians thought it would be a long time away, if you included the weeks spent on the warm-up tournaments for the French Open. In the sixties, there were some who would have chosen Wimbledon over Roland Garros: the US players have generally never done well on clay, with only Andre Agassi and Jim Courier having notched up any success in the Open era. That tended to mean that they would not rank it amongst their favourite events.

The tide turned again with the arrival of a new French president, Philippe Chatrier. It is not overstating it to say that he almost single-handedly turned Roland Garros around. Chatrier was a good player in his own right, and played Davis Cup for France, but his contribution to tennis went far beyond his ability on the court. He took over as president of the French Federation of Tennis (FFT) in 1972 and remained in post until 1992. Chatrier worked hard at marketing the French Open better through television, and getting the commercial agreements in place to secure more investment. He refurbished the facilities at Roland Garros, which were looking tired. He improved the practice facilities, prize money, medical facilities, and all the elements important to players. Once the money is flowing, and the infrastructure is in place, you are in a position to get the players back on side. I am sure he did a lot personally to attract the best players. He was a generous and gregarious host, and would have dinner parties that he and his PA Regine Toures organised in Paris every night during the French Open. They were held in beautiful restaurants, and he would provide some fine food and wine, generally for overseas visitors.

From 1977 to 1991 he was also president of the International Tennis Federation (ITF). He ordered a fact-finding mission to be sent to study tennis in West Africa, out of which came the African Junior Championships. The ITF created an international tennis development programme, through which it collects funds and tries to improve tennis in poorer regions of the world, particularly Africa, South America and also Eastern Europe, by setting up coaching schemes, buying rackets and balls, and sponsoring minor tournaments. There are a number of players who have come through that scheme and won junior and senior titles, notably Cypriot Marcos Baghdatis.

The Grand Slams contribute towards these goals, from funds raised through the Grand Slam Development Fund, administered by the ITF. In 1986, under the chairmanship of Buzzer Hadingham, Wimbledon initiated the Grand Slam Development Fund with a $500,000 contribution. The other Grand Slams subsequently followed and the funds are administered by the ITF. When the Compaq Grand Slam Cup, the end-of-year tennis event, started in 1990, each of the Grand Slams agreed to put a certain amount of the profits from the event into the Development Fund – around $2m. The Grand Slam Cup offered huge amounts of money, something like $1m, to the winner from a sixteen-man tournament, which made it subject to a fair amount of criticism. People assumed that it was a very profitable event, from which the proprietor made a lot of money. As part of it, we were able to say that Yes, it is a lot of prize money, but we are putting a lot of money into the Fund, and therefore a lot of good is coming out of the event. Up until 2004, the Grand Slams had put around $30m into the Fund. Whilst the Grand Slam Cup no longer exists, we now have the Tennis Masters Cup. Through that, the Grand Slams continue to give money to the Development Fund, up to $1.5m a year.

When Chatrier retired from ITF, he went onto the International Olympic Committee (IOC) and was very much the front-runner in getting tennis back into the Olympics. Tennis had in fact been one of the nine original Olympic sports, in Athens in 1896. It then dropped out of the games after 1924, and it was thanks to a concerted campaign from Chatrier that it re-emerged at the end of the century. One of his great joys before he died in 2000 was having tennis back as a full medal sport in the Seoul Olympics in 1988. He was elected onto the IOC with a view to assessing the eligibility of existing and potential Olympic events, but shortly after contracted Alzheimer's, so was never able to fulfil all that he would have liked to do for the Olympic movement. I have a feeling that as a visionary, he would have wanted to do so much more. The main centre court of Roland Garros is named after him, and No. 1 court after Suzanne Lenglen. I am sure he was the most influential president of the FFT, and probably the ITF, to date. I admire the sort of people who are not looking at today or tomorrow, but way beyond that. I am much more of a today man, adept at dealing with the nitty gritty detail. I like to be in the presence of someone who has that contrasting outlook, and can see the pros and cons of a long-term strategy. I wish I had known him better and worked with him more. He seems to have created a foundation that his successor can build on. The basis of French tennis at the moment, particularly amongst the men, is second to none. They have a very good squad of players, with at one point seventeen in the top 100.

Another huge plus to Chatrier was that his English was excellent, unlike his successor in 1993, Christian Bimes. Communications with the president have been difficult, and not just because of the language barrier. The Grand Slam Committee meets just five times a year, but when the French president sometimes only turns up for two, maybe three meetings a year, it does not help, in my opinion, with getting decisions and views fairly exchanged.

With the channel to the president not fully open, we were fortunate in having two very good chief executives: Patrice Clerc, and then, when he left to help run the Tour de France, Stephane Simian, a former ATP player and a great guy. They have been very good friends, particularly to Wimbledon. They were honest, trustworthy, and always got things done. Our link with both men has proved essential. We never wanted Roland Garros to do anything that we had not been forewarned about, which might have had an impact on us given the proximity of the two tournaments. It never happened because of the good relationship we had with the chief executives.

Regardless of who is at the top, the French system seems to run very differently from Wimbledon's. It has always been a very tightly controlled regime. I barely met anyone beyond the president and chief executive of the FFT, yet when people came to Wimbledon, we thought it was helpful for them to meet a number of the key senior people. Also, if the Grand Slam Committee decided to action something, we would take it back to our committees. I did not get the impression that that happened in France, where everything seemed much more autocratic.

With the French Open being just two weeks before Wimbledon,

I always felt uncomfortable when I visited it. I didn't like being away from the shop so close to our event. My discomfort was not helped by my total lack of grasp of the language. Because of its proximity, especially when Eurostar left from London Waterloo, many more of our team would go to Paris than the other tournaments, but I have never been there at the end of the event. I tended to go for three or four days in the second week, and come back on the Friday, so I never saw the finals. Leaving before the climax does not help you fully appreciate the whole thing, and my time was so limited, I did not get much of a chance to see any tennis.

I am sometimes asked if I can imagine a time when there might be a fifth Grand Slam, and my answer is No. For starters, I cannot see the justification for it. We have four Grand Slams, the end-of-year events, the Davis and Fed Cups, and the Olympics. How many more peaks can there be in a calendar? We have Grand Slams on different surfaces at the moment, and another on clay, hard court or grass would add little. The only other surface that would test a player and provide a different environment would be an indoor tournament, but that would be pretty difficult to achieve with a draw of 128 men and ladies, and doubles. It is more than simply the facilities. The fact that a country is growing fantastically in the sport, for example China, would not to my mind warrant their consideration as a fifth Grand Slam. To get to Grand Slam status, there is so much history and tradition involved. For some new tournament to come on the block, it would be very difficult for everyone to comprehend. Traditional tournaments who have participated in the sport for so many years would have more cause or claim, for example the Italian and German Opens. Even these countries to my knowledge, have never come forward with a hard and fast case for a Grand Slam, and the longer it has been left, the less chance there is, I am sure, that we will ever have another.

Chapter 6

A Year in the Life of . . .

People judge the success of Wimbledon by the matches and the weather. Whether the event was run well or not will generally only hit the radar if there has been an incident. Given that we could do precious little about the tennis or the rain (I would have if I could!), my team and I spent fifty weeks of the year making sure that we did not end up making the headlines for the wrong reasons.

My mental and physical diary, for obvious reasons, did not run to a calendar year. All efforts were pinned around the two weeks at the end of June and beginning of July. I guess the start of the natural transition from one Championships to the next was the Champions' dinner (which used to be the Wimbledon Ball, but was changed in 1977). The dinner was held on the final Sunday at the Savoy. The Championships were over, and we could relax and reflect on, hopefully, a job well done. I say relax, but I was still on duty. Normally I would sit near the door, ready to deal with late entrants or even gatecrashers, usually from the media. I would have a table of ten comprising tennis writers, broadcasters, overseas guests, and people associated with The Championships, but all friends. The chairman would have the men's and ladies' champions, although in my last year, he kindly invited Jenny and me to sit with Roger Federer and Venus Williams at the top table. The chairman and the two singles champions say a few words, which is pleasant, if a little unmemorable. I do, however, remember Pete Sampras struggling through a couple of obviously unprepared lines in the first years that he was champion. I said to Mark McCormack, 'He's your client, he's won here three times and will do so again – could you have a word and tell him what is meant to happen?' I assume that he did, as the next year it was far better.

The dinner took place on the Sunday, irrespective of whether we had to come back to play any finals on the Monday. I hope, with the roof installed, that will never have to happen again with the main finals. It is a pain and a terrible anti-climax. It is far better that things run to schedule and the Club is closed on the Monday, with most people permitted the day off. After that the disassembly operation starts immediately, and systematically. The major broadcasters would try to get their equipment out as soon as they could, but otherwise we phased people coming in to clear up, to avoid chaos.

On the Wednesday, the chairman would invite the Club committee and the senior executives for a game on the Centre and No. 1 Courts. It is one of only two times that Centre Court is played on outside The Championships, and so is really quite special. The only other occasion is just prior to The Championships, when four lady members are invited to play, to ensure that the grass is behaving as it should, to check that all technical equipment is functioning, and to allow the ball boys and girls a final rehearsal. Our annual game meant that I can say I have played on Centre Court thirty-three times, which is probably more often than Boris Becker. The atmosphere, however, was slightly different. There were no crowds, just an empty Coke can rattling around and the odd contractor coming in to do a bit of jeering. The Court felt very big, much bigger when it was empty, as I think the crowd tends to bring everything closer. It was also not in its pristine condition at that stage, but it was good fun none the less and a real thrill just to be playing on Centre Court. The day was always rounded off by our Championship staff reunion cocktail party. Many people who have worked at the tournament, including our own staff, and representatives of all groups of people who have helped at The Championships together with their partners, would come to the cocktail party held in the former members' enclosure, now the Café Pergola.

The rest of that week I would spend dealing with correspondence. There were my personal thankyou letters, of which there were probably about thirty. Then it was time to tackle the postbag full of mail from people commenting on the event. They were mostly letters on the ticketing front or stewarding incidents, but I think some people find it easier to put pen to paper than others. One year a pied-wagtail landed on court and we were slightly surprised by the number of wagtail devotees who felt compelled to tell us that we should not have tried to shoo it away. There were letters every year from people who could not get in, or wanted a refund because of the rain, or TV viewers who had not liked watching players spitting, or Venus Williams's clothing, or McEnroe's swearing. McEnroe definitely created a big postbag during his time, generally from people saying, 'He should have been chucked out, why tolerate it, it sets a bad example . . .'

Every letter was answered by the appropriate person. Most of them fell to the Championships director, as they were specific to his area. Some related to the broadcast coverage and were passed on to the BBC, but it was useful that they came to us in the first instance, in order that we could monitor the broadcaster's performance. That said, we were very content with the BBC. My only criticism remains that the daily highlights programme should be at 10 p.m. rather than at 8 when play may not have finished. With a lot of letters, it was simply a matter of acknowledging the type of complaint and saying you would take it on board and look at it. Generally, that was the end of the correspondence, although sometimes insurance and lawyers got involved, if someone had fallen down some steps for example. We also had the odd letter that was best passed to the police.

I think that given we had 470,000 people coming over the Fortnight, and 8–9,000 temporary staff every day, we did not get too many problems. Take the catering operation, which is a huge exercise. Wimbledon is the largest single annual sporting catering operation carried out in Europe. Each year, around 130,000 lunches are served, 190,000 sandwiches sold, 28,000 kilos of strawberries eaten, and 150,000 glasses of Pimms drunk. Yet in the whole time that I was there, I think in total I had about ten letters of complaint.

We would usually have a courts sub-committee meeting during the fortnight after The Championships. We would invite the head groundsman and go through how the courts had been playing and whether there were any issues on any particular day. We would also be interested to hear what renovation programme he was suggesting for the following year. We would get feedback from the players, and the head groundsman would monitor the courts very closely. We also got help from the Sports Turf Research Institute in Bingley, Yorkshire. They would measure the hardness, dryness, and dampness of the courts daily. We were looking for perfection, and in an ideal world we would like all the courts playing identically. The head groundsman's remit also covered all the other courts and the croquet lawn. (Despite our title, we did not have a croquet lawn at our current site until 1960, and then it was not full size. Following the redevelopment of the grounds, the croquet lawn has now been relocated to our land at Southlands College and is full-size.)

This was also the time for a Club committee meeting to discuss any urgent matters arising from The Championships. We would look at any crises or things that people wanted to get a mandate to work on improving for the following year. The first time that we played on Middle Sunday, for example, gave us a great deal to think about and provided lessons to be learned. Usually, there was also something on the security front that needed to be addressed, or the starting plans for a new building project. It was a relatively relaxed meeting, coming so soon after The Championships.

The All England Club is very much a committee-driven organisation. We have a Club committee of twelve, comprised entirely of members, and elected by the membership at the AGM. They are the equivalent of non-executive directors and have a non-executive chairman, currently Tim Phillips. They make all the decisions relating purely to the Club. The chairman of the day tries to get a balanced committee. Being a tennis club, it is easy to find people who are keen and knowledgeable on tennis, but now running The Championships is much more than that. We need accountants, lawyers, businessmen, heavy hitters, or people who may have IT and media capabilities. We do not get too many champions available these days. Ann Jones is on the committee, and Virginia Wade was our first lady committee member. Tim Henman joined in December 2008. In terms of business contacts, we have done a little better. We did have Sir Ronnie Hampel, former chairman of ICI, until fairly recently. He knew so many people, which is very worthwhile in our business. In 2007, Mervyn King, chairman of the Bank of England, came on board. In terms of financial acumen, I would say he would be a pretty useful person to have on any committee, although I suspect that given the implosion of the financial markets in 2008, he has been kept rather busy elsewhere. He is a keen tennis player none the less, and I have seen him, rather charmingly, walking along to the Club with a rucksack on his back, having taken the tube and seemingly spurned all offers of chauffeur-driven luxury.

Then there are a number of Club sub-committees dealing with issues such as staff, fixtures, rules, and courts. In order to run The Championships, the twelve members of the Club committee are joined by seven representatives from the LTA, including the LTA president, to form the committee of management of The Championships. The chief executive of the LTA is also present. The main Club committee generally meets seven times a year and the committee of management six times. They arrange various sub-committees covering all items relating to The Championships, such as catering, tickets, marketing, or transport. Each of these sub-committees is chaired by an All England Club member, with, generally, a 2:1 ratio of Club and LTA representatives. I would attend all the sub-committees where possible, but I did not have a vote, on either the sub- or the main committees, and neither does my successor. It was essentially a non-issue as most matters were never put to a vote in any event, consensus having already been reached.

As an example of the operation in practice, we introduced price differentials on Centre Court tickets in 1979. The system was similar to a theatre, with the best seats, closest to the court, costing more than those under the roof. We kept the system for about five years, but in the end disbanded it as it was not working for us. The decisions to both implement and then end the system were first debated by the executives, then put forward to the appropriate sub-committee who said Yes, and then passed to the main committee. Once they had said Yes, it was back to the executives to press ahead with the actual implementation. That was generally the procedure. It is quite long-winded, but it has proved to be the best way. That level of discussion is important as, by so doing, we reach consensus.

I do not think I ever attended a debate that was heated. People may not have agreed, but it was always discussed in a calm, rational manner. We made the right decisions nine and a half times out of ten, which might not have happened otherwise. There were of course, the odd exceptions. One decision, which I disagreed with at the time, was allowing William Hill to have a betting tent on the tea lawn for the 1975 Championships. I did not think that it was very 'Wimbledon' that we should be encouraging betting, particularly on our own site. The committee soon changed their mind, and the following year we told William Hill that they could come back, but in a different location miles away, and paying significantly more (ten times as much). Unsurprisingly, they declined the offer.

It is true that a chief executive of a mid-sized business could find the committee system difficult. I certainly did not have the authority that the majority of chief executives up and down the country would have. There is no doubt about that. It was one of the concerns when they were looking for my replacement: could they find a top-class person who could work within the committee system? They did go to great lengths to explain the scenario to candidates. I was involved in the first round of interviews and it came out in that, as well as, I believe, the second and third interviews. It was explained that one of the reasons why we keep the committee system is because of the partnership with the LTA. Their views need to be considered on all major decisions. Any fears there may have been have clearly been dispelled with Ian Ritchie's appointment. Ian, I am sure, has taken on more responsibility than I had. Similarly, I took on more than my predecessor, as is the way with an evolutionary process. Confidence has grown in the executive. The committees are not meeting any more often now than they did ten years ago, but as Wimbledon has grown, there are more decisions to be made, which means more are taken out of the committee forum and handled directly by the executive. That said, the underlying structure remains as strong. It is not an easy system, but not unique – the LTA and the Football Association are both based around nineteenth-century administration models, and the Royal and Ancient Golf Club of St Andrews was run in a very similar way in managing The Open. At the end of the day, it was not something that worried me. All I wanted was to get the best results for the Club and The Championships.

Committee members worked (and continue to work) very hard, the individual chairmen of sub-committees even more so. While we may not have increased the number of meetings over the years, the chairmen had close links with the executive, who were more inclined to ring up and say, 'I've got this idea, what do you think?' We would already have discussed the matter, and by and large, we all knew what the others were doing and worked well as a good close-knit team.

What is going to become harder is finding an honorary chairman who is willing and able to give the amount of time that his predecessors have done. I found it amazing the amount that Tim Phillips, the current chairman, and former senior executive at British Airways, gave – and still gives – to the Club.

The committee season would kick off from the time we got back from the US Open in September through to the end of the year. It was principally a time for the Championship sub-committees to meet. They would look at all aspects of maintenance, catering, and marketing. The media sub-committee would look at logistics, photographers' technological require-ments, whether there were enough press writing desks, or what the complaints were from the year before. A lot of suggestions would come from British tennis writers who we would meet a few times a year. Then there was IT, and order of play, consider-ing all aspects of The Championships' playing side, including scheduling, use of Hawkeye, officials, refereeing staff, rules of the game, and so on. Generally the sub-committees meet twice a year, once in the autumn and once in the spring, but the order of play sub-committee also meets every day at The Championships. In total, there were probably around forty-five sub-committee meetings a year. The first meeting is most import-ant as that sets out any changes for the following year, except for the ticket sub-committee spring meeting, which determines ticket prices for the following year.

Each sub-committee is chaired by a Club committee member

and administered by a Club executive. When I first came to work at the Club, there were just two executives – the club secretary and assistant secretary. That did not change until 1981 when we added a financial controller (Tony Hughes, who subsequently became finance director and retired in July 2007). Since then, the executive has steadily grown, in recognition of the growth of The Championships. In 1984, Roger Ambrose joined as Club secretary; in 1985, we took on Rob McCowen as marketing director; in 1989, we appointed a TV marketing director (Ian Edwards), who was replaced by John Rowlinson as director of television in 2002; and in 1995, Jeff Lucas joined as IT director. Richard Grier became Championships director in 1985, but had already been in post, first as assistant secretary in 1979 and then Championships secretary. I mention these people for two reasons. Firstly, they were all of invaluable assistance to me, and without them I would have been dead in the water. Secondly, it is a reflection of the Club environment, that, bar John Rowlinson, there was no change in personnel in these posts. Very few people leave Wimbledon. It is a very pleasant place to work, dealing with congenial people, all working towards the same goal. You are doing something that you believe in and that has a high point – something tangible that you can aim for and from which you can derive a certain amount of satisfaction if it all goes right. It is not like churning out insurance all day long (I would imagine, having no insurance expertise). It engenders a certain degree of loyalty and that element of longevity stimulates a very strong team atmosphere.

During the course of the period leading up to Christmas, there was a visit to the men's end-of-year championship, the Tennis Masters Cup, wherever it was being held (in Shanghai in 2008, in London in 2009). The Grand Slam Cup when it started in 1990, was an ITF/Grand Slam event. As of 2000, as the Tennis Masters Cup, it became a co-owned event between ATP, the Grand Slams and the ITF. As co-owners, we found it useful for us to attend. The chairman and I would also sometimes go to the WTA tour-end event, now in Doha.

Every December, we also had our AGM. This and the Club dinner are always in central London, as we are not just an SW19 club. We welcome people from all over the country and internationally.

As we moved into the New Year, the pace would hot up, certainly psychologically. This is when the public ballot is held, started originally in 1924. Some of the tickets are given to the LTA for distribution through their club system, the rest are distributed in the ballot. No matter how much we have increased the seating capacity over the years, the public ballot is always hugely over-subscribed. Some might say that we should try to share the tickets out to give everyone a chance to attend. We should perhaps put in a system whereby people who have been unlucky several times before are prioritised next time around. However, I think the public ballot should be open to everyone, regardless of whether they have had tickets before. It would be hard otherwise to call it a public ballot. It would be similar to stopping someone from entering the lottery because they had already won it. At least people have less time to wait to find out, now that the operation is conducted by computer rather than by hand. The lucky applicants are notified in February. If they cannot come or do not respond, the Club does subsequent ballots from then on, to try and keep as many people as possible satisfied.

During this time, the Championships departments would be having literally hundreds of meetings with the contractors who have some involvement with The Championships. I would sit in on those occasionally, but it was a well-oiled machine. I was probably busier in the months leading up to Christmas than in the spring in some ways. I was not involved in the small details, although I was always very interested. There were some elements, such as the coin-tossing ceremony, which changed each year. Since

2000, two youngsters come onto Centre Court and toss the coin before the start of the men's and ladies' finals. The youngsters are nominated on behalf of charities chosen by people associated with the Club or tennis in some way. The year after I retired I was asked to choose the charity for the men's singles, and so seven-year-old William Caines, who suffered from cancer, tossed the coin on behalf of Cancer Research. It is a nice touch, and provides a memorable day for the coin-tossers who are given lunch and tea and meet some of the top players. In terms of preparation for the more structural elements, however, the closer we got to The Championships, the more we relied on contractors and suppliers to deliver, be it a new scoreboard, new signs, new tentage etc. It tended to be The Championships team that were chasing to make sure everything was done.

What took up much more of my time and energy over the last fifteen years was the Long Term Plan. There was all manner of internal planning at varying levels. With the architects, it was a question of sorting out size and layout of rooms, who is going to go into what room, crowd circulation, queuing arrangements . . . the list went on. Then there were the logistical hurdles of the different stages of the work, liaising with everyone from our building and services manager, John Cox, right through to head groundsman Eddie Seaward who had to have access to the courts at key times, with the necessary equipment. It all took a lot of planning. A lot of time was also spent with our agents, IMG and TWI. To get the best out of an agent, you need to manage them, especially in a continually evolving market such as television.

It was one of the joys of my job that no week was ever the same in terms of the matters to discuss or to be dealt with. One look at a random week demonstrates this.

Each day of that week, and every week, at 8.30 a.m., I would meet one of my executives, though I did not see Roger Ambrose or Richard Grier at that time because generally we would be at lunch together in the member's dining room and I would see quite a lot of them during the day. Once a week every week, I would also get all the executives together over lunch for a short agenda looking at specific things coming up. Lunches on the other days were a nice, informal way of ensuring that the whole team knew what was going on. We did not always talk about business, but it helped with team building. It all depends on the type of CEO you are. I am not a dictatorial person. I prefer to do things through consensus and bring the team with me. I am not proud – if they have a better idea than mine and we adopt it, it does not worry me in the slightest. To have regular informed lunch meetings where ideas can be exchanged is good, and we in fact ate together most days of the week.

After the 8.30 meeting on the Monday morning, I had a meeting with the HR manager so that I knew what was going on staffwise, and in the afternoon, I saw one of the designers for the Long Term Plan. We were looking at the main turnstile at gate three to see how that should be arranged, as part and parcel of the new design of the museum building. We wanted to see how many turnstiles could be incorporated – just one of the countless details at each stage of the plan. Early that evening, we had a staff pensions meeting.

On Tuesday, I had a meeting at Queen's Club. I talked to Richard Grier about his targets, some financial, some not. We had put in place a new arrangement for the management of the qualifying rounds at Roehampton, so we needed to ensure that it all went very smoothly.

Back at the Club, a journalist from *Ace* tennis magazine wanted to have a walk around, so I gave her a tour. It was a good opportunity to get out and about and check that all was in order around the grounds, something that I liked to do regularly. I thought this was quite important, but was put in my place one winter morning by one of the maintenance staff who was stripping down some wood. 'Jolly cold today, isn't it, Ralph?' I shouted across. 'Not if you're working, sir,' came the reply. I scuttled back inside to my office and got the pen out.

I finished Tuesday with a meeting with Johnny Perkins, who is in charge of our public relations, and was formerly with the LTA. We first started using PR experts in 1981, and have become more reliant on them as the years have gone by, particularly during The Championships if and when crises arise. Johnny and his predecessor Sue Youngman have been a great help in arranging quick and important communication with the media. As well as dealing with news stories as and when they arrive, Johnny would organise invitations to editors of national newspapers to come to the Club for an informal lunch. We would invite the editor and tennis journalist from one paper at a time, to have lunch with the chairman, chairman of the media sub-committee, Johnny, and me. There was no agenda; it was more of an opportunity for them to get to know us and what we were up to, and us them. It showed the editor that we took the tennis writer seriously and as part of the team, and had the additional benefit of providing us with a link to the editor if we had a serious problem with a story that could blow up.

On Wednesday, we had an emergency services meeting. That was when all the services would come together: police, royalty protection, ambulance service and fire brigade. The royalty protection team would have their own special thoughts on how, in the event of a crisis, the royals should be evacuated. They would want to know if there had been any changes in the royal box area, or any changes in the transport system around the grounds.

Then there were a series of meetings involving the grounds and our security people, and finally one with Roger Draper, who at that time was with Sport England, and wanted to know more about the workings of the All England Club – a fairly prescient meeting, given his current role as chief executive of the LTA.

The following day, I had a long session with IMG and we

had our pensioners' lunch. Every other year, we hold a lunch for all our retired staff and their partners, which is a good way of keeping everyone in touch – as I am now discovering as one of the beneficiaries! I also had an Olympic torch meeting, to discuss the route the torch would take around the grounds, and other arrangements. We spent a good deal of time planning the event, which was to happen during the 2004 Championships, but in the end could do nothing about the fact that it rained all day. Carrying the torch was certainly the only action that Tim Henman saw that middle Saturday.

My week ended when I went with Richard Grier up to a meeting at Silverstone with a group called Major Events Organisers Meeting (MEOM). The group was formed in 1986 in response to the threat from unofficial suppliers, over whom we had no control, selling corporate hospitality. It brings together representatives from fifteen events, venues and organisations such as Henley Royal Regatta, St Andrews golf, Wembley, Glastonbury, the Brit Oval, Epsom Racecourse, the Rugby Football Union, the Royal Horticultural Society and the London Marathon. The idea is to share a diverse range of experiences on issues such as ticketing, the cost of policing, which can vary hugely, traffic, and IT matters. We would go to different locations each time, and it was a useful exercise. We subsequently introduced a similar concept for facility managers where our clerk of works and head groundsman could go to different venues and share best practice. We would meet twice a year and two of the perennial discussion areas were unofficial corporate hospitality and ticket touting.

When corporate hospitality is arranged through an official event organiser, there is no problem. We can work with the hospitality company in allocating the correct number of tickets, provide them with an official marquee, and keep control of what is going on. However, with the growth of hospitality in the mid to late eighties, unofficial suppliers started entering the market. They would go to other landowners, asking to put up a marquee, and then acquire a large number of tickets through the black market which they would package together and sell at a vastly inflated rate. It was a very negative influence on any event, and we wanted to take prompt and decisive action, so in the nineties, the Club started imposing much more stringent ticket conditions than we had ever had before. We took a lot of legal advice and did a lot of testing, both in and outside the grounds. We would stop, at random, people coming into The Championships and ask them a series of questions to check that they were being truthful that the ticket had been allocated to them. If they were not, they were dismissed from the grounds. If someone said it came from Stan Smith in Haringey, they would be taken off to a room until we could verify the source, and if the two did not match up, the person would not be allowed entry. Even if they did not know that they had received a ticket from a tout, we still would not let them in. If that person had an issue, they had to take it up with Stan Smith or whoever had sold them the ticket, not us. The clampdown cost us a lot of time and money, and is an ongoing battle. Many other events do not scrutinise the tickets in quite the way that we do. We also have anti-tout squads going up and down the queue, and at Southfields tube station, trying to see if there are touts selling tickets. We would rather stop the transaction happening in the first place than have to deal with it after-wards. It is embarrassing for people if they have bought the ticket innocently, and their day is ruined.

Word has got around, and we probably have less need for people checking up and down the queue now. Forgeries have also become less of a problem because we have introduced pretty sophisticated tickets. They have a watermark and thread running through them, rather like a five-pound note, making them hard to copy. We spent quite a lot of money on the design, partly because we wanted to make them forgery free, but also because we knew that people like to keep them as a souvenir.

We might not have needed to go to such lengths had the government intervened with anti-touting legislation. That would certainly have pleased the representatives of the MEOM. It would have helped us enormously if the government had said, that all touting was illegal, as they did for football, but they were not prepared to go as far as that. Their main concern with football was that rival fans could end up in the same part of the stadium. They are not necessarily anti ticket touts per se, the argument being that if someone wants to sell a ticket and someone else wants to buy it, then that is capitalism for you and perfectly fair; it is not doing anyone any harm, provided the ticket was not stolen. We would counter that it does not make for a free market because, if you inflate the prices, you exclude a portion of the public who are not able to afford them. Touting also takes money out of tennis. This issue was looked at most recently in 2008, but again the government has decided against making new laws to combat the problem, instead suggesting that parties work together in creating a voluntary code. *Plus ça change.* As Ian Ritchie said, following the announcement, 'It is deeply disappointing that after all this time we still appear to be no nearer a proper regulatory solution to this problem. The long-term future of the sports and entertainment industry ultimately depends on the integrity of the partnership between fan and event. We firmly believe that a voluntary solution would be totally impractical and the best way forward is through effective legislation.'

Dealing with ticket touts is certainly an issue that will come up with the sale of tickets for the Olympics in 2012. I, and I am sure the current committee, can only hope that that moves the debate forwards.

As the countdown to The Championships began, the pressure would mount. The builders had to finish work and make good what was a building site, while the temporary marquees, walkways and toilets were erected. Landscapers were hard at work adding aesthetic touches, and there were hundreds more contractors on site. I would have to take time out to attend the French Open at Roland Garros, which, as I've said, was always something I felt uncomfortable about. Once Roland Garros finished, there would be a two-week gap before The Championships. While the Stella Artois was being played, we would have our wild card meeting, where the order of play sub-committee met with the referee to decide who we would invite as wild cards into the main events, and into qualifying. Generally they are British players, with two or three overseas players who might have dropped out but are back playing, though lacking fitness. There are eight wild card places, in both the men's and ladies' singles.

At this time we would have quite thorough site inspections to check that everything was progressing smoothly and in a satisfactory manner, and conduct final briefings with, say, the stewards and security teams. The Assistant Commissioner and the chief superintendent of police in Wimbledon would keep me up to date with the current threat level in terms of terrorism or, for example, the proactive Fathers 4 Justice campaigners, who were keen on climbing up walls and demonstrating from the top of buildings.

Security was a huge issue for me, and my biggest worry as chief executive. We never wanted to do anything that would discourage people from coming, but it is only right to make people aware of their responsibilities, in, say, not leaving bags unattended at any time. Pretty much ever since 9/11 we have been on high alert. That is not because of any specific threat, but because Wimbledon, as with most major sporting events, is a reasonably obvious target. We are watched by a global audience, and we have a big US presence, as well as players from over sixty countries. Being on high alert means extra vigilance and extra checks, with sniffer dogs walking the buildings and grounds every morning.

We would also have emergency exercises. We would have a day when police from Scotland Yard came down and met with senior key staff, stewards, and the emergency services. They would build up different scenarios, asking us to imagine, if things were happening in one part of the ground, what we would then do if something else started up elsewhere. It is never a very joyful day, I can tell you.

We have only had to evacuate Centre Court once, late on a Saturday afternoon. There was a suspect package, which the bomb squad had to examine. We did stop the match, sending the players back to the dressing rooms and the crowds out of the arena. We never had to do a total evacuation of the grounds.

Ultimately, it was my decision whether to evacuate or not. Primarily, it was the IRA that posed the biggest threat during my time. We had five bomb alerts in the space of fifteen minutes one year. While you get all the advice and help you can from the police, it is your decision whether to evacuate the Centre Court or the whole ground. There is the obvious risk that if you ignore it, it may prove to be a real bomb, but if it is a hoax call (as proved to be the case every time) and you evacuate, there is a risk of people panicking and being injured in the rush to leave. You also play into the hands of the hoaxers, who would take huge delight in watching Centre Court being evacuated and would more than likely try it again.

It is important to stress that we never did find a bomb, and that our security checks and drills, practised rigorously, gave me satisfaction that we were as prepared as possible for any eventuality.

Streakers posed their own security threat, and were therefore something we took very seriously, not flippantly at all. I felt hurt whenever a streaker or protester got onto any court – it was a breach of our defences. We liked to think of the court area as being completely secure, and having people able to get onto court posed a security risk. We also wanted to manage things the way we wanted to, not the way other people might have wanted to. The good thing about a streaker as opposed to any other type of court invasion was that at least we knew with the former that they were not carrying a weapon! If someone made it onto court, the police or service personnel would have to take that person out. That is why on the show courts we did our level best to ensure they never got there in the first place. We had service personnel courtside, who made sure that they were facing the crowd and that they were far enough forward to see everyone on the front row. They would spot someone trying to get on court and try and apprehend that person so that there was not an ungainly rush – we did not want someone with army boots doing a huge rugby tackle on the court, which could damage it. We had our first female streaker in 1996, prior to the men's final, and a male streaker in 2002, again during the men's final. After each incident, the papers quickly pounced on speculation that we would move the public away from the side of the courts or have some form of netting. Despite what was said, it was not something we ever seriously contemplated. It would be a hugely retrograde step. Part of the joy of Wimbledon is being so close to the action, and long may it remain so.

The week before Wimbledon is the qualifying tournament, during which we would do the seeding for the main events. The system has been quite controversial in its time. The seeding used to be decided by the order of play sub-committee, but this was changed for the men's singles in 2001, following objections from the ATP. With our new seeding system for that year's men's singles, a player's ranking was amended by how well he did at Wimbledon in the two previous years, and at any other grass court events. If he had done well on grass, he was more likely to have a higher seeding than someone with a higher ATP ranking but who had never played on grass. The ATP were being lobbied hard by clay court specialists, who tended not to fare so well on grass, and therefore came out the least favourably in our seedings. The association stated that they wanted us to follow the ATP rankings. We pointed to Tomas Muster, an Austrian player, as an example. At the time, Muster was ranked No. 1, but every time he had played at Wimbledon, he had never got beyond the first round. Similarly, Patrick Rafter, who lost to Pete Sampras in the 2000 final, could have met him in the first round had he not been bumped up from his ranking of No. 23 to be the No. 12 seed. We argued that that was not the point of a seeding. It is about literally planting your seeds in a place in the draw in which they will flourish and come through.

As a compromise, the Club now uses an objective surface-based seeding system for the men, which we had hoped the other Grand Slams would follow, but they did not. The Club produces a seeding list based on those weightings. The only people to be included are the top thirty-two in the ATP ranking. The system would often make some small adjustments to the ATP rankings, for grass court players such as Pat Rafter or Andy Roddick, for example. The women did not want the surface-based system, so we agreed, on condition that we retained the right to alter the seedings if an adjustment needed to be made in obvious circumstances. By and large, we kept to the women's rankings. Whenever we did tests on women's seedings, and applied the same objective formula as with the men, it worked out that there would be very little change, whereas with the men there were quite significant fluctuations. The service is not such a dominating factor with them. In truth, even with the men the gap has narrowed, as there are not so many natural serve and volleyers.

From the Wednesday onwards, the players can practise on The Championships courts, but only on a limited basis unless they are a member (normally by virtue of being a previous champion). Then on the Thursday before The Championships, we would do the draw. That involved the referee, the secretary of the LTA, and me.

Saturday would be the International Club of Great Britain's dinner dance.

The day before the start of The Championships, the chairman

and I would go to the players' meetings. He would welcome them to Wimbledon, explain any new changes, and say that we were there to help with any questions. Once the tournament started, I would go around the competitors' restaurant and lounge, just to check that everything was all right. I would chat to one or two players, and perhaps look into the dressing rooms from time to time, but I would not spend a lot of time during the Fortnight with them. I would spend more time with the seniors. For the likes of John Newcombe, Stan Smith, or Mansour Bahrami, it is a totally different atmosphere. They are much more relaxed if they are playing in the senior events. They are there for a bit of fun and happy to socialise. I would see more of the top players at the Tennis Masters Cup in Shanghai or at the other Grand Slams where I had no responsibilities. I think if I have one regret, it is that I have not been able to spend more time with the players, but it was hard with so much else to do, coupled with the fact that the players were so focused, they did not really want to be inter-rupted by me. I think it would have been easier if I had played at Wimbledon myself or been a great player. We could have talked a similar language. Plus the age difference got steadily worse!

Monday morning, and The Championships start. Breakfast time would be a whirlwind of media involvement:

  7.30–9.30 Broadcasters' breakfast
  8.15 Radio 5 Live interview
  8.25 Radio 4 interview
  8.40 Radio Wimbledon interview
  9.00 meeting with the police
  9.20 Sky News interview
  9.30 Sky Sport interview

The interviews tended to follow the same lines every year. Inevitably there would be questions about the weather, and I

would often be asked who my tip was to win. It was an opportunity for me to be able to say what we were doing differently
that year, the change in queuing arrangements and in the size of
hand luggage for example, and get that message across. I had to
do quite a lot of interviews, particularly if there was a crisis or
something was out of the ordinary, like a tube strike. There was
a clear division of labour for dealing with media matters: I would
speak on logistics, the referee Alan Mills on order of play or player
issues, and the chairman on international issues.

There would then be briefings with the umpires and super-
visors before organising the annual photograph with the Mayor
of Merton and the Duke of Kent, which is framed and then sent
to the Mayor as a keepsake. The Mayor is elected for a year and
is invited to the royal box on the first Monday.

After the daily 6 p.m. security meeting, I would attend, if
possible, one of the cocktail parties hosted on the grounds almost
every night. These are essentially a means of the Club thanking
all those who have been involved in some way, like the umpires
or honorary stewards. The honorary stewards party is a thankyou
to those who manage all the queues and help people to their seats
on the show courts. They are not paid, but do it for the love of
it. They are invaluable to us, acting as a softer version of the
service stewards, and because they have been doing it for so long,
they are not fazed by whatever question might be thrown at them
by the public.

On the second Wednesday, I would host the chief executive
cocktail party, with Jenny. I would invite overseas guests, a number
of members of the Club, some Grand Slam officials, former
presidents of the USTA and some players, including all of the
participants of the senior events. We could always guarantee
a good attendance from the senior players as we would have a
formal photograph taken of them, which always went down
a treat, and which I would then send to each player. Entertaining
people was very much part of the job, both during The

Championships and throughout the year. It was part joyful, part interruption. It was nice in theory to attend the cocktail parties but most of the time I would just dip in, if I went at all. Sometimes I was not even able to stay for my own, if play was continuing and I needed to make some PA announcements.

As chief executive, I was the direct link between the chairman, the committee and everyone else. I felt this quite keenly during The Championships. I would base myself in the office, but try to get out as much as I could, armed with my walkie-talkie. This was harder in the early days, before we had a security office. The emergency telephone would sit between my office and that of my PA, Paula McMillan, and had to be manned at all times. Thankfully it never went off, but my regular absences, leaving Paula shackled to her desk, may have caused her some uncomfortable hours.

There were a number of meetings that would be set up during the Fortnight, generally with important customers to check that everything was to their satisfaction, or with people who had come to Wimbledon who would not normally be in town. There were also Grand Slam committee meetings in the second week and Grand Slam executive meetings prior to those meetings in order to set the scene.

I would also make public address announcements. It was very time-consuming but I felt that I needed to let the spectators know what was going on, especially if things were not going routinely. It was certainly not for the love of hearing my own voice. I dread to think how many times in my life I must have listened to myself say: 'Ladies and gentlemen, may I have your attention please?' The reason why I decided to do the announcements – I am not sure anyone did them before me – was that I genuinely felt that the public needed to know what was going on at certain times. So, for that matter, did I. I did not want to be craning to hear someone else making an announcement if I had not been involved in what was being said. If I was the boss of the organisation, I wanted to know precisely what was being said and when, and if it was wrong, I would take the can. There was once an announcement over the PA system at a tournament in Arizona, US, which went: 'Would the guy with the pea shooter knock it off?' Fairly unlikely I grant you, but I did not want that sort of thing going out in my absence.

The announcements were not necessarily all about the weather. They could have been the daily morning welcome, plans for tomorrow, or security issues. Nowadays, all weather announcements are made from the referee's office. That may be a good step forward. Personally, however, I just wanted to be in control and to know what was going on the whole time, and I felt I needed to make a balanced assessment of conditions. The referee's office would have a tendency to put the players' interest foremost without necessarily thinking about the public. The two need to be looked at together. For example, if a match is moving slowly on No. 1 Court, the referee may decide to move the next scheduled match on that court to No. 2 Court. On the face of it, it seems sensible, but people may have bought their tickets on the day in anticipation of seeing that particular match. That sort of change may result in a lot of aggravated fans either rushing to No. 2 Court or to the ticket office or to the referee's office, trying to get some sort of satisfaction. Similarly, if you are going to abandon play because of rain, you need to tell the players first so that they can get out, then our own key staff, the police, and main car parks, and only then tell the public. There is an order to these things that, if not followed, could lead to confusion.

I saw the announcements as an essential, if intrusive, part of my fortnight. Others had a slightly more charmed view. I was very flattered to hear BBC presenter John Inverdale say: 'If the world was coming to an end, so long as I heard Chris Gorringe make the announcement, I'd know everything was going to be all right.' Perhaps less flattering was the NBC broadcaster Bud Collins's description of me as 'the voice of moist doom'.

My other very public role was at the presentation ceremony. Walking out onto Centre Court for the first time in 1980 was an experience – a good one, I should add. It gave me an incredible sense of the atmosphere. I had played on Centre Court when it was empty, but to walk out there when it is full is really quite special. The court is where the action is, and you are one of a few people in the centre, as opposed to one of thousands when you are watching, so you feel the atmosphere from an entirely different perspective. There were always a few butterflies, fears about tripping on the carpet, or getting my timing wrong. From where I stood, tucked away at the back behind the wall, it was impossible to see the carpet being laid out or the table being set up. I would just have to make a mental note of how long it had taken in rehearsal, and hope that it was ready when I set off prior to the presentation party, which would include the Duke of Kent our president, the Club chairman and the president of the LTA. The alternative would have been for me to keep coming and going, peering around the corner in a hesitant, dithering manner, which would not have looked good. Once everyone is safely assembled on court, the presentation is relatively straightforward. I was also responsible for making sure that the players walked around past the professional photographers, and gave them enough time to take their shots. This was a very special moment, and a privilege to be part of it. As Martina Navratilova said, 'He walked you round with the trophy, so I think the happiest moments of my life have been spent with Chris Gorringe!'

We have replica trophies for the men's and ladies' champions, and I can honestly say I do not know which is which. One set sits in the museum, and the other in the trophy cabinet in the clubhouse. I never wanted to know which was which, as I always wanted to imagine I was dealing with the original. I am sure the champions would have felt the same had they known.

There has been one presentation ceremony in which I played

more than a supporting role. In 1999 I received a letter from Buckingham Palace, telling me I was to be awarded a CBE in the Queen's Honours List. The letter said that I was to keep the news secret and, never having been one for breaking rules, I did not tell a soul, not even Jenny. A month or so later, I was listening to the news on the radio at midnight and they started to mention those who were to be knighted or receive other honours. I quickly shouted down to Jenny, 'Oh by the way, I forgot to tell you, I got a CBE in the Queen's Honours List.' I thought I had better tell her in person before she heard it on the sports report. I'm not sure she was convinced by my display of poor memory.

Once the award was made public, I received 324 letters of congratulations, ranging from the Duke of Kent and Princess Margaret to the headmistress of my daughter's high school. It was very warming, although I suspect that some of them – the one from the Garter King of Arms perhaps – may have been automatically generated.

It was a very enjoyable occasion going up to Buckingham Palace. I was able to take Jenny and our two daughters, and we were joined by my mother for lunch afterwards. I cannot remember what the Queen said to me, as it all passed by in a bit of a blur. All I really remember was that the person in front of me was responsible for making the Queen's hats. I was quite nervous. Some people say that the CBE was for my services to tennis, others rather unkindly suggest it was for my services to underarm tennis. I know that I accepted the CBE on behalf of Wimbledon and the whole of my team. I felt honoured, surprised and embarrassed to have been singled out, when running Wimbledon is such a team affair. The CBE is an honour for the Club. There were so many people involved every year in making The Championships the event that it is, that I could not possibly take credit without passing credit on to them.

Chapter 7

Building the Club

Nowhere is the contrast between maintaining tradition and leading on innovation more apparent than in the infrastructure and landscaping of The All England Lawn Tennis Club. Maintaining our status as the premier tennis tournament in the world has meant that in each and every one of the last thirty-five years, there has been some form of alteration or improvement. For ten months of the year, the grounds look more like a building site than a tennis club. The voices emanating from the courts are more Polish than Home Counties, and the dress code is predominantly fluorescent yellow, not white. Not that the outsider coming to the Wimbledon fortnight would have the first clue on this aspect of the Club. Every year, by the first day of The Championships, the building work stops, the machinery is removed, the flowers return, and the grounds revert to the typically English garden setting.

The Club started life in 1868 as The All England Croquet Club, off Worple Road in Wimbledon. In 1875, tennis was added to its activities, and two years later, the name was switched to The All England Croquet and Tennis Club, and the first Lawn Tennis Championship created, in recognition of the growing popularity of the sport. 'Croquet' was actually dropped from the title at one point, but was restored in 1899 for sentimental reasons, when the Club became The All England Lawn Tennis and Croquet Club. The facilities were expanded to meet the ever-growing public demand prior to the First World War, but it was clear that a bigger site was needed. The Club moved to Church Road in 1922, acquiring the 13.5 acre site for £7,870. Building the courts cost a further £140,000, financed by Club funds and debentures. Many thought that the new ground would prove to be a white elephant, but any such criticism was quelled by the number of ticket applications in the first year. Demand was so great that the tickets had to be issued by ballot, the start of the system that exists today. The creation of a Centre Court designed to hold 14,000 people probably did more to popularise tennis than any other factor.

Since 1922, the site has grown to over forty-two acres through further acquisitions, but in truth it is still not enough land – 100 acres would be better.

Throughout the seventies and eighties we carried out piecemeal alterations to the grounds, under the direction of Knight Frank, the Club's surveyors. They did a very good job for us, and gave us some good ideas, particularly relating to improving facilities on Centre and No. 1 Courts. Together with Bell Buttrum and Partners, they came up with an idea for a new roof structure to Centre Court, which would enable us to reduce the number of supporting columns from 26 down to four. That meant that over 3,600 seats would now have a perfect view, whereas before it had been restricted.

One of the saddest alterations to be made was the replacement with seating of the two free standing-room areas on Centre Court. This followed the football tragedies at Bradford and Hillsborough stadia, following which we were forced by the authorities to move to an all-seated stadium on safety grounds. It meant that the only people allowed on Centre Court would be those who had seat tickets. We felt that some of the atmosphere and freedom for spectators would be lost, and it was not a change for the better. We were clearly not alone, judging by a letter written to *The Times* in

February 1990, which read, 'Sir, the House of Commons has been "all-seater" for some time now. To the best of my knowledge this has resulted in no improvement in crowd behaviour whatsoever.'

By the late eighties we had decided that, rather than doing things on an ad hoc basis, we needed a far-reaching co-ordinated plan as to how things would develop. We had a feeling that if we were to retain our status, we needed to keep the grounds updated, and not just on an annual basis. We were running out of land and space on our current site. We needed to know whether we could produce improvements without having to move grounds as we had in the 1920s. The US and Australian Opens had already moved to their new sites, and we were conscious of a need to stay ahead of the game.

With the great help of our consultant Keith Maplestone, we went out to a firm of architects, Building Design Partnership (BDP), gave them a detailed brief as to where we thought the Club needed to go over the next twenty years or so, and asked them to come up with a master plan.

We did not give them a budget, but we had a good idea of our limitations. We knew that what we had to do would have to be phased over a number of years, and we were dependent on debenture income. All of our capital improvements are funded from this, and not from TV, merchandising or ticket sales. The debenture income goes to the All England Ground Company, which is responsible for the capital improvements. Assuming the value of debentures did not go down, we knew that a set sum of money was going to come in every five years. We initiated debentures on Centre Court back in the 1920s when we were moving to our present ground. For about £46,000, current holders acquire the right to two seats on Centre Court for each day of The Championships for five years, plus access to the debenture holders' lounge, and the right to acquire a parking ticket. The current issue, due to expire in 2010, raised £46m. When we decided we were going to go ahead with a new No. 1 Court as part of our

long-term strategy, we introduced a debenture scheme specifically
for that court. It was done partly to raise funds, but the timing
was also right. It made more sense to launch a No. 1 Court debenture scheme for a new No. 1 Court itself, rather than launching
No. 1 Court debentures because we wanted to put a roof on
Centre Court. These debentures run for the first ten days of the
Fortnight, and are limited to 850 seats (plus benefits such as their
own lounge) as opposed to 2,300 on Centre Court. They therefore raise significantly less money but are nevertheless helpful.

In our brief for what we had now dubbed the Long Term Plan
(LTP), we wanted to have better facilities for players, spectators,
media, and officials, while creating benefits for our neighbours.
It tends to be the case that better means more space. If you want
a better kitchen, you ideally want a bigger kitchen. BDP said that
to a certain extent that was true, but there were ways of managing
it to maximise what you have.

One of the things that we felt was wrong was that Centre and
No. 1 Courts were built next to each other and No. 2 was just
across the main concourse from No. 1. The vast majority of spectators were therefore all tightly knit together, whereas in an ideal
world, taking into account safety and ease of circulation, we really
wanted to separate and spread out spectators across the estate.
The priority was to disengage the old No. 1 Court, and build a
new No. 1, north of Centre Court, in Aorangi Park. The Park
was land we had bought from the London department store
Barkers for £150,000 in 1967, but had immediately leased out to
the Wimbledon New Zealand Club, with the right for our Club
to use the grounds for car parking during The Championships.
Once the lease was up in 1979, we were able to use the whole of
Aorangi Park, and it featured prominently in the plans. Aorangi,
incidentally is the Maori term for Mount Cook, the highest moun-
tain in New Zealand, and translates as 'cloud in the sky'.

We kept the name Aorangi for the grass bank terrace, really
through want of a better suggestion. We did not like the idea of

naming places, courts or rooms after players, as players change and new ones come along. The irony that Aorangi Terrace is now commonly known as Henman Hill or Murray Mount has not escaped us.

The theme was 'tennis in an English garden', and we put emphasis on landscaping to create a garden atmosphere, with reduced impact from television and hospitality. We wanted people to enjoy the experience more – whether through better circulation space around the courts, better catering, or greater comfort from their seats. However, we also wanted facilities for advanced TV coverage, better media coverage, and enlarged player changing, leisure and fitness space. Better conditions for watching tennis would include the new No. 1 Court, two additional outside courts, 25 per cent extra seating and more spectator space around each court. Improved transport facilities, by bus, train and car, would set the right tone from the outset, and separate 'back of house' circulation for top players, organisers, and service vehicles would help with efficiency to everyone's benefit.

There were also the neighbours to consider. Our plans would involve a phenomenal amount of building work in a residential area. They needed to be shown the benefits of the LTP, such as less traffic congestion around the grounds, progressive reduction of queue impact, and enhancement of the park setting, while also seeing how we would minimise disruption along the way.

One measure we had to consider was the amount of time we would spend in setting up the grounds, for example in putting up marquees, in preparation for The Championships. Despite the work that has gone on, and the growth of the site, we do not allow any additional time in setting up that might disrupt the neighbours further. The first marquees are erected no sooner than April, and must be removed by the end of July.

BDP seemed able to accommodate pretty much all of our demands, other than being able to host the qualifying competition on our own land rather than at Roehampton. At that time, we had fourteen practice courts and since then we have created a further eight. That would be enough for the qualifying competition, but the courts are too close together. You cannot get the umpires' and linesmen's chairs to fit around the courts. Even if we could, we would not then have the space for the top players to practise on site in the week prior to The Championships. We would not have been keen on the idea of sending them elsewhere – the players even less so!

Once we had the report back from BDP, we shared the findings with all major stakeholders, particularly Merton council. We took them with us, and kept them consulted on our plans well before we put in an official application. A very good model of what we wanted done was made. Richard Saxon, who headed BDP, made some excellent presentations, and we followed up with more presentations to neighbours, the media, and the members, so that there were no surprises. We knew the plan needed to be sold in advance. Quite frankly, if we had not got the planning permission, we would have seriously had to consider moving site. Around this time I did a BBC interview on Centre Court with Gerald Williams and was asked if we did not get planning permission, what would we do? Move to Basingstoke, I replied, which sent a few shockwaves around the Court! Happily it never came to that, although a week later I got a letter from Basingstoke council's chief executive enclosing a video espousing the merits of the place. There was no question of us ever being at loggerheads. We had a good relationship with Merton, who wanted The Championships to stay here. I suspect, but have no proof, that the Labour council did not have too many voters around the area of the Club, so they were less than worried about the impact.

To our relief and not a little surprise, we received permission from Merton very quickly. What took longer was the section 106 agreement, which had to be negotiated between the council and ourselves. It is in effect a planning obligation, but common practice with larger building projects, and a way for the local authority to raise funds for good uses. There were a number of points that the council insisted that we did within the local community. We put money into refurbishing the forecourt of Wimbledon station, and did some improvements in Wimbledon Park with the addition of things like toilets and floodlights. Other areas included paying for a tennis development officer in Merton. The overall amount involved came as a bit of a shock, and was more than we had budgeted for. We had had experience in this area with an earlier application, but on nothing like the same scale. Subsequent planning applications have also attracted section 106 agreements, but to a much lesser degree, so perhaps the council believed they had had their two pennyworth in stage 1. It was negotiable, so we did get it down by a considerable amount, but it was still more than we had bargained for.

With the costs and amount of work involved, the project was to be split into three stages. We had just announced our plans and put the application in, when, totally separately and coincidentally, Merton decided they wanted to sell the freehold of Wimbledon Park Golf Club, just across the road from us. It came as a total surprise, and completely threw us, given how much resource we had committed to the Long Term Plan, but it was an opportunity so large that we thought we should try and buy it with the future in mind. Cash flow was an issue, but with the aid of a temporary bank loan (long since repaid) we put in a successful bid of £5.2m, and are the landlords of the 73-acre golf club, which has a tenancy of 33-odd years left to run. We had hoped to buy the Wimbledon Club also, a sports club which sits in the middle of the golf course on a ten-acre site. They had approached us with a view to selling, and we acquired the twenty-acre site in Raynes Park to rehouse them. However, in the end, I think they felt we were trying to push them out, and they walked away, which left a bad taste in the mouth for all concerned. We now use Raynes Park for grass practice courts, and outside the Wimbledon period it is let out to clubs and schools who do not have adequate playing facilities.

Chairman John Curry was instrumental in pushing the golf club purchase and the Long Term Plan forward and deserves a lot of credit for his foresight and perseverance. Both he and Peter Jackson, who chaired the LTP sub-committee, were hugely influential in fulfilling the LTP's goals, devoting inestimable time and effort to the project.

Work on stage 1, the key point of which was the creation of a new No. 1 Court, started immediately after the 1994 Championships. The new court, with a capacity of 11,500 seats compared with 6,350 on the old, was ready for play in 1997. Hosting The Championships in the intervening years was incredibly challenging. To maintain its status as younger brother to Centre Court, the new No 1 was countersunk into the hillside in Aorangi Park. That meant removing over 100,000 cubic metres of clay, not to mention all the work that was obviously necessary in stabilising the ground when removing that much material. For the 1995 Championships, the first two levels were constructed, in as much as we had two enormous flat slab areas around the court that we had to use as a platform for marquees and various other public facilities. The following year was a little better, with parts of the stadium open to the public, once they had been temporarily fitted out. During this period we had two cranes in operation, but had to remove one for The Championships, as it severely affected the players' sight-line and impaired the vista across the grounds. Those two years were the worst examples of Wimbledon being held in a building site, and the dust and noise created by the removal of the earth for the underground tunnel and stadium was a source of aggravation for our neighbours.

Our neighbours know now that we do our best to minimise the disruption and they appreciate that. They also see how the place is enhanced once we have finished our work. For example, the homes by our new practice courts have benefited enormously. They used to look out over a rough old patch of grass, but now see six perfect courts with good players in action on them. Not only is a good view good for the soul, it is good for house prices.

When the new No. 1 building, complete with improved public and hospitality dining facilities, was ready in 1997 it was cause for celebration. The inaugural event was in fact a non-tennis affair. Prior to the official opening, No. 1 Court played host to a special edition of *Songs of Praise*, which was an interesting diversion. The court was officially opened by HRH the Duke of Kent, our President, who came out and ceremoniously measured the net before play started with Tim Henman. The Duke presented silver salvers to ten former champions who had each won the singles title at least three times, and the three British singles champions – Angela Mortimer/Barrett, Ann Jones and Virginia Wade – were also introduced. Having seen the complexity of the creation and development of the court, I found it immensely satisfying to have been part of the Opening Ceremony and to look forward to the years to come.

Stage 1 also saw the building of two additional grass courts, 18 and 19, and a new broadcast centre for TV and radio, which became the first permanent sports media building in the world. In order to maintain the levels of income and interest we were attracting from the media networks, we needed to provide good facilities for them. It is not as if they are covering a one-day event; it is fourteen days on the trot. Before, they had been camped up in the car park in Portakabins and temporary marquees, and it was a little bit ramshackle. Now we can say that no other sporting organisation in the world can currently match the range of studio and production facilities provided in the Wimbledon Broadcast Centre. All the Club's international broadcasting customers were able to provide input into the design and shape of the building, and we have ended up with a state of the art centre tailored specifically for its users' needs.

Despite the problems with the old set-up, it was never the case that building the Broadcast Centre was a no-brainer. After all, we were talking about putting up a massive building that was really only going to be used for two weeks a year. The cost of the building and the amount of space it took up inside the ground were big factors, but we knew that in the long term it made sense.

We built Aorangi Park Terrace with a vehicle tunnel. It meant that all the broadcast lorries could go down the tunnel and not have to go into Somerset Road, which is residential. That did a lot to improve life for our neighbours, in terms of reduced noise and traffic congestion. Another advantage was that all the catering lorries could come into the grounds at gate 1 and go down the tunnel to discharge everything. The food is then distributed via underground buggy routes. Previously, all goods had had to be carried through the main thoroughfares, already over-congested because of the proximity of Centre and No. 1 Courts.

The other aspect of the first stage was the landscaping of the whole of the northern end. I think this landscaping of the grounds is one of the elements of the LTP of which I am most proud. We stayed true to our aim of 'tennis in an English garden'. When budgets were tight, it would have been easy to cut back in this area, but we did not, and the results are much the better for it. Aorangi Terrace is mainly grass, banked in tiers leading down to the big screen at the bottom beside No. 1 Court. It would have been very easy for us to have made it all concrete terraces with benches, but aesthetically it would not have looked half as appealing. There is also a water feature, which almost did not make it through on safety grounds, but it has proved to be a real asset. I also have to give credit to BDP, who advised us that having a car park at the highest part of the grounds meant that we were not using the land to best effect. We changed the plans and now spectators can enjoy beautiful views over the estate and to the London skyline.

In 2000, we opened the Millennium Building, which represented stage 2 of the LTP, on the site of the old No. 1 Court. The aim here was to provide better facilities for the players, members, press and photographers, officials, stewards, ball boys and girls. A quick glance at some of the facilities provided within the building demonstrates how the face of tennis has changed in the open and commercial era. As with the other Grand Slams, players have access to physicians, physiotherapists, masseurs and other treatments because, generally speaking, players cannot bring their own trainers in. It would be chaotic. We could easily end up with 200 trainers on site, each with their own specific requirements for their clients, not to mention room and equipment demands. We use ATP trainers who are on the circuit all year, and are therefore already familiar with the players. Players are free to, and do, bring their own trainers for use outside the grounds.

One of the most unfortunate elements of the modern era is drug testing. It was first introduced at The Championships in 1986. Tests are conducted randomly for the first few rounds, meaning that probably half of the players are checked once they come off court. From the quarter-finals onwards, every player is tested. It is now standard procedure at Grand Slams, with each Grand Slam mandated to contribute by providing facilities and a sum of money towards the testing. The tests first came about by agreement of the Grand Slams and player associations as it was in everyone's best interests that the game is kept clean. Since 2007, the ITF has managed, administered and enforced the Tennis Anti-Doping Programme at all the events sanctioned by the ITF, ATP and WTA Tours, which includes Grand Slams and Davis and Fed Cup matches. There have been very few high-profile incidents. Having won the Australian Open earlier in the year, Petr Korda tested positive for nandrolone at Wimbledon in 1998. He was banned for a year, and although he was cleared of knowingly taking the substance, his subsequent appeals failed. More recently, and after my time, Martina Hingis tested positive for cocaine and, while vehemently denying the results, retired from the sport. By and large, however, despite the considerable expense involved, I think that the lengths that are taken have proved worthwhile, and drug abuse is not the problem in tennis that it is in other sports. It is a view shared by many of the players, with Andre Agassi,

Andy Roddick and Martina Navratilova all having publicly stated that they believe that the system is comprehensive and rigorous enough. Agassi's view was that, 'It's not possible to get more aggressive with the goal of maintaining the integrity of our sport.' His comments came following eleven urine tests and eight blood examinations, while playing in just thirteen tournaments.

Alongside new treatment and testing rooms, we were also able to upgrade the players' dressing rooms. Taking down the old No. 1 Court allowed us to put an additional 728 seats on the west side of Centre Court and underneath those, we have dressing rooms on three levels. The main ladies' and men's dressing rooms, used by members and top players, are at ground level. Above them are two dressing rooms that are identical, where the rest of the men change. At basement level, it is the same for the ladies. Again, we consulted heavily with the players here. We went around to various events, asking players whether they wanted horizontal or vertical lockers. The men wanted horizontal and the women vertical so that is what we did. We queried whether they should be lockable or not, given that we have dressing room attendants there all the time. Following consultation, the decision was made that they should not lock, as it would be complicated if people lost their keys. Whether to have baths or showers was another discussion point. Baths, it transpires, are a peculiarly British institution, and not that popular in the US or on the continent. Consequently, the non-members' dressing rooms have showers, while the members' have baths and showers.

The Millennium Building is laid out in almost a W shape, with roughly one end devoted to members and the centre to players. The other end (nearest to the broadcast centre) is for the press. We have around 800 international writers and radio reporters attending The Championships each year. There are three writing rooms, one on each of the three floors of the building, with enough desks for 350 journalists. A paper such as *The Times* would be allocated four desks, two for tennis correspondents and two for features and news writers. Each desk has closed circuit TV,

incorporating 33 channels as well as all Championships information and up to the minute results. All interviews conducted in
the press interview room are relayed live to the writing rooms on
their monitors, and transcriptions in several languages are available as soon as possible afterwards. We consulted frequently with
the Lawn Tennis Writers' Association when designing the press
facility, which helped in terms of the fine-tuning of the space. Little
things can make big differences – one suggestion was for an under-
desk compartment in which to keep research books and documents,
so that they were close at hand and could stay there overnight.

The completion of the Millennium Building tied in nicely with
our Millennium Championships celebrations, one of the nicest
presentations I have ever seen or attended. While the Duke of
Kent had officially opened the Millennium Building earlier in
June, we also had a Parade of Champions on the first Saturday.
We invited back all those who had won one or more singles titles,
or got to the final of the singles twice or more, or had won four
or more doubles titles, for a presentation on Centre Court. We
were concerned on several counts. People come to watch tennis,
not ceremonies, and we had a lot of champions to get through.
We wanted to respect them, but were conscious of how long it
all might take. We were also worried about the weather, which
had not been behaving as we would have liked. If it rained, we
were not sure how to get fifty-nine Waterford glass presentation
plates, a red carpet, and a cluster of champions off the grass
without damage or injury (primarily to the court!) and in quick
time, otherwise we might not have been able to use the court at
all that day. In the end we decided that we would just have one
token plate that would be presented to each person and then
given back, with the champions able to collect their own later, off
court. John Barrett acted as master of ceremonies and the Duchess
of Gloucester, honorary president of the LTA, carried out the
presentation. It went very well, judging by the letters we got.
Everyone watching had his or her own hero or heroine who came

back, which provided spectators with a wonderful trip down memory lane.

While the completion of the Millennium Building was the focal point for stage 2, we also renewed the south end of Centre Court in 2002, and managed to open six new grass practice courts, giving us twenty-two grass practice courts in addition to our eighteen Championship courts in 2003. Our head groundsman at this time, Eddie Seaward, made some excellent contributions to the Long Term Plan. He was able to ensure that the courts were designed in the right way with the right specifications. His man-management skills and maintenance of the courts to a consistently high standard were two further reasons why he thoroughly deserved his MBE in 2008. His predecessor, Jim Thorn, was also excellent. Jim came from St George's Hill, Weybridge, which, as you will remember was my club. It is nice that they still treat me as a friend there, given that I pinched their head groundsman, and their head coach, Alan Mills, to be our referee. Jim came to us in 1982 and stayed for nine years, in the meantime revolutionising the way the grass courts were prepared each year.

The focus of the third stage was supposed to be building a new No. 2 Court. It would be half sunk into the ground. In that way it would not be too much of an eyesore for residents looking across the estate or from the Clubhouse. We would also widen the passageways to improve crowd circulation and provide better viewing for spectators. However, we decided to put all of that on hold and concentrate on Centre Court – our Crown Jewel. When we had first laid out the LTP in the nineties, a retractable roof had been possible in as much as the technology was available, but what had not been proved to our satisfaction was that you could have a sliding roof that would work for grass court tennis. We had not seen a roof design that would: retain the grass at a quality that would withstand two weeks of play, and that would not make it sweat and be slippery; that would provide the right ambience for the spectators; and that would allow the grass to grow for the rest of the year. It was a contentious issue. We did not have all the answers, but certain members of the media and our committee wanted it as they had been to the Australian Open and seen the roof in action there. However, the Australians had a different set of circumstances. When they moved from Kooyong's private members' club to Flinders Park (now Melbourne Park), in order to finance the set-up, the main centre court had to be a stadium design, not just a tennis arena. They needed the stadium to be used for as many days a year as possible, for concerts or whatever, which meant adding a roof but saying goodbye to grass. Once grass is taken out of the equation, the addition of a roof becomes very much easier. Theirs is infinitely heavier than ours, is not translucent in any way, and is presumably specially designed in order for it to work well for concerts or musical events: there is no escape of noise or light through their roof. As well as having the roof over the main stadium at Melbourne Park, they have also built an adjacent stadium – again another multi-purpose building with a roof on it. It is something that I think all the Grand Slams are keen on in theory. The US would like to do it, but Flushing Meadows is such a vast stadium, it would be an incredibly complex exercise, not to say an amazing engineering feat. Roland Garros would also have liked to add a roof, but the failure to win the bid for the 2012 Olympics put paid to that for the time being.

Ten years ago, the debate was also about the pros and cons of having a roof over just one court. It was good for spectators and TV, but not necessarily great for the players, who are used to playing a grass court event outdoors, and would suddenly have to adjust to playing under a roof with artificial lighting. Also, logistically, it is not going to help you through a huge backlog of matches, and it will not help the balance of the schedule or draw. On the first day, we would try to play thirty-two men's matches in one half of the draw, with the other half being played on the second day, and the same with the ladies. In that way we continue to go through the draw evenly. You would want all your players to be playing the same stage matches at the same time, so that no player is given an unfair advantage by having an extra day's rest. However, if it rains all day and all play is wiped out save for five or six matches on the covered Centre Court, those players would have the upper hand by having progressed to the next stage a day earlier.

The significant advantage would be the guarantee of playing the semis and finals on Centre Court on the days stated, come rain or shine. The epic men's final between Federer and Nadal in 2008 would not have needed to go to the wire, with fears of bad light stopping play after rain interruptions earlier in the day. It certainly added to the tension, but it would have been a dreadful anti-climax if they had had to come back the next day to play, say, just two games. It would also help at least some spectators at Wimbledon and our global TV audience to see live tennis every day. As time has moved on, these arguments have taken precedence. The debate has shifted away from concerns over the draw towards the entertainment side, and I think even the players appreciate that this is not only a major sport, but also an entertainment industry that we are now in.

By the turn of the millennium, tests and expertise on roof structures had improved. We were now using HOK as our architects, who are the premier builders of sports stadia in the world, and who, incidentally, were behind the Millennium Stadium in Cardiff. Although that stadium had different requirements from our own, grass on a rugby pitch being less sensitive than grass on a tennis court, HOK were able to prove to us that the roof would work with no detrimental effects to the court. One of the points we made clear was that we wanted as good if not better growing conditions for the grass.

With the technology proven, our priorities changed, and we deviated from the Long Term Plan, creating instead a new three-year plan for Centre Court. In addition to the roof, we would extend (and upgrade) the seating from an existing capacity of

13,800 to 15,000. We would also have extended and upgraded catering and hospitality facilities for the public and debenture holders. The first two levels on the east side would hold both canteen-style and waitress service restaurants for the public, the latter being 25 per cent bigger than the existing Wingfield restaurant. There would also be a new, large Wimbledon shop in the south-east corner. The third level would be for debenture holders, and would include self-service on the east side and table-service dining areas overlooking courts 14 and 17. There would also be private suites and bar areas on the fourth level.

We made the decision early on that in the Centre or No. 1 Court buildings, we would not have hospitality suites which overlooked the court they were on. If play could be seen from the suites, there would be too much temptation for people to linger there rather than go down to the court, and there is nothing that aggravates the public more, quite rightly, than rows of empty hospitality seats.

Corporate hospitality is very conspicuous and takes up a lot of space. We wanted our users to have good locations, but not necessarily where the public would see too much of them. That was quite straightforward when they were in marquees on the hard courts at the sharp end of the grounds, and I think that we have achieved the same now that they are in the upper levels of Centre Court. Even though we have gained some space in Centre Court, hospitality will remain under 10 per cent of our ticket allocation, as the new No. 2 Court takes up some of the old outdoor hospitality area.

Before we could start work on the Centre Court and its surrounds, we had to remove everything that was currently inside the building, including the museum, with all its artifacts, and the Championship offices. That meant having a new museum building, which now accommodates all the office staff for The Championships on one level, with the ticket office and shop, museum, library, meeting rooms, plant rooms and storage rooms all on the ground floor and below.

Throughout the Long Term Plan, and in fact, for the last thirty-five years, we have used Galliford Try as our builders. They have done all the construction work, bar three new indoor courts opened in 1990, and the Aorangi Park Pavilion. Such is the extent of the work that some of Try's staff have rebuilt parts of the site that they had themselves built years earlier! Throughout the process, they have been excellent partners, directed by some able contract managers, such as Barry Luckett and Mike Bridges.

For the 2007 Championships, the roof had come off and the Centre Court was entirely exposed for the first and only time. One side of the building was a pure shell. There was no shelter from the weather in the stadium, so temporary rain cover places had to be created under the structure where people could get out of the rain. Temporary benches were put in the shell that was later to become the debenture holders' area. As much as possible had to be done to minimise the building site effect.

Getting ready for The Championships when there has been ten months of major buildings work going on is not just a question of putting up extra pot plants. This is where the skill and experience of our building and services manager, John Cox and his deputy Ah-Heng Turner helped us so well every year. We had to plan meticulously and tell the builders very carefully which spaces were needed for catering, or merchandising, or where temporary toilets needed to be plumbed in. Then, of course there were also temporary portaloos which had to be camouflaged and, for example, the concrete platforms on which the cranes sat had to be screened off for safety. The amount of timber the builders used was phenomenal.

It is incredibly expensive stopping work, clearing up and starting again. When Royal Ascot underwent a major transformation of its grounds, the event upped sticks and went to York, so that the works could continue uninterrupted. We did not have that option, as there is nowhere in the UK that could replicate Centre Court. It just meant that we had to be ready each year, and we had to find a way round any potential problems. The LTP had to stick to deadline, no ifs, no buts.

Normally we would try and get the builders to stop work by the opening of the grass courts, around the third week of May. That then allowed us a month to get ready, although on occasion, particularly of late, I think it has been nearer 1 June. Before leaving, the builders do a thorough clean throughout, and make safe in conjunction with health and safety, and it gets pretty tight each year. Most years, I did have a slight queasiness in my stomach, a slight sinking feeling that this was the year that it would not happen in time. There is small comfort in saying. 'We have always done it before.' It does not mean that you can do it every year. For starters, the amount and complexity of the work varied so much. Legal obligations also change. The local authority come round to inspect the grounds, before giving it the go-ahead from a health and safety perspective. That can be a uniquely stressful event, particularly after the Hillsborough tragedy. We had to make substantial alterations to the free standing areas, at a time when the authorities were at their most alert.

In 2009, this latest immense building project will come to fruition. The most visible, and I am sure most discussed element will be the roof. A few facts. The roof is made of a special waterproof fabric that is very strong, translucent and highly flexible. Its translucency will allow natural light to reach the grass, although artificial lighting will also be necessary. An air-conditioning system, supplying 143,000 litres of conditioned air per second to the bowl, will provide players and spectators with the optimal internal conditions. The roof will fold concertina style, which allows it to be stored in a very compressed area when not in use. It will take about ten minutes to close (less than half the time needed by the one at the Australian Open) and then it will be between ten and thirty minutes before play can restart, depending on climatic conditions. The new roof will be ten times heavier than the old, weighing 3,000 tonnes. If you consider that just four columns support the whole roof, it is quite amazing – but it is well within all tolerance levels, so there is no cause for concern! For those who love their statistics, apparently it would take 290 million tennis balls to fill the stadium with the roof closed. How that has been assessed, I have no idea.

Ten years ago, it was right to be wary of the appropriateness of a roof for Centre Court. In 2009, I think we can be proud of another hugely innovative step forward that will help retain Wimbledon as the premier tournament in the world, and still on grass.

What comes next will I hope, for all concerned, be a bit of a breather! That being said, plans are underway to accelerate stage 3, not only because it is less disruptive to our neighbours and members if we can get it all out of the way in one go, rather than over a number of years, but also to be sure that all work is completed in time for the Olympics. There is already a new No. 2 Court, located towards the southern end of the grounds to continue the policy of spreading spectators more evenly. The Club has also repositioned some of the southern outside courts, in order to provide wider walkways for spectators, and has also completed a new brick wall and railings around the Club's perimeter. New workshops and groundsmen's quarters are being constructed, and there are ongoing discussions as to what to do with the old No. 2 Court.

The LTP has taken up all of the debenture income since its inception. How future debenture income will be spent remains to be seen. I would never discount more building works of some kind or another, and there is the possibility of a roof over the new No. 1 Court. There is always more to be done.

Seeing the Long Term Plan come to fruition has given me probably my greatest sense of satisfaction. It was an additional workload over and above running the Club and Championships and took up a considerable amount of my time, and that of many of my colleagues. Mainly, that was in the planning stage. Creating a new No. 1 Court was not just about the court and its seats, but all the facilities around, all the restaurants and suites upstairs, and the crowd movement. The same was true with the Millennium Building – how would we fit it out, what proportion would we give to the press or players, what did the players actually want, and would all of that fit into the design of the building? Plans have changed along the way. Originally, the Millennium Building was going to be rectangular, which would have been functional and easy to adapt. The switch to a W configuration allows for a nice summery-type building with good views for most of the users in various directions. Also, the Fred Perry statue was originally going to be in the middle of the main concourse, but then there were fears for his safety, given the amount of heavy machinery used during the work on Centre Court. And the roof had not been contemplated at all in the first plans. There are niggling areas yet to be sorted, but these are small concerns in light of the major hurdles already overcome.

I have already paid tribute to Peter Jackson, but his successor as chairman of the LTP sub-committee, John Dunningham, is also owed a huge debt of gratitude by the Club, for all his voluntary work over a number of years. Both John Curry and then Tim Phillips have so ably led the whole plan, together with a team of consultants and advisers, including especially Ian King, a Club member. At the same time, the executives and first line managers have contributed greatly, on top of an already full workload. The Club is so grateful to them too.

It has been very exciting to watch our paper plans and papier mâché models become reality, knowing the positive impact they have had and will continue to have for players and spectators alike. It gives me particular satisfaction to know that there will only ever be a few of us who appreciate the full extent of the work that was required. For everyone else, it has always just been 'tennis in an English garden'.

Chapter 8

Broadcast Around the World

For the majority of the year, large parts of the All England Club lie dormant, eerily quiet and uninhabited, the odd sheet of paper with tournament statistics left abandoned on a journalist's desktop. Walk around the grounds and the biggest gathering of people you will see will be a group of construction labourers, kitted out in uniform hard hats and yellow jackets. Our members quietly go about their business, enjoying a mixed doubles here, catching up in the bar there. Then we hit June, and the transformation is unimaginable. When it comes round to the first day of The Championships, this private members' club in a leafy suburb of SW London finds itself broadcast into the living rooms of some 750 million homes worldwide. The Championships are the largest annual broadcast of any sports event in the world, with footage distributed to over 170 countries. I suspect it would surprise a few people to know the pioneering role that the Club has played in the advance of television; there have been some significant landmarks in our past.

Wimbledon was covered by BBC radio as far back as 1927. Permission for the broadcast was only given on condition that the commentator, Teddy Wakelam, whispered, and that the BBC also paid for a pane of frosted glass to prevent their hut having a view of the players' lavatory. Television followed in 1937, with half an hour a day coverage. The day after the first broadcast, the *Daily Telegraph* reported in some wonderment: '. . . people could observe from some miles away every movement of the players . . . There were also scenes of spectators in the stands and some of the faces could be seen quite clearly.' In 1967, the very first colour television transmission in this country took place on the first Saturday of The Championships, when a four and a half hour programme was aired from Centre Court. The BBC then chose to sponsor the first major professional tournament at the Club in August that year, in order to mark the introduction of the colour transmissions and of BBC2.

Fast-forward to today, and the BBC, as host broadcaster (as well as the UK rights holder), acts for more than forty other international networks. ITV covered Wimbledon alongside the BBC from 1956 to 1968, but then decided it was not worth competing. The BBC's coverage of every moment of play on nine courts (seven for the last eight days) effectively amounts to nine separate outside broadcast operations. To help them in their task there is a range of studio and production facilities provided in the Wimbledon Broadcast Centre that is currently not matched by any other sporting organisation in the world.

Television revenue is hugely important to the Club and therefore the LTA, and provides the bulk of its income – more so than ticketing, hospitality or merchandising. Its financial significance has increased over the years, although the climb has been erratic, due in part to variable rates of exchange and in part to fluctuating interests within each market. We had a hugely beneficial period in the eighties in Germany, for instance. Their satellite stations were coming on board and vying for supremacy. There was a lot of competition and we rode on the back of that, happily for us right at the time that Steffi Graf and Boris Becker were at their height and causing unprecedented interest in tennis in Germany. But then the bidding wars died down, and the players' dominancy receded, meaning that income from that one country significantly reduced, to be replaced elsewhere.

Some broadcasters have done better than others. Thirty years ago, NBC were paying ten times more than the BBC, while the BBC were getting more hours coverage than the US. NBC, the free to air broadcaster, have always said that paying rights fees at the level that they did, did not generate income for them, so the contract was accepted on the basis of prestige. The US was the key market for many, many years, but as we had negotiated a premium fee from the outset, income from that quarter, while sizeable, has not escalated rapidly. However, we are now getting much more realistic fees from the BBC, the host broadcaster.

In 1957, the BBC paid us £5,000 a year. That was by no means the lowest figure. In 1960, Eurovision, representing the whole of Europe, paid us £1,500. We suspected that we might be able to do a bit better. The opportunity came in 1968, a real watershed in the history of tennis when the sport moved into the Open era. The advent of colour was increasing television's appeal, and there was the potential for real money to start coming into the sport. Ironically, however, the dawning of professionalism also meant that costs went up considerably. The surplus in 1968 almost halved, partly because we had to pay prize money for the first time.

With change around us, it was time to think about getting in professional help. It was not a hard decision that we should make use of an agent to conduct our negotiations. We were a private members' club that essentially ran one event a year. By contrast, the other Grand Slams were run by their national associations, which meant that they tended to be putting on more events and were therefore dealing with the world of television more frequently than us, a fact that may have warranted their having their own inhouse negotiator. The growing commercial nature of tennis and sport in general also meant that there was a new breed of sports marketing agent around, adept at exploiting the opportunities. I have already mentioned the hugely significant role that Mark

McCormack played in Wimbledon's development, but it was in negotiating television contracts that he particularly excelled.

The complexity of television worldwide developed. There was satellite, cable, and terrestrial, but there were also all the other ingredients that you could put into a TV package apart from just the rights fee. Generally, media technology was getting pretty complicated, and more components were getting linked or bundled together. In the end, the figures really spoke for themselves. We had not been doing particularly well in Europe in terms of TV revenue, and it led Mark to turn round to us and say, 'If you give it to me, I guarantee I'll double what you're getting from Bagenal.' It was a pretty aggressive call, but he was absolutely right.

Mark's IMG got involved in Europe in 1982, the same year that we officially decided to schedule play on the second Sunday. That was no coincidence. We had initially been reluctant to make the change, for all the historic reasons of Sunday being a day of rest. We suspected that it would not go down well with the local community or the local churches, but Mark was very persuasive. He pointed out that quite apart from the benefits, from The Championships' point of view, of having more spectators able to watch finals on Saturday and Sunday than on Friday and Saturday, he would be able to get us an additional £400,000 of income purely from television. Again it was a punchy call, again he was absolutely right, but it was no straightforward task. It took almost two years for the decision to come to fruition with the amount of consultation involved. Compromises had to be made. With the neighbours, for example, we agreed not to sell any on-the-day Centre Court tickets for the last four days of The Championships. Queues for on-day sales were getting so long that they were trailing around all the private roads leading up to the grounds, which was a constant source of aggravation for the residents.

Although we had now taken on board a hard-nosed negotiator to deal with our TV rights, the revenue generated was never our only consideration. We were equally concerned that Wimbledon be carried to as large an audience as possible. We looked closely at the hours of play that the network was going to cover, and how that would be divided between live coverage or tape-delayed coverage. We also looked at the coverage within the territory. We did not want rights to be sold purely to a satellite channel, where fewer people might be able to watch if it was on a pay per view basis. Satellite and cable TV were usually able to offer higher rights fees than terrestrial, yet in most parts of the world we aimed to place at least part of The Championships on national, free-to-air television.

In Europe, originally, we sold the rights through Eurovision, a conglomerate representing the European countries. The money was adequate, but we could not guarantee that Wimbledon would receive good airtime in terms of live coverage. Eurovision only dealt with national broadcasting companies, which meant that we were not necessarily getting all the hours of coverage. In France for example, they might be showing the Tour de France.

From Eurovision we moved onto UFA and then Prisma. These German companies again were bodies that represented Europe-wide rights, but this time, although the money was very good, the problem was that they primarily dealt with satellite companies. We made a fundamental decision in 2000 that we would sell the rights on a country-by-country basis in Europe. That would allow our agents, Trans World International (TWI, a division of IMG), to go from one country to the next negotiating with the various networks, as we wanted more terrestrial, or free-to-air, coverage. Generally speaking, a free-to-air broadcaster gave one a wider coverage of one's sport but paid less relatively than a satellite or cable network. We were fairly sure, however, that taking this step, would have a significant downturn effect on our income, and it did. It was also time-consuming and so an expensive thing for TWI to do, which obviously we had to contribute towards. It has however, proved itself worthwhile. We now have greater coverage, and, once we had a network on board, income has also steadily grown.

Then there was the question of quality. On a basic level we needed to be assured that the type of channel that we were selling through was focused on sports rather than on, say, pornography, to take an extreme. Also, the quality of the production team, and whether or not they had experience in tennis events was important. We wanted Wimbledon to be seen in territories where its image was enhanced rather than reduced as could happen with poor or amateur coverage.

And then there was the money. In some years, with New Zealand and Switzerland for example, we did not do a deal, as we did not think the money being offered was sufficient and we did not want to set that sort of precedent. They came back the following year. However, it was not always a question of selling the rights to the highest bidder. Both the BBC and NBC have become loyal partners. We have been with the BBC since 1937, and the Club has renegotiated the contract, which incorporates TV, radio, broadband and BBC iPlayer, until 2014. The multimedia drive forward has been good in that it has enabled the Club to offer a broader package to viewers and listeners around the world, and has made Wimbledon more accessible. People, wherever they are, can now follow The Championships any time of the day or night. The financial benefits are less clear, given that media rights are bundled together, but accessibility has been the key driver. Technology was not my forte, and I think my greatest contribution towards the multimedia revolution was in surrounding myself by people with greater knowledge than I had.

The government, unwittingly, hampered us in our ability to negotiate better UK rights fees by the elevation of The Championships to 'Crown Jewels' event status, alongside the likes of the FA Cup final, the Grand National and the Open golf. These listed events are ring-fenced, meaning that the exclusive sale of UK broadcasting rights to pay TV is prevented by the Broadcasting Act. We, along with the other listed events, tried to consult with government on this, stating that we wanted a free hand to be able to negotiate with whomever we pleased. Our aim was always to have Wimbledon covered on free-to-air channels, but it hardly put us in a strong negotiating position with the terrestrial channels when they knew that our hands were tied by statute. The government has not changed its view on this, and in the meantime, it is quite possible that less money flows through to British tennis as a result.

Wimbledon has been with NBC since 1968, despite having had discussions with others such as CBS and ABC. By and large, it has been a happy union and we have been lucky to have them on board. We thought we might come to blows at one point, when one NBC executive had the temerity to ask if we could extend the changeover time by thirty seconds so that they could fit in extra advertising. I relayed the request to John Curry, our chairman at the time, who, once he had come down from the ceiling, replied, 'If they ever ask that question again, we will not extend the contract.'

Given their importance to Wimbledon, NBC did and do receive special treatment. They have their own cameras on Centre Court, which is not ideal as they take up space and are intrusive. It is a constant battle balancing the needs and demands of the television network and the level of intrusion for the spectators trying to watch the game. However, NBC had slightly different production techniques from the BBC, and often used to want tighter shots of the players, honing in on the faces, which was something the BBC did not tend to do so much. At the end of games, they would want different shots of the players, whereas the BBC tended to go to the scoreboard more. As far as we were concerned, it was not great if the NBC camera was not being used, and was sitting unmanned with a cover over it, while the BBC were covering the action. It could often happen if, perhaps, it was a doubles match that the US audience might not be so interested in. The image of an unmanned camera on Centre Court was one that we would rather not have sent around the world, but unfortunately, insisting that the cameras be removed would have been more trouble than it was worth, and could have caused a fair amount of disruption.

NBC are also the only network allowed to do a separate interview with the champion and runner up. Bud Collins interviews the players in the anteroom before they go into the Clubhouse after they have come off Centre Court. That concession was in fact the catalyst for the on-court interviews that are now a part and parcel of Wimbledon. The BBC asked whether they could do a live interview on court, given that an interview, playing only to a US audience, would be happening just off court. We resisted it for a while, thinking that it was 'not Wimbledon'. Our experience of hearing those interviews at other tournaments was not very encouraging. Not surprisingly perhaps, given that the players have just finished a final, the comments were not particularly erudite or insightful, and they tended to say exactly the same things.

In the end, in 2000, we relented, as it was the way things were going. We have increasingly become an entertainment business and we are living in a world obsessed by personalities. You can understand that people want to hear from 'the stars', and find out a bit more about them. We also had to think about what the players might want, but I do not think there was any objection there. They are obliged to do an interview after every match in any case. I think even now it has mixed responses. By and large people do like it, although it depends on the players and how composed they are. Federer was very good, and very gracious, as was Roddick. My problem with it was that I could never hear what was being said. The PA system goes into the stands rather than out on court, so it was very hard to hear what Sue Barker was asking and what the responses were. I found an enigmatic smile was the best way forward in those circumstances.

We are lucky with the broadcasters we have used. In the forty years we have been involved with NBC we have only had to deal with two bosses, Arthur Watson and Dick Ebersol. Similarly, the US cable station HBO did a fantastic job for us for over twenty years, through their devout Wimbledon fan Seth Abraham, especially given that they are primarily a film network in the US. HBO did live coverage all the way through, but did not have the rights to the finals, which went to NBC along with first choice over the semi-finals. HBO did more hours of coverage than NBC, who only started on the Middle Sunday with a wrap-up programme of the first week. However, having NBC on board was vital, regardless of how good HBO's coverage was. In the US, most people would turn to NBC if they were looking for tennis, and to HBO for films. To us, that was an important distinction.

Kerry Packer's Channel Nine in Australia, was another stalwart. Whatever one might say about him or Rupert Murdoch – and people say a lot – he loved his sport, particularly cricket. It was his more flamboyant gestures that often courted attention. I remember Mark telling us a story about one of Kerry's polo outings while staying in his home in Hampshire. One Sunday Kerry and his friends had been playing and it was now about seven or eight in the evening. Kerry called his wife and asked if the chef could cook something for ten people, and she replied that the chef had been given the evening off. So Kerry drove to the local village to a restaurant that was shut. He rang the bell and said, 'I wonder if you would open up. We'd just like ten steaks and some wine. Keep it simple, but I'll make it worth your while.' The owner declined, saying that it was a Sunday night. So Kerry went off to the next village and asked the same thing from another restaurant that was shut. This time he had more luck, and they had their steaks and a nice enough meal. At the end, Kerry Packer wrote out a cheque and said to the owner, 'I hope that you think this covers what we had, but I'm only going to give it to you on condition that you go down to the next village in the morning and tell the guy there how much I've written this cheque for.' It was £10,000.

I only met Kerry Packer once. We had dinner at the Club, and Kerry got a helicopter to Battersea and then changed to a chauffeur driven car. This was accompanied by an ambulance, which followed him everywhere. In October 1990, he had suffered a near-fatal heart attack in Sydney and was clinically dead for six minutes before being revived by ambulance officers. In his own inimitable fashion, he went on to buy portable defibrillators – nicknamed Packerwhackers – for every ambulance in New South Wales. He seemed all right the night I met him, in fact on very good form.

Our broadcast centre was built in 1997 and remains state of the art. Prior to that, the media centre was a temporary structure that had to be erected each year. It was designed by Buzz Hornett at TWI, who was key in acting as the chief link between the BBC and the countries with whom rights had been negotiated. The centre, complete with satellite dishes sending images out to the world, overlooked Court 14 and was affectionately known mainly by Buzz and Mark McCormack – as Buzz's Tower.

The new centre can accommodate fifteen foreign television companies, who can each produce their own programmes directly from the site, in addition to the BBC as host broadcaster. NBC, for example, will take one or two presentation studios with production studios beneath, which means that they can put their own gloss on their output. It is a significant financial outlay, as they have to pay for the space, and send an entire crew over to stay in London for two weeks. In 2008, the BBC made over 10,000 hours of tennis available to the Club for distribution to 173 countries around the world. The BBC itself aired 140 hours of coverage on BBC1 and BBC2 plus their interactive service. In addition, over 2,000 television and radio people were accredited over the Fortnight.

Radio over the years was slightly taken for granted. It did not feature in our financial agreements with the BBC for many years.

It was a matter of 'Draw up the contract for the television rights, oh and don't forget to put the word radio in there too.' Its lesser status was certainly something that John Inverdale picked up on. When talking about the Radio 5 Live studio, he said, 'A bit cramped? When Dame Kiri Te Kanawa came on as a guest during the rain delay, she said it was the first time that she had ever been interviewed in a coffin.' The fact is that radio studios will always be seen as the poor relative to TV studios, as they lack the necessity for good aesthetics.

Radio has become more of a financial contributor of late. The first radio agreement in the US was with Golden Gaters in California in 1979. Now it is with Sirius. Sad to say, in my entire time at Wimbledon, I never listened to any of the BBC's radio commentary, as there were so many other things needing to be done. I understand it was very good, and am certainly taking the time to appreciate it now.

We started Radio Wimbledon in 1992, which only broadcasts over a four or five mile radius. We were approached by two guys who were doing a radio show specifically for the Le Mans 24 hours sports car race each year. We could see that there might be a benefit for us, particularly for people coming to The Championships, who could be kept up to date on which car parks were full or which trains were not running. It started with trying to help people getting to The Championships and has developed to include chatty interviews and coverage.

It has grown very well – it is now on the internet and therefore worldwide – and provides a good service, although it is a cost factor and does not make any money for the Club. It broadcasts from 8 a.m. to 10.30 p.m., and so needs a lot of presenters and engineers. At least the station now has the same wavelength on the radio each year. Before that, it made it difficult to advertise the service, as we did not know which frequency it would be on.

Television was becoming sufficiently important to us that in

1989, we introduced a television marketing director, Ian Edwards. He left in 2002 and was replaced by John Rowlinson, with a change in title to director of television. John was the former assistant head of sport and outside broadcast at the BBC, so a very high calibre recruit. Despite at one time having his eye on the top job at the BBC, Head of Sport, John came to us not so much as a career move, but because he wanted a post that he knew he would thoroughly enjoy. And he does. He advises TWI, who do the negotiations on our behalf, and makes sure the contract, when finalised, is executed properly in terms of all the detailed arrangements. He has done a good job and is well respected amongst the broadcasters and by TWI.

Opening the doors to television and allowing the Club, the players, and our official suppliers to be viewed by millions the world over was inevitably going to increase pressure on us to become ever more commercial. Marketeers were certainly not ignorant of the potential opportunity that such an audience would bring. It was a constant battle, and there were times when it felt attacks were coming from all angles. Wimbledon was not the only venue to be targeted by opportunists. It happened at all events, and was one of the things we discussed at our Major Events Organiser Meetings. Ambush marketing was one particularly hoary thorn in our side. The only branding permitted on court is on items essential to the court activities – the Slazenger balls, or the Rolex scoreboard for example. In my time, I think the idea of oncourt advertising hoardings probably came up no more than three times. That was how strongly we felt against it. When Lord's went down that route by putting advertising on its perimeter boarding, if anything it made us more determined not to do the same. Although it was understandable, given the lesser funding in cricket, I have never got used to seeing them there, and I think it's a shame that the home of cricket was not able to hold out as the only ground to have totally clean boards.

Imagine then, the reaction from our official suppliers, who are told the strict limitations on their own advertising and branding, if they should witness a rival company giving out free T-shirts and products to spectators queuing outside. Suddenly, thousands of Centre Court spectators could be wearing T-shirts or baseball hats with the rival's logo there for all the world to see. It is a very tricky situation, as everybody likes a freebie, and the Club does not want to come across as a killjoy, but the damage it can do to existing suppliers and the integrity of the ground is obvious. If official suppliers are not allowed to give out free T-shirts and hats, then nobody else should be. It is a question of degree: a free cushion or pens and pencils from the hospitality marquees are fine. Anything that will be conspicuous to the cameras, like branded umbrellas or items of clothing, is not.

One way of dealing with it is to confiscate any offending items at the gate and tell people that they can be picked up at the end, but it is easier said than done and is not ideal. It holds up the queue for starters. The better solution is to try and stop it happening in the first place, but it is an ongoing problem, and also quite delicate to deal with, as it is not an illegal activity, just undesirable.

There have been some quite imaginative attempts at free publicity. During one Championships, I was walking around and I heard on my walkie-talkie that there was a pink elephant in Somerset Road wanting to come into the grounds. I was a long way away and tied up, so I asked Richard Grier to investigate, thinking it was clearly nonsense. However, there was indeed a real elephant, all decked out in pink, advertising a local circus and marching towards gate 13. With no ticket, he was refused entry.

Worse are the planes or helicopters that fly overhead with some banner trailing after them. You then get the unwanted marketing *and* the noise of the engine directly overhead. We have called through to the Civil Aviation Authority to get planes cleared away and to try and prevent a repeat performance on the odd occasion when it has happened. They were not the noisiest visitors, though. Concorde flew over to do a large sweep on one of her last flights in 2003, which was something we had not expected at all. The Concorde officials had the good grace to ask permission to do it a second time, and we were happy for that to happen, as long as it was before play started. Concorde was a beautiful machine, and it was quite poignant that she should include us in her farewell plans.

Players' clothing is another area where it felt as if we were being subjected to a constant war of attrition. Every year, manufacturers would try to push the boundaries on colour on white outfits, and have had some success with logos. There is no question that the amount that is permitted has grown, and the beneficiaries are the players and the manufacturers, with no benefit at all to the venue. But what is done is done, and there is no turning the clock back. We just did not want the players to become sporting bill-boards. The Grand Slam Committee has agreed with both the male and female player associations what is permissible at the Grand Slams. There is a limit on the number of square inches that can be taken up with a logo, where the logo can be placed, and what rules apply if, for example, a player is wearing a sleeve-less dress. It is all very detailed – the rules on logo positions take up an entire page of the Grand Slam rule book.

I was interested to see that the rules were most recently tested by Adidas, when the use of its three stripes was queried. Adidas uses three distinctive bold stripes as one of its symbols. The big debate was whether those stripes constituted a design, and were therefore not affected by the logo restrictions, or were a manu-facturer's logo. The Grand Slam Committee had held them to be a logo, and as such, Adidas would have to comply with the rules restricting the size, like all other clothing manufacturers. The company was given a grace period in which to comply, but instead, chose to sue all four Grand Slams and the ITF. First round went to Adidas, who, when the Club sought to enforce the rules, went to the High Court and were granted an injunction. That left them free to ignore the restrictions for the 2006 Championships, until the High Court was able to conduct a full hearing later that year. It was resolved in an out of court settlement before the full hearing, with all parties accepting that it was a manufacturer's logo, but agreeing to an amendment to the dress code, which would increase the space allowed for such logos, where the manufacturer's name did not appear.

The Grand Slam rule book also covers what players are permitted in terms of logos on bags, towels and other accessories. To avoid any problems, we did not allow players to bring onto court towels other than our own, even though this proved to be an expensive exercise. Each year we would lose literally thousands of towels, which I found extraordinary. One year, we tried to stop players' forgetfulness, shall we say, in popping the towels in their bags and taking them home, by providing a souvenir towel, nicely wrapped in a presentation box. However, when the towels kept disappearing through the door at the same rate of knots, that was one idea we knocked on the head in pretty quick time.

Alongside our restrictions on the size and location of logos, there were the rules on 'predominantly white' clothing. This is an area that remains very important to the Club, but can be really quite difficult to police. Several years ago, in order to reduce confusion, the phrase was changed to 'almost entirely white', and that wording is now in the entry form and Grand Slam rule book. We would write to all the clothing manufacturers, enclosing a number of guidelines and asking them to submit to us the clothing range that they were proposing to give to their contracted players for the upcoming Championships. They were not obliged to do so, but if they did, it gave us all a chance to work together to reach agreement prior to the event. I was in Australia one January, and was asked by Nike to come down to their hotel by the river and view their ladies' clothing range. They were working with Maria Sharapova on designs, while she was at the tournament, and were hoping to get agreement from all sides there and then.

The majority of players do not get involved with the clothing decisions, frankly just being pleased to be given free kit. However, the top female ones, like Sharapova and the Williams sisters, would play a large part in the decision process.

At Wimbledon it was my role to check the range, as the referee is not in situ at that time of year. While it would normally fall into the domain of the referee, he or she is not a permanent member of staff, but a contract employee who works for us for six weeks a year. I would look at the clothing to assess whether, in my opinion, it was predominantly white. Unlike the limitations on logos, there is no hard and fast rule as to what 'predominantly' means, which makes it a subjective, grey area.

It has been an issue on quite a few occasions. By and large I would say it was fine. Otherwise, if it clearly infringed, I would say that it was unacceptable and that it must be taken out of the range, or, if there was time, be modified. As with all other areas, there was a degree of seeing how far the boundaries could be pushed. Most manufacturers, when they submitted a whole range, would include about half a dozen that I would chuck out immediately. Then there were other areas, where it was not so cut and dried. We were in favour of a bit of colour, which can break up the severity of an entirely white outfit, but it was a question of degree. We had quite a few instances when the umpire called the referee's office and said, 'I think we have a problem.' Usually, that would have been spotted in the warm-up so that it could be dealt with then. Nobody wanted to create a scene, which actually played into the hands of the manufacturers. They would have loved the publicity of a player being sent off court for having too much colour, and it was not they who were responsible for paying the fine. We did not normally escort players off court, but warned them that the offending item could not be worn again and that they would be inspected before coming out onto court. We did have to escort one player off: John McEnroe came out onto Centre Court wearing blue shorts. I actually think that that time, it was a genuine mistake, and that he had been wearing them for a warm-up outside.

Then you get clothing that may be logo free and predominantly white, but is just inappropriate. Two classics were Anne White in her all-in-one body suit, and Mary Ann Eisel who, embarrassingly for all, fell out of the front of her outfit. The former was told not to wear the outfit again. The latter had no need of such advice.

Appropriateness is again subjective. Jack Kramer was allowed on court to win The Championships back in 1947 wearing a white T-shirt with no collar, which was certainly not normal attire at the time. Today's equivalent is the sleeveless T-shirt favoured by players such as Nadal. That caused us a few anxious moments when it first appeared. No one liked it, and everyone agreed that it was not normal tennis attire, but having allowed so many extraordinary tennis dresses through the years – just look at some of the Williams sisters' outfits – why should we not allow these sleeveless tops? There was also the problem that every other tournament in the world was allowing them. The compromise was that we allowed it with a restriction on the size of the armhole, which cannot be gaping. I do not think there is any such thing as normal tennis attire any more, and the interest in fashion brings tennis to a wider popular appeal, and is another way of drawing in the audiences. It also makes tennis a game of the moment, which is better than the perception of it being outdated, stuffy and staid.

At one time, Christian Bimes, president of the French Tennis Federation, was contemplating going down the same route as Wimbledon with the predominantly white ruling. He was horrified by some of the outfits that were appearing at Roland Garros. I have to say that I am pleased that he has not followed the Wimbledon route. I certainly told him that it was quite a difficult one to police. It takes up a lot of time and you do not win many friends by telling people that they are not allowed to wear certain things. It is a subjective area, not done on percentages, so they might have allowed something through which we would not or vice versa, and that would have caused unnecessary aggravation. As you never get all the manufacturers to submit their clothing in one dump, it is even harder to be consistent. Over the years, I think we have kept a fairly good hold on the situation.

Much of the importance of preserving traditions such as predominantly white clothing lies in the enhancement of Wimbledon as a brand that appeals to a global TV audience. Yet in the last few years, there has been sensitivity over the fact that television rights around the world are not increasing at the rate they did, and the knock-on effect that this has had on revenue generated from the Championships. TV rights have generally plateaued. At the same time, costs have gone up a fair amount, particularly with the new buildings we have had on stream since the nineties. The whole estate simply costs more to run. While the structural costs of erecting the buildings come out of debenture income, the running and maintenance costs are taken from money raised from television and other income streams. The surplus has only increased once in the last five years, due largely to massive interface costs arising from the Long Term Plan, i.e. the huge costs incurred in stopping building work and making the grounds presentable before each Championships, which have to be written off. The £25m raised in 2007 is the lowest it has been since 1993.

There are continuing efforts to do more in China and India, certainly on the merchandising. There are thirty-four Wimbledon shop-in-shops in fourteen locations in China, but television is proving to be less easy as the different dialects mean that the market is regionalised. India should also be better than it has been, and that may well be a legacy of the fact that Mark McCormack was never strong there and had not built up much expertise or many contacts. Tennis also has a battle on its hands when pitted against cricket, which is practically a religion across the country. Vijay Amritraj has tried to be helpful, promoting tennis and being a commentator for Star TV, which covers a lot of countries in South East Asia.

Interest is growing in Eastern Europe, but finance was always an issue there. I would hope that the successes of players such as Novak Djokovic, Jelena Jankovic and Ana Ivanovic would mean that tennis is undergoing a transformation in the area and pressure for more coverage will rise as a result.

The Club has always said to the LTA that it cannot guarantee income will rise, and they should look at other ways of increasing their income, not just from Wimbledon which in the past has provided about 75 per cent of their funding. It is very pleasing to see that the LTA has secured a multi-million-pound, five-year sponsorship deal with Aegon. It is the biggest in the LTA's history, and has to go some way to helping ease the pressure on Wimbledon to maintain or exceed current surplus levels.

I suspect that the advent of the Centre Court roof will bring added pressure for night sessions as a boost to income. In the US and Australia, having an additional session for which tickets can be sold has been helpful in raising revenue. On the downside, it will put tremendous pressure on the grass, and then there are all the problems with car parking, and people leaving at eleven at night or later and the amount of disruption that will cause the neighbours. Time will tell how long that one will be resisted. It was certainly never contemplated in my time, or even discussed, as we were all in agreement. Wimbledon is a daytime event and we only wanted a roof for inclement weather, and particularly to guarantee that we could complete the semis and finals to schedule. However, the committee should quite rightly re-evaluate old decisions and it may come up in the future. Maybe the technology to improve the durability of grass will move on even further. If we could be assured that the grass would cope with a second session, then I suppose it is a possibility, but it is the old debate of money versus tradition. Wimbledon is an open air, outdoor event played in natural daylight. That has been fudged to an extent with the addition of the roof. How much further would you take it?

There has been the odd extraneous activity that has provided additional funds for the surplus, while also helping retain Wimbledon's profile. One such was the use of the Club as the location for the 2003 Working Title production *Wimbledon* with Paul Bettany and Kirsten Dunst. That was in fact the third cinema film on The Championships in my time. In 1979, we had *Players* with Ali MacGraw and Dino Martin, including a cameo role from Pancho Gonzales, and directed by Anthony Harvey. We also had *Rough Cut* in 1980, with Burt Reynolds, Lesley-Ann Down and David Niven.

The Working Title producers approached us, saying that they were doing the film and would like to use Wimbledon as the setting. Originally, we said No, as we thought it would be too disruptive. They wanted to use Centre Court and the area around it during part of The Championships and they wanted to be on site for six or seven weeks after it was over. When you have anything up to 600 extras and the film crew and the rest of the entourage, you are talking about a vast amount of people who really can take over a place. In the end we agreed they could do it. We could see that there would be good opportunities to introduce Wimbledon to a whole new audience, and as the film was going to be made regardless of what we did, it would be better for us to work with them. We were swayed by finance, but the fact that Working Title make fantastic pictures that appeal to a very wide audience, and that this one could bring tennis and Wimbledon to the masses, were also big selling points.

We got on very well with the production company, and although we did not have ultimate rights, they wanted us to be involved in looking at the script, and working with them in terms of where they could go and what they could do. It was quite interesting to see a film being made from the other side of the camera. It was well understood that the stars would not be convincing as players in terms of their ability to play shots. The solution was for them to mime their actions on court, and to have the ball super-imposed later. Having witnessed Kirsten Dunst's attempts to catch a ball that was thrown to her by a ball boy, I think that was a wise decision. After countless balls had been dropped, the ball boy eventually gave up, came over and put one in her hand.

For some of the crowd scenes, they used thousands of dummies. I remember seeing them for the first time on Court 2. They looked like humans, but were all swaying slightly in the wind, which was really quite eerie. There were some crowd scenes involving live beings. My daughter Anna had applied and been selected as an extra. I popped over to Centre Court one day to see how the filming was getting on and spotted her in the royal box. She was reading a newspaper, much to her father's horror. For another of the crowd shots, one day in the first week, we delayed play on Centre Court by half an hour, so that they could film a full stadium just before the start of the day's play. I said before that every-body likes a freebie. A little taste of Hollywood thrown in with your Centre Court seat is not bad!

Tim Phillips and I saw the final draft and the director, Richard Loncraine, asked us if there was anything we wanted to change. They would have changed it if at all possible, as the relationship was very good, but I think by that stage we had learned to appreci-ate that a little bit of poetic licence was acceptable and why let the truth get in the way of a good story?! The producers had done a good job of making us accept that it was not a document-ary, but an entertaining light-hearted romantic comedy. There were a few factual things that were clearly not right but, in the context of the storyline it did not really make that much differ-ence. There were not as many rounds in the tournament, for example, and they did not play the semi-final on Centre Court, as they wanted the full impact of Centre Court left for the final. The players did not walk onto the court from the usual direction,

The Wimbledon Junior Tennis Initiative carrying out a demonstration on Court 14 during The Championships.

Ian Ritchie and Tim Phillips enjoying an easy question at a press conference at the Club.

Myself with Regine Toures and Ted Tinling, in one of his more sombre outfits.

Most of the Club Committee and Executive taken in 2002

My last Chief Executive's cocktail party in 2005 with Stan Smith, Jenny, myself,
together with many of the senior players.

The men's dressing room as it appeared at our Worple Road site,
now recreated in the museum.

The Millennium parade of champions on the Centre Court, from the right: Billie Jean King, Roy Emerson, Margaret Court, Sir Ronnie Hampel (all in the background), Rod Laver, the Duchess of Gloucester (Hon. President of the LTA), Malcolm Gracie (President of the LTA), Tim Phillips and myself.

Jenny and myself relaxing with Dan Maskell (left) and Gerald Williams (right).

Left) The Doherty Gates in Church Road; an iconic part of the Wimbledon landscape.

One of the three press writing rooms in the Millennium Building.

OVERLEAF: An aerial view of the Club before the new roof was installed.

Venus and Serena Williams receiving a quiet word of advice.

With my family supporters: Jenny, Anna and Kim,
at my farewell party given by the Club.

and the dressing rooms were mocked up, as ours did not have sufficient height for the lights.

The whole film was lighthearted and quite enjoyable. The members were given a private showing in a cinema in Curzon Street, and it went down well with the majority. The film was shown throughout the world and I do not think it did our reputation any harm at all – in fact it did well in the UK and Japan. In the event, it was worth doing, despite the enormous disruption.

Another event on an altogether different plain was the 75th anniversary of the Diocese of Southwark in 1980. On the Sunday after The Championships, a service was held on Centre Court. The sight of a multitude of bishops and clergy in their surplices wandering around the grass in their bare feet was wonderful. The more mundane reason for their shoeless state was that they did not want to ruin the turf, but maybe they thought it was hallowed ground – who knows?

One of the most exciting, albeit non fund-raising events to which the Club will play host will be the 2012 Olympics. This will be the second time the Olympic tennis event has come to Wimbledon, the first being in 1908. The Club members unanimously approved of the Olympics coming to the Club again at an AGM in December 2004. The Olympic tennis tournament will be smaller than The Championships, with fewer competitors and events. Therefore we will only need ten courts as opposed to eighteen or nineteen, which will mean reducing the capacity of the grounds. Hosting the event will not require any changes on the Club's part, other than those involved in handing the International Olympic Committee a blank canvas. The IOC will have brokered their own licensing and supplier agreements. Any branding that would normally appear at The Championships, such as the Rolex clocks or IBM speed of serve indicator, will therefore have to come down, if the companies are not IOC suppliers.

In February 2005, the IOC Evaluation Committee visited the

Club and seemed to enjoy having a behind the scenes visit, albeit on a pretty miserable day weatherwise. They went into the dressing rooms, the press writing rooms, and other areas of interest, but they did not raise any substantial questions. Once we had won the bid, it was decided that the Paralympics would not be played at Wimbledon, but on a newly constructed site in East London. The reason is that there will be both men and women competing, and for disabled female athletes, playing on grass in a wheelchair is just not possible. The friction is too great, and women do not have enough upper body strength. For the same reason, although men's wheelchair doubles is played during The Championships, it has not been possible to have women, although a trial doubles event is planned for 2009. The benefit of the Olympic decision is that the creation of a new site in East London will provide a better legacy for British tennis.

I am very enthusiastic about the idea of the Olympics at Wimbledon, but I know that there are a lot of people who question the appropriateness of having tennis in the Olympics at all. Most people would say that to win an Olympic gold at whatever sport is the highlight of their career, but possibly a tennis player would think that winning a Grand Slam is more prestigious: if we already have our four pinnacles, why bother having tennis in the Olympics? The main reason why Philippe Chatrier and others at the ITF pushed for its reintroduction was that an Olympic sport is more likely to receive funding from governments worldwide. Tennis is a global growing sport, and to get the money it needs, it would do better if it were an Olympic sport. It is as simple as that.

The second important reason was that the Olympics is a fantastic climax every four years. It is the ultimate sporting event and as such, the sport of tennis should be involved. It is also worth remembering that tennis was in fact included in the inaugural 1896 Games. It also provided the first female gold medal winner in any discipline in the 1900 Games. It was dropped in

1924, primarily because the arrangements were a disaster, but made a re-appearance as a medal sport in 1988. I think a lot of the objections to tennis being in the Olympics stem from the outdated perception of the Olympics being an amateur event. The restriction on professionals was dropped many years ago, and now there are many competing, not least in athletics and football. While each sport may take a different stance as to whether amateurs or professionals will take part, within that sport it will be the elite competing against each other on a level playing field.

I started on the other side of the fence on this issue, but now that I understand Chatrier's reasoning, I have come round and would tick the box saying it should happen. I think it enhances the sport of tennis to be included. To have someone like Nadal winning is good for the Olympics and good for tennis. Granted, the initial fields were not particularly strong, but with each Olympics since tennis was reintroduced in Seoul, South Korea, they have improved. The fly in the ointment is fitting it into the calendar. Sadly, I think a lot of it depends on the timing, and on which continent the Olympics is held, as to which players will attend. For London 2012, players will be kicking their heels in Europe for three weeks waiting for the event, and there is a risk that they may choose to go on to America to start the hard court season in preparation for the US Open.

The inclusion of tennis in the Olympics, will mean exposure to the sport for billions of people, including, as with China in 2008, those in the host nation. That can only be a good thing. While we have done our level best to ensure that The Championships is seen by as large a TV audience as possible, there are parts of the globe that even Wimbledon cannot reach.

Chapter 9

The Stars on the Court

Ken Fletcher was no slouch. He and Margaret Smith/Court were the only pair ever to win all the Grand Slam events in mixed doubles in one year. Yet when he was in his prime, and third seed in the singles, his training regime extended only as far as making sure that he was in bed by 3 a.m. during Wimbledon. That was his one concession. Fletcher epitomised a bygone era, when those at the very top of their game did not take themselves too seriously and were still able to have a lot of fun – and not just in tennis. Dennis Compton used to turn up to test matches still in his dinner jacket from the night before, and yet put in a sublime performance. Those days are long gone, and the focus of a modern day player, let alone the team of support staff, would never permit such frivolities.

Martina Navratilova was perhaps the first to symbolise the dawning of a new era. When she first came on the tennis scene, she was a Czech citizen. At the age of seventeen, she was already winning thousands of pounds, of which she saw nothing. 'I have to give all my cheques to my country,' she explained in an interview. '[They] give me $7.14 a day for eating in the US, and here [Wimbledon] I get £5.' By the eighties, and after her defection to the US, the story could not have been more different. Her back-up team, known as, Team Navratilova, even included a nutritionist who was able to analyse her dietary and training needs from computer data, leading to claims that she would be the first bionic tennis player.

Having a sizeable entourage has since become the norm for any player in the top ten, and possibly the top 20, in the world. As well as the usual range of coaches, dieticians, trainers, and physiotherapists, Venus Williams even takes a lawyer around with her. Many players also have a good number of family and friends who will travel with them. When they were surrounded by so many people, it made it ever harder for me to talk to and get to know today's players. They are still just as nice as people; it is simply very hard to get close enough.

The commercial element to tennis has changed things completely. When Maria Sharapova won Wimbledon at the age of seventeen, it caught everyone on the hop. The thoughts were that it might take her another couple of years to reach her full potential and land a Grand Slam title. Sharapova's excitement that day was a joy to watch, as she scrambled around borrowing a mobile phone from someone to call her mother and share the moment. Those shots were relayed to an audience around the world, and within weeks, Sharapova had a contract with Motorola worth hundreds of thousands of pounds. Her combination of good looks and talent made her a marketer's dream, and many more deals have followed. The following year, Nike were to provide her with shoes studded with 18 carat gold. She told reporters that she might ask for a safe in the locker room, although the request never made it to my office.

For the players, the amount of money involved has undoubtedly come at a price. They have become more commercial beings, and to an extent, greater public property. All players are now obliged to conduct press interviews after each of their matches. It used to be that if you had a core of seven or eight journalists you could ask the press liaison officer if you could interview a player, but this now happens as of right. Strictly speaking, the player gets a $10,000 fine if they do not attend an interview, as stipulated in the Grand Slam rule book. We have invoked it, but have occasionally let people off. We once turned a blind eye to Jimmy Connors exiting sharply when he had had a very surprising loss. However, the players now are so used to it that they do it automatically. Andre Agassi was particularly good as he always said something interesting or constructive. Roger Federer always seems to be in control of himself. Some players have difficulty with the languages, so at the end of the eight or nine minute interview, there is a time – about three minutes – when national press can ask questions in their own language. Certain players talk much more fluently than others and are comfortable doing so, people like Billie Jean King or Martina. It was difficult to end their interviews after nine minutes. Others however, have clearly resented the press involvement. Ivan Lendl once said to an interviewer, 'If you ask about my dream, my dream is to play tennis, come off the court, shower, change, go back to my hotel room alone, and never have to answer these sorts of questions.'

A member of the committee always escorts the players to the post match interviews, which is a way of building a relationship between Club and player. It can also be important to make sure that it all goes smoothly and that the questions are appropriate. The press have in the past tried to ask Anna Kournikova, for example, a number of questions totally unrelated to tennis.

A greater public profile has also increased the need for security for some players. I suppose it was inevitable, and not just in tennis, but sad none the less. There can be differing reasons for it. When Björn Borg appeared at Wimbledon in 1973, he was a new phenomenon as far as British tennis was concerned. They were exciting times and there was understandable enthusiasm from younger fans. He was a sort of Viking god, with his long flowing golden locks. There has never been anyone who attracted the young supporter in quite the same way, either before or since. We had to lay on police escorts for him, not so much because he was in fear of his life, more of losing his clothing to adoring female fans.

The higher the profile, the greater the security a person needs. It can happen that a player, or celebrity in any walk of life, can say things that will upset people, especially if they are speaking on sensitive issues such as faith or race. However, I am not aware of the people we have had to protect having spoken out in that way, or there being any rhyme or reason as to why they were targeted. It is generally just one deranged person who has an obsession with a player. They see them on TV now more than they used to and this raised profile is the problem. It is not cheap to follow a player around the world, yet these obsessives do. The worst example was the stabbing on court in Hamburg of Monica Seles by an ardent supporter of Steffi Graf. I cannot believe her attacker was never properly punished. It was such an open and shut case, and yet he received a minimal sentence. People who do these things in high profile should be punished more than others to set an example, although, that being said, there thankfully has not been a repeat performance. After the attack on Seles, we decided to set out the players' chairs in a different position. We would normally have had them facing out across the court, either side of the umpire's chair. Following that incident, we turned the chairs so that they faced down the court with their backs to the umpire's chair. That way, players and officials would be more likely to see an attacker coming. But nine times out of ten, the players will come out and turn the chairs back again, as they feel there is then less distraction for them during the breaks.

With all these things, there is a balance. You do not want to cut the players off from the fans, or stop the fans from having a good view. The Club now provides an escort to take a player from the dressing room to the court to make sure that they get there safely. Players have good access to Centre Court, and with No. 1 Court they can be taken there via an underground route, but the other courts provide greater public access. We started doing player escorts for seeded and high-profile players, but now it is done for all. If there is nothing untoward, they are escorted only to and from court, unless they are such a popular player, as with Borg, that there is a need to protect them to get them out of the grounds at the end of the day as well.

Occasionally, players would bring their own security, not that we encouraged it. However, if there were good reasons – for instance, if someone had been targeted within the last twelve months – then we would want them to feel comfortable, and if they had brought someone on board to deal with that threat, then we would try and work with them. We would encourage them to use the same security firm outside the ground as we use inside, to ensure consistency.

Threats do happen, possibly more often than people realise. Certainly, in my experience, it has been the female players who have had problems with death threats and stalkers, mainly the latter. We would usually get this information from the WTA or ATP, and I would pass the information on to the local police and our security firm. I would work closely with them, and we would look after the security of the player within our grounds at our cost.

Security was just one of the issues that Richard Grier and I would discuss at our periodical meetings with the ATP and WTA. In the late seventies, the player associations would help out with the players' needs, and play much more of a handholding role than they do today. Now, they organise tournaments – the Tennis Masters series – on the one hand, and on the other, look after the players' interests, deciding on how many tournaments a player should play, the rankings system, prize money, marketing of the tour, finding sponsors, and TV contracts for the tour. They are big organisations, looking at the bigger picture – it has been a subtle shift from looking after the players' needs to looking out for their interests. They provide official ATP and WTA hotels in London, and players can sort out themselves whether or not they choose to stay there. A growing number choose to rent accommodation in the Wimbledon vicinity.

Top of the players' demands are good practice facilities, and as I have described, we have increased these enormously. Catering is obviously also important. Caterers have had dialogues with the player associations from time to time, as requirements change over the years. The competitors' restaurant is not just for the players, and other users do not always want to eat highly nutritional food, so there has to be a fairly broad menu. We prefer to talk to the player associations rather than trying to liaise with each individual nutritionist. We get so few complaints about food that it seems to work. The Club cannot or will not pander to every individual need, but we know what they want. The players come first and the menu is not that complicated – essentially a lot of pasta, carbohydrates, and bananas. There are the odd requests for something more specific. Tim Phillips and I were at the WTA Championships in Los Angeles, when Anastasia Myskina, a top Russian player, told us that what she really wanted was some prawn sandwiches. We duly passed the information on. What is more of a challenge is for the players to juggle lunch to fit in with playing, and rain delays can make it more difficult.

The Club also provides a bar, but nowadays the players do not drink alcohol and so it is used primarily by their guests.

The provision of medical services is something that we have had to give much more space to in recent years. When I first came, we had the dressing rooms, and attached was the physio room with three beds in it, and that was about it. The ladies only had one or two beds. There was no gym. The facilities for the physio, gym, doctor, physician, and drug testing are at present very satisfactorily accommodated in the Millennium Building, and within the dressing rooms, but will inevitably get too small, as players will want more gyms, stretching areas, etc., etc., as focus on fitness continues to increase. We have also found that increasingly, there are specialist singles and doubles players, which means that there are more players registered for each tournament and more space required.

The medical and changing facilities were matters on which we consulted closely with the players and associations. We tended to get suggestions from them on things like the number of cabinets, types of bed, sheets or paper towels on the bed, passes for more providers, or the virtues of saunas over jacuzzis. We had discussions on that latter subject, as we were finding the saunas under-used.

Talking to the players on matters that might materially affect them was important and within my remit. When Hawkeye – which tracks the flight of the ball through the use of a series of cameras high up in the stands – was introduced on Centre and No. 1 Courts, there was a lot of discussion. The system was thoroughly tested for many months, if not years, beforehand to ensure that it would not be affected by things such as wind, dark, overcast conditions, shadows and artificial light. Still, I know Federer is not really a fan of it. He thinks it is a distraction, and the linesmen should be calling the lines to the best of their ability. However, he does make his challenges, even if in a rather disdainful manner, and seems to be accepting it. As with Cyclops, which was introduced in 1980 and monitors the service line on serve, I think we will find there are fewer problems now that it has been introduced. Provided it has been set up properly, it is very hard to argue with a machine, although some have tried – notably Ilie Nastase.

Equal prize money was, of course, a discussion point throughout my entire time at Wimbledon.

To recap on the facts: when tennis went open in 1968, the ladies' champion received 37.5 per cent of the men's prize money. Rod Laver won £2,000 and Billie Jean King won £750. Incidentally, the previous year, the ladies' winner was given a £30 gift voucher and the man received nothing, so inequality predated the Open era! The US Open went to equal prize money back in 1973. The Australian Open went equal in 1990, then for a period went off it and is now back on. In 2007, Wimbledon and Roland Garros went to equal prize money throughout the singles and doubles events.

The basic argument was always market value versus sexual equality.

On the one hand, men play a minimum of three out of five sets while women play two out of three sets. Because of this, women are better able to play singles *and* doubles, so top women could take away more prize money than the men, on average.

TV ratings are generally higher for men's than women's matches. Ticket prices for men's days are higher than for women's. In 2008, for example, a Centre Court ticket for men's finals day was £91, and for the ladies', £84. White market debenture tickets were sold back for £2,750 for the men's final and £1,750 per person for the ladies'. The difference in prize money at the top of the ATP and WTA tour events has been quite marked, although it is getting closer. And finally, Wimbledon public surveys have consistently said that people prefer watching men's to ladies' tennis. In 2005 it was 73 per cent.

On the other side lies sexual equality. Women always felt it was wrong that they couldn't win the same amount. They trained just as hard as the men, played just as hard in competition and deserved the same status. In 2007, the Club acquiesced to the WTA demands. The Club statement on prize money said that tennis was 'one of the few individual sports where men and women compete at the same event at the same time. It will be a boost to the game as a whole recognising the enormous contribution women have made to the game and to Wimbledon. It should also encourage girls who want a career in sport to choose tennis as their best option. Therefore the decision is good for tennis, good for women players and good for Wimbledon. Every year the committee analyses all the relevant information and then makes a judgment. In February 2007, the committee took account of overall progression and the broader social factors and decided that the time was right to bring this subject to a logical conclusion and eliminate the difference.'

I think it was a no-win situation. The longer the Club said No, the more women would get agitated. The majority of people who raise this, if asked themselves, say women should not get equal prize money, but I honestly do not know whether you can go on fighting this year after year. In the end, there was not a huge difference in the amounts, and I think that that was the point the committee arrived at. The women were too close to the men in terms of the money they were receiving. They could not make any closer alignment without going the whole hog.

I do have sympathy for the women in that there have been some amazing women's matches, far more interesting than a swathe of men's matches. Playing the best of five sets does not necessarily make the match any more enjoyable to watch. The person who wins the 100m is better remembered than the person who wins the 400m, so it is not quantity but quality that counts.

But I can probably also say that I witnessed only one ladies' match that was a particularly good match at the 2008 Championships, and that was the ladies' final. Over time, I can probably remember far more riveting men's matches.

Equal prize money was something that we looked at every year, but we always thought the market value argument outweighed sexual equality. What did surprise me was that over the years, the ATP never came out with the view that the men deserved more prize money than the women. The word boycott was hardly mentioned, although there were threats from time to time and a lot was written about it in the press. Billie Jean King was an obvious driving force for change, but she was certainly not alone. When Chris Evert won in 1976, she promptly pledged that she would not be back to defend her title unless there was equal pay, another threat that thankfully came to nothing. There was no doubt they took it personally and were very serious about it. I am afraid I fanned the flames at one point with a totally flippant remark on Radio 4's *Today* programme some years ago. I had said that if the ladies' champion did not get less than the men, 'we wouldn't have so much to spend on the petunias'. It was a quote that came back to haunt me when Pam Shriver ran with it as she thought, quite rightly, that this was a poor excuse.

Another, slightly less protracted point of discussion was the optimum time at which to open the cans of balls. We always opened the cans the day before they were to be used on court. We were concerned that if it were left to the ball boys and girls to do it on the day, they might cut themselves. There is quite an art to opening the cans, and we felt that they could panic on Centre Court in front of so many people. We were told by Slazenger that the timing made no difference. This became a bone of contention with Tim Henman, however, who thought that the timing was critical and our approach was wrong. He felt that by opening them a day earlier, they were slower, had less life and furred up too quickly. He came into my office and we talked about it. When we analysed it, we found that we were probably the only tournament that did open its tennis balls in advance, so in 2005, we opened them on the day.

Tim was in fact to fly across my professional radar much earlier in his career. He had the ignominy of being the first person to be disqualified from Wimbledon, in 1995. A more unlikely person to be in the record books for this particular offence you could not imagine. During a first round men's doubles match, Tim had fired a ball down to the other end in frustration and had accidentally hit a ball girl running across the net. He was automatically disqualified, following the Grand Slam rules, and did not finish the match. One or two of us thought at the time that the rules were more he 'may' be disqualified rather than he 'should' be disqualified, but I did not see the incident so it is not easy to judge. In any event, the deed had been done, and you have to support the referee to the hilt after that. It would have been the last thing that Alan Mills, who was summoned by the umpire, would have wanted to do. However, all parties took it with good grace. Tim was quite shocked by it. There is no doubt it was an accident, and I am surprised that it does not happen more often. The following day he saw the girl out on a practice court and presented her with a bunch of flowers.

It was quite an extraordinary year for disqualifications, given that we had had none before. It happened to Murphy Jensen of the US because he failed to turn up for his second round mixed doubles match. We never learned the real reason why he did not appear, but one rumour was that he had gone fishing. (As a complete aside, his brother Luke served equally well left or right handed, which I always found amazing.) Then to complete the hat-trick, Jeff Tarango, also of the US, was disqualified from his third round singles match for three offences. He was fined $15,500 compared with Henman's $2,000, which shows how poor the behaviour was. Tarango was notorious for it, but perfectly nice off court and good company. His wife was a very feisty character, as demonstrated by the fact that she slapped the umpire in the press interview room after the disqualification. The umpire did not press charges – it was probably all in a day's work for him. He has though, retired from umpiring and now works for Lacoste. It is safer.

It is all the more surprising that the dubious honour of first disqualification fell to Henman, when we had already endured the McEnroe and Connors era of play. John McEnroe was a hot-head and still can be. In the late seventies and early eighties he would often be punished, but was never disqualified. I think he should have been. I was never there on court to see his worst offences, but I saw them on the news afterwards. Seeing what I did see, I would have thought it should have been a red card – and if any event can give a red card, it should be a Grand Slam, because no player is above the event. I understand why it is more difficult for other tournaments that rely on direct sponsorship. If the star of the show gets disqualified, the sponsors and player might walk away the following year. However, a Grand Slam like Wimbledon should have the power and muscle to disqualify if it believes it is right and the decision is fair.

McEnroe had the ability not to allow his outbursts to affect his game, although more often than not it certainly affected his opponent, who was an innocent bystander in all this while the rampaging was going on. The interesting thing is that he never appeared to have any major outbursts when he played Borg because, he says, of the major respect he had for him. That suggests to me that he must have been able to turn it off and on somehow, and it does not say much for his approach to the other opponents.

When McEnroe first won Wimbledon in 1981, we decided that we could not make him an honorary member as we had recommended that he be fined the highest amount for his behaviour. Up till then we had invited all champions to become honorary members of the Club, but in this instance it would have been hypocritical and inappropriate. The move certainly stung, and it is fair to say that there was no love lost at that point between the champion and the Club. McEnroe declined to attend the Champions' dinner, pleading exhaustion. My suspicion remains that one reason for his declining was that, had he attended, he would have had to make a speech thanking the committee. Chris Evert, the ladies' champion, stood up and joked that she had been told that she would have to make two speeches, to cover McEnroe's absence. 'Unfortunately I can only make one, as I haven't John's vocabulary,' she quipped.

The following year, McEnroe lost to Connors in the final, but was elected an honorary member that year. Connors gave as good as he got in terms of aggressiveness, and McEnroe has described the pair of them as two prize fighters squaring up to each other. In some ways, Connors was worse than McEnroe in that he was crude. McEnroe was worse to officials, whereas Connors was worse with language and gestures. In any event, I do not think either should be put up as role models for younger players. We had a lot of comments, asking how we could condone this behaviour among the top players.

Buzzer Hadingham, who was chairman at the time, wrote

McEnroe a letter at the beginning of the 1983 Championships asking him to behave himself well and correctly. He said that he was asking as a friend, but also said that if he stepped out of line, he would personally have him thrown out of Wimbledon. Buzzer felt he could write that sort of letter, as he knew the players well and was a wonderful communicator. That year McEnroe beat Chris Lewis in the final and he certainly did not behave on the same scale as previously.

I think money does play a part in all this. If a modern day player feels they have been cheated out of a linecall, just maybe they feel it is justified to have a stand up argument with the official because there is so much money involved. That said, I cannot believe that anyone tried any less to win Wimbledon because they were not being paid to win it. It is also fair to say that the vast majority of the players are very well behaved.

Despite all the problems, there were major positives to McEnroe: to my knowledge, he never criticised his opponent after a match; he played doubles as well as singles, which was a real bonus; he also played Davis Cup, which players like Sampras and Connors were not prepared to do regularly. He was a catalyst to ensuring that we had an infinitely better code of conduct, covering how the game should be administered on court. It was as a result of his era that the standard of umpiring and line judges began to improve significantly. So, out of the bad came good. I think he probably did have a good case on some of his calls, but so did many other people who chose not to argue about it. It is universally accepted that the standard of officiating is much higher now than then. For a start, they did not have Hawkeye.

People ask how I sum up McEnroe. I would say 'graceless', simple as that. He now plays on the seniors' tour and has done remarkably well. There is no question that he is a quite incredible player, but his behaviour, even when I saw him play recently at the Royal Albert Hall, was in my view just as bad, if not worse, than it was in the eighties, and I found that quite frightening and disgusting. People say that there is probably now an expectation and hope that he will behave badly when playing at somewhere like the Royal Albert Hall, and that it is probably in his contract. That is not true, I have spoken to the tournament's founding director John Beddington, and he confirmed that it *never* was in his contract to misbehave at that event. Contrast that to saying, as I believe, that he is the best tennis commentator there is in the world, and it seems amazing. I have read his book, and it seems to me that he is aware that he has behaved badly and almost apologises, but is not able to rectify it for the next tournament. Although his bad behaviour at Wimbledon is all water under the bridge, I find the fact that it continues incomprehensible and very sad.

We are incredibly blessed by having people like Roger Federer and Rafael Nadal at the top of today's game. Roger is such a delightful man. We all see his wonderful skills on the court, and he is a genuinely nice guy off it. He never turns an interview down, and is always courteous. If ever you were to have a role model, it should be him. Nadal is also very pleasant, and very courteous. I have spent more time with Federer than the others because he is that sort of person. Also, I guess, his generally speedy progression through the tournament has meant that he has a bit more time during the Fortnight. On the back of that, I have had some good times chatting with him at the Tennis Masters Cup. He would talk to us for an hour or so and I would be thinking, You have to go to bed, you are playing tomorrow.

Borg was an idol for so many people, including myself. When he started to lose his drive, he said to the Men's International Professional Tennis Council that he did not want to play in as many tournaments as he had previously. However, at that time, there were something like fourteen compulsory tournaments a year, and the Men's International Professional Tennis Council stipulated that players who did not play in the stated amount would have to play in the qualifiers for the events in which they did play. That would mean Borg playing the qualifiers for Wimbledon, a tournament that he had won five times, which was disgraceful. Sir Brian Burnett went down to see Borg in Monte Carlo to try and persuade him to return to Wimbledon, but sadly it did not come to anything, and he had made his decision to retire.

It was tough for Borg. His whole game was based on fitness, focus and determination. A bit like Nadal, he did not earn many cheap points. That took it out of him. He was a quiet introspective type, and there was no release for it all. He just could not put himself through the pain of continuing at that level.

Most of the players who say the nicest things about Wimbledon tend to do so because they have won here. Ivan Lendl was an exception. His dislike of grass as a surface was well known, and something that he was the first to admit. He has said on occasion that grass is a great surface – to play golf on, and that even his grandmother would take a set off him on grass. Yet I remember walking around the grounds with him telling him what we were planning to do with No. 1 Court, and he told me that if we made the new court similar to Centre Court, we would not go far wrong, as he thought Centre Court was the best tennis stadium in the world.

He could count on at least one ardent supporter on each of his attempts to win Wimbledon. My daughter Kim had a banner saying 'Go Ivan' hanging from her bedroom window, which overlooked the practice courts. Seeing such blatant favouritism on display at the chief executive's house prompted Tony Pickard, Stefan Edberg's coach to say, 'I'm not sure I like that!'

Lendl felt he had to curry favour within the family on another occasion. It was a rainy day during the week before The Championships, so all the grass courts were out of action, but Lendl and Guy Forget decided of their own volition to wind up the net on one of the practice courts backing onto our house and start practising. Jenny happened to see it and called me at the office, asking whether they should be playing. I said no they should not, and could she call for them to come off, please. She leant out of the window and asked them to stop, as the courts were too wet. They did not take too kindly to this at all, but eventually obeyed. Word later got back to them that the woman at the window was actually the chief executive's wife. They obviously felt guilty at some of the words they may have used, and brought her some flowers the next day by way of apology.

I have always thought that it is nice that we can invite our champions to become our fellow members of the Club. I think that they also appreciate it. For some, like Martina Navratilova, it is like coming home, and she has become part of the furniture. Very few champions make it back to the Club outside The Championships, but I remember Agassi coming out of season. We had depicted him on our Christmas card – we normally have a picture of the two champions on the card, either taken at the Champions' dinner or holding their trophies. That year, it had been him and Steffi Graf. He saw the card on the noticeboard and said, 'That's nice, can I get one?' I replied that he was a member, and therefore of course he could. He said, 'Great, I'll have one hundred.' That was years before the pair started dating, but I suspect it was not our choice of festive colours that had caught his eye.

We like the Club to feel welcoming to former players and encourage as many as possible to come back. When he was chairman, Buzzer Hadingham initiated the Last Eight Club, which has been a great benefit to us and The Championships. The club, formed in 1986, is for those players who have got to the last eight of the singles, the semi-finals of the doubles, or the final of the mixed doubles. Those players can be a forgotten breed, unless they are a member of the Club or are playing in the senior events. Now they are welcome back and are provided with a hospitality suite to meet fellow members and entertain guests, and are given a number of tickets to Centre and No. 1 Courts. It feels nice for them to come back to a place where they have done really very well. It was something that the other Grand Slams later copied, with mixed results.

Past Wimbledon champions get a ticket allocation as would any member, although if they do return, they do not need to pay. Players have access to the competitors' stand on Centre and No. 1 Court where we have players' seating. Players on Centre Court are given match tickets, in order that their family and friends can watch from the players' box. The type of people who might ask us for extra tickets are those who played at Wimbledon, but who are not in the Last Eight Club, and are coming back for the first time in say forty years with their wife and family. We try and help where we can.

The commitment, dedication and single-minded focus required for today's players to succeed is phenomenal, and does not come without cost. The demands of the training regime and the number of events in the tennis calendar year put an incredible amount of pressure on them, particularly younger players. It is a pressure cooker environment, made harder by the fact that tennis is an individual rather than team sport. The number of tournaments that youngsters play is controlled by the tour, particularly for the women. Laura Robson, the fourteen-year-old British winner of Junior Wimbledon in 2008, has wonderful career prospects ahead of her, provided she is not driven too hard, too quickly. She needs time away from the intensity of the tour to avoid the burnout that we have seen too many times before. This does not seem to be as much of a problem in the men's game, where players come through at a later age, once they have developed physically. It gives them more of a chance to mature mentally and withstand the pressures. There are obviously exceptions on both sides. There are many boys who have won Junior Wimbledon who are never heard of again. Conversely, when Boris Becker won Wimbledon aged seventeen, he was younger than the boy who won Junior Wimbledon. Becker was also meant to be playing Junior Wimbledon that year, but pulled out when, to everyone's surprise, he found himself in the last sixteen of the main event.

Many of the players coming through at an early age can attribute part of their success to the will of their parents. So many of the female players coming out of eastern Europe have had dominant mothers. The Williams sisters pay tribute to their father, as did McEnroe and does Sharapova. You have to give credit to Judy Murray for the way that Andy is playing. Perhaps a dominant parent is key to success. Certainly Martina Hingis was lost without the support of her mother, with whom she had temporarily parted company, when playing at Wimbledon in 1999. Her mother had made her face the booing crowds at Roland Garros the month before, after her surprise defeat to Steffi Graf, and Martina's response, to take a break from parental influence, resulted in a shock first round defeat for the top seed, who was beaten by Jelena Dokic.

Dokic was herself no stranger to wilful parents. Her father was aggressive both to her and the people around her, to the extent that we felt she needed more protection. We monitored the situation very closely so that if things got out of hand, we could whisk him out of the grounds as quickly as possible. That did happen, on at least one occasion. He was abusive to a photographer, and the police moved in pretty quickly to remove him. Yet most of the time, she did not want to have him away from her. It is difficult, and shows the complexity of the relationships on which players rely, but there were certainly times that it was in her best interests that he should not be present. In that instance, a player liaison officer talked to Jelena. These things are mainly best sorted out through the WTA as they are dealing with players on a day-by-day basis, and know them personally – far better for them to get involved than for a less familiar face to try and intercede.

I think one unfortunate side-effect of this increasing pressure on players young and older has been the loss of stature of the Davis and Fed Cups. The players say that the most important things in the calendar are the Grand Slams, then the Tennis Masters Cup, and then they would love to play Davis Cup – but only 'if it fits into my schedule'. It is not the highest priority for the majority of players.

The Davis Cup is run by the Davis Cup committee, under the auspices of the ITF. On an annual basis they look at how they can change the format to make sure all the players, rather than just a majority, want to play. For the first time, they will be putting in ranking points, which should be an incentive for top players to play for their country. However, there is a degree of unfair-ness with linking ranking points to Davis Cup performance. Imagine three US players ranked numbers 1, 2 and 3 in the world. The top two would get ranking points for playing Davis Cup and the third would miss out. It is also a shame it has come to this. It never used to be the case that incentives were required, but today, the calendar is increasingly full, as the ATP and WTA want their players to take part in as many events as possible to main-tain the credibility of the tour, and to retain sponsors' interest.

How best to retain player support for representative tennis is fraught with problems and there are no easy solutions. There has not been any significant change to the events in years. The prob-lems did not arise in the fifties and sixties when the Davis Cup was relatively small, and it may have got a little unwieldy now. Possibly, the world group could be cut smaller and seeded, so that the top countries and therefore the top players would have fewer rounds to play. But that has not yet been agreed by the ITF.

Would running the Davis Cup every four years, like the Olympics, or every two years like the Ryder Cup be a good idea? The Ryder Cup route would certainly have been a good option for the Wightman Cup that used to be played between the women of the USA and GB, which died in the early seventies because of the lack of strength within the British team. However, I do not think the Davis Cup should go down that route. It is steeped in tradition going back over 100 years, involving over 120 coun-tries in the world. It is difficult to imagine it as an event being played every other year. I do not think any calendar is helped by an event that drops in from time to time. When we have the Olympics, it puts a lot of pressure on the calendar, and there are inevitable losers – those who run a tournament very successfully for three years but then have to lose it or double up.

You have a feeling that something has to happen with the Davis Cup. It is still a very significant part of the tennis world. The finals have been fantastic over the past few years, drawing the biggest crowds ever, and there is no reason to consider its demise, but how to elevate its status in the minds of already over-stretched players, I do not know and neither, seemingly, does anyone else. It has at least been more successful than the Fed Cup, which I think does not benefit from the same cachet or public support. That is possibly because we are not as successful in it as some of the other countries, but I am hardly likely to advocate that as the benchmark by which to judge the impor-tance of an event. On that basis, the British public would have written off Wimbledon in 1977!

It is always nice, given the immense pressures that the players face, to see the odd glimpse of their lighter side. The public tends to forget that they are, underneath it all, quite normal people. My PA Paula commented that she had once been over with her nephew to watch the players practising. They saw Sampras and Henman sitting on a bench laughing and joking and poking fun at each other. Her nephew was amazed, saying that he had never seen either one of them laugh before.

Some of that light-heartedness came to the fore in 1996, on the day 'The Supremes' hit Centre Court. During The Championships, Jenny was sitting next to Cliff Richard in the members' stand on Centre Court when the rain came and there was yet another delay. Jenny suggested to him that the crowd would really like it if he sang for them. Nothing more was said, but she told me about the conversation that night. The following day we had another deluge, so I thought: Let's try it. I put out a call for Cliff, asking him to come to my office. He duly appeared and I asked him if he would be prepared to do it. His acceptance might have been based on relief to find that that was the reason for my call. He says that he had felt as if he was being summoned to the headmaster's office. His first thought was, 'Oh dear, I've lost my membership!' Cliff agreed to sing and then asked if we had any instruments. I said not, this being a tennis club, but that we could sort out a microphone. We took him up to the back of the royal box and he started singing, which went down tremendously well. Presumably word got back to the ladies' changing room, as soon we had Pam Shriver, Virginia Wade, Martina Navratilova, Conchita Martinez and several others standing behind him and singing along as his backing group. As Cliff and the Supremes (his words) treated the crowd to classics such as 'Summer Holiday', and 'Bachelor Boy', the audience started singing and clapping with him – including the Duke of Kent. Cliff was revelling in the moment and at one point shouted out, 'I never thought I'd play on the Centre Court.' As he launched into 'Congratulations', the clouds parted and the sun shone through.

I think it was very courageous for someone with his reputation to sing to a live audience without any rehearsal or instruments or (professional!) backing. He was putting his reputation on the line, given that it was broadcast globally. There was a lot of excellent feedback, but, predictably, some less favourable comments also. I had one letter from someone saying that they had tuned into watch tennis and did *not* expect to see Cliff Richard singing. A Club member said it was disgraceful that a fellow member of the Club should be used in this way. Personally, I think it was a splendidly British way to deal with a thoroughly British problem.

Chapter 10

Where Does All the Money Go?

Every year, the cry is the same. Just as the dust settles on the clay courts at Roland Garros for another year, attention turns to Wimbledon, with headlines screaming, 'Where are our champions? What is wrong with British tennis?' Among the edifying headlines written recently was 'Wimbledon: British hopefuls have no chance.' And as we enter week two of the tournament with invariably not a single British female still in contention, and hopes resting on, at present, just the one male, there are calls for drastic action to be taken and for the LTA to be called to account. To a degree, the criticism is fair, for all is not rosy in the garden of British tennis. Just one look at the statistics will tell you as much. We have not had a female champion at Wimbledon since Virginia Wade in 1977, or a male since Fred Perry in 1936. While Tim Henman, Greg Rusedski and Andy Murray have spent much of their careers comfortably in the world's top 100 rankings, our Davis Cup performances have not been impressive either. Our highest ranked female player is, at the time of writing, Anne Keothavong, ranked 48th, which is the first time we have had a female player in the top 100 for a number of years. It is not just at the very top level that the problems are felt. As Barry Flatman reported in *The Times*, 'Compared to 80,000 youngsters actually competing regularly in France, latest figures show there are just 8,400 doing the same in this country although there are more than 6,000 licensed coaches.'

Yet if it is fair to point out the shortcomings in our tennis success, it is equally fair to look across the board at sport in this country in general. Our footballers have not won the World Cup since 1966 or any other major trophy and failed even to qualify for Euro 2008. In rugby, recent World Cup success flew in the face of poor performances in the four previous years, and poor performances since. Success in the Ashes series at home in 2005 was followed by a whitewash for our cricketers down under and an ignominious early exit from the World Cup. Yet it is tennis that grabs the headlines. In their defence, people say that the footballers may not have qualified for Euro 2008, but they did at least get to the quarter-finals of the three previous tournaments and have performed consistently well, even if not to tournament-winning level. Then what about Tim Henman? Equally he did not win Wimbledon, but he reached the quarter- or semi-final eight out of nine consecutive years, which is a phenomenal achievement.

Much of the reason for tennis's bad press is that it is perceived as a wealthy sport in this country. Each year, all profits, or 'surplus' funds from The Championships, after expenses, are handed over to the LTA for the furtherance of British tennis – currently around £25m. Just how much is handed over is information in the public domain as, for tax reasons, the LTA is obliged to report the sum. The same obligations do not apply to the FA or the RFU, for example, nor, for that matter, to the other Grand Slams which are run by each respective country's national tennis association. Without any obvious comparison, tennis stands out as a wealthy sport.

The agreement between the All England Club and the LTA dates back a long time. When we first started The Championships, back in 1877, when the Club was based in Worple Road it was

primarily to raise funds for a new pony roller for Centre Court
– perhaps not the loftiest of aims that our predecessors could
have set themselves. It would be fascinating to see their reaction
now to the global phenomenon they created. From then until
1912, the Club promoted and managed the event and kept all the
profit. In 1913 it was agreed that the Club would pay the LTA a
percentage of the gate receipts, although in practice the LTA
either waived or, more often than not, took a minimal percentage
of the sum over the following years. By 1920, the increasing popularity of tennis meant that the Club had outgrown the Worple
Road site and had its eyes on Church Road, where it is now
based. In order to finance the move, The All England Lawn
Tennis Ground Company was formed, which bound the Club
and the LTA together. The ground company formed debentures,
which provided the capital to buy the ground and buildings.

In 1922, our first year in Church Road, the surplus of £7,009
was shared between the two parties after deducting the expenses
of the Club.

The big turning point came in 1934, when we formalised
arrangements by signing an agreement with the LTA. In crude
terms, this said that once the Club had paid for the running of
The Championships and the Club, the whole surplus would be
passed over to the LTA for the furtherance of British tennis, and
the LTA would be responsible for tax payable on that sum, which,
that year, was £24,413. The Club also gave to the LTA one half
of its shareholding in the Ground Company.

Amazingly, that agreement has stood the test of time very
successfully. Running The Championships was in the best interests of both parties, and continues to remain so. Since 1934, there
has been just one amendment of note following a review of the
1934 agreement, and the changing commercial complexities of
running such an event. A deed of variation was created in 1993,
which brought into play All England Lawn Tennis (Wimbledon)
Ltd, alongside the All England Club, the LTA and the Ground

Company. The fourth company exploits the commercial use of trademarks, the money from which goes back into the pot for the LTA. The deed also recognised rather more meaningfully the part played by the Club in staging The Championships. Under its terms, the Club could retain an element of the surplus (capped) for contingencies, something that had not been permitted before. By their very nature, it is not stipulated what the contingency funds would be used for, but if, for example, a major catastrophe befell the LTA leaving it under financial pressure, the Club would be able to help out for a year or two until it was back on its feet. For our part, it has been reassuring to have an element of protection that did not exist before. If, for example, the LTA had decided to end the agreement and take The Championships elsewhere, perhaps to the new national tennis centre, we could in theory have just been left with half our ground, which would be pretty poor recompense for all the work that has been put in over the years. Perhaps given the longevity of these agreements, and partly the sensitivity of the subject matter, that deed took about seven years and some hard negotiating on the part of our chairman John Curry to complete. The 1993 Deed of Variation was a twenty-year agreement, so is due to lapse in 2013.

During 2008, the Club and the LTA negotiated a new agreement – the 2008 Renewed Deed – that received the blessing from both organisations last December and comes into effect in 2013. As a result of this agreement, the Club will regain total possession of the Ground Company at a cost of £55m and receive ten per cent of the Championship surplus. The LTA will be guaranteed 90 per cent of the surplus from 2013 to 2053 and at least 70 per cent for a further twenty years as well. The Championships will continue to be run on the same lines as they have been in the past.

The agreement underpins our relationship with the LTA, a relationship that has had its ups and downs but remains strong. The LTA have a significant presence on the Championship committee, with seven representatives sitting alongside twelve from the Club. Whilst they currently also provide three of the six members of the Ground Company, although the Chairman is always from the Club, in 2013, there will be eight directors, of which six will be from the Club and two from the LTA. To an extent we direct rather than control the way The Championships should be run. The LTA could put spokes in the wheel, particularly on financial matters, if they chose to do so. Votes are carried on a majority, but I could count on one hand the number of times things were put to a vote. If you were not winning an argument, it was a question of taking whatever was the point of debate away and looking at it in a different way. I have never had a problem with the LTA's involvement – you can understand why, if there are major financial implications, they need to be involved. The impact after all, is directly to their bottom line.

For their part, the LTA are very happy provided The Championships are successful, which they have been. The more success, the more money they get to help fund British tennis. The relationship between the two sides is always good while the surplus is going up nicely. If it plateaus or goes down, that is when harder questions are asked by the LTA about new revenue streams and expenses.

During my time, the surplus figure steadily rose which meant that the relationship between the Club and LTA was very good. There have been a few fireworks over the years, given the characters at the top, but generally it was a good working relationship.

That has not always been true. In the old days after the Second World War, we used to have our committee meetings in London rather than at the Club, and relationships were so bad that, even though the two groups were in the same location, the Club people would have a very nice dinner, and the LTA would have their sandwiches in the back room. It was very much an 'us and them' scenario. Back then, and this was the fifties, before my time, the attitude among Club committee people was very much, 'Let's do this, and don't worry about it. It doesn't matter because the LTA are paying for it.' Now, thankfully, there is much more respect between the two parties. I have to say I do not really understand why that was the attitude, but I am glad it changed. I think people grew up a bit, and took a more responsible approach. There has also been a definite improvement in communication. I think that there is a better understanding now of what each side is trying to do. Members of the LTA would come over to us to meet with the committee, and give presentations on what they were doing which demonstrated how the surplus received from The Championships was being spent. They would talk us through plans for the development of tennis or facilities in the regions or whatever. More recently, the president and chief executive have been coming over to the Club and talking to the members, which has also been a good thing. If people are kept informed, it builds up a much greater element of trust.

Both the LTA and the Club are singing from the same hymn sheet in as much as they are both driven by the desire to further British tennis, to see tennis develop throughout the country and to help deliver a British champion, ideally at Wimbledon. The Club's role in achieving this is to optimise the amount of money it can raise at The Championships, which can then be passed on as surplus to the LTA. The potential conflict here is that we have never been prepared to compromise the integrity of The Championships in order to achieve this goal. The LTA appreciate this and there has never been any real trouble on this point. However, I sense that change could be in the air if the surplus were to fall significantly.

During my time there has been a surreptitious but distinct increase in the LTA's involvement with The Championships and consequent desire to use it as leverage for their own aims. The LTA have for years allowed us to run the event as we wanted, but towards the end of the nineties and onwards, they have tried to use The Championships as a means of promoting the LTA more and helping their sponsors. One example was Aerial, a major LTA sponsor that had put a lot of money into junior development. Aerial wanted to arrange an event that would be televised, which would involve the best juniors playing at the Club, with the champion present and Aerial's advertising boards all around. It does not surprise me that the LTA want to help their sponsors in this way, and it is understandable from their point of view, but we have to be careful that no form of promotional activity impinges on our ideals. Why would we allow advertising hoardings for Aerial when we have scrupulously avoided them for The Championships themselves? In the event, we permitted a more low key affair to take place on some courts that we own just outside the grounds.

Sponsors offering promotions with the tagline that the prize is two Centre Court tickets is another bone of contention. We would monitor that sort of activity very carefully at our end, as we do not want to give the impression that tickets are easy to come by through corporate sources. We want to keep tickets in the public domain and accessible to all, rather than available through promotional elements. We would only allow companies that are senior in stature as far as the Club is concerned, in that they have contributed a lot to the Club and to tennis, to have tickets for this sort of promotional activity.

Our official banker for many years was Barclays, but right now, if you drive down to the Club, you will see the HSBC logo just inside the perimeter fence, and clearly visible from the road. That is pretty high profile. There is a question in my mind as to whether it is appropriate for us to do more advertising. But the Club is more commercial now than it was ten years ago, and will be even more commercial in another ten years. It is the way of the world and tennis is certainly no exception. Sponsors contribute more, but demand more in terms of exposure. The Club has to accept this, while ensuring that the balance is kept right. I would hope that permission for the HSBC logo to be displayed so prominently was given for the right reasons.

During my last ten years as chief executive, we handed over to the LTA almost £292m before tax. Most national associations would be very pleased to get that sum of money coming in, and I think there have been no complaints from the LTA in our direction. Where there is more of an issue is with government funding. Other national associations, lacking the equivalent of an annual international championship, get better funding from government. I do not think that the fact that we have to make the information public helps here. Yet even taking into account the fact that tennis is one of the more poorly supported sports by the government, sports in general in this country do not receive the same funding as our rival sporting nations.

This was a view shared by many at top level, and certainly at the LTA. I remember when John Crowther was chief executive of the LTA, during my time as chief executive, he was very critical of the view that the success of Wimbledon meant that the LTA did not require any additional funding. He tried to say you should look at the whole picture, not just The Championships. In April 2005 he wrote an impassioned article in the *Observer*, in which he called on the government for better assistance. He pointed out that 'Government investment in sport is 40 per cent less than in countries such as France, Canada and Australia. In tennis, France's long-term, sustained investment means that they have 5,000 more indoor courts than us and more in Paris than in the whole of Britain. Tennis and other sports are perceived as "cash rich" in Britain. This is not the reality. The LTA's total investment in the game, combining commercial income and government money, is £31.3m, or £6.80 for every participant.'

The Lottery has helped to a degree, but when you compare the UK with other countries like France, government attitude is definitely found wanting – at all levels. John pointed out the contrasting figures with regard to facilities available within towns and in particular to covered courts. When we applied for planning permission for three more covered courts at the Club in 1989, we had to go to a public inquiry. It was a lengthy process involving lawyers, and we ended up having to change the initial planning application. The additional costs, both in terms of time spent and professional fees, were very unwelcome. More to the point, at that time, we were eleventh in Europe in terms of the number of covered courts we had, alongside Denmark. Ten others were doing better than us, just in Europe.

However, there is something more to this than simply the issue of government funding. We are significantly better off than most countries around the world. It does seem surprising that we do not provide a better depth of player when you look at countries like Argentina and Spain, let alone Serbia, and how successful they have been in consistently providing a number of people who have reached the top 10, 20, or 100 in the men's game without having a major tournament in their country (apart from the Tennis Masters event in Madrid). I remember Rex Bellamy, the *Times* tennis writer, saying you can make money out of tennis players, but you cannot make tennis players out of money. That said, it has got to be better to have the money than not!

Part of the problem is that sport is not emphasised sufficiently in schools here. In France it is not emphasised either, but after school, children go off and play sport with the local communities and clubs in a structured environment. That is the culture of the country. Here, once the school day is finished, they go home. The government's target is to try and get two hours of sport a week. Well, I cannot be the only one to think that that is no great achievement. The government perennially talks about the importance of sport and the dangers of obesity, yet its apathy in dealing with it seems to mirror the armchair loafers that it is happy to point the finger at. Think how much money the NHS would save if more people were playing sport. The government is culpable in not engendering a sporting culture from an early age. For years, there was also an anti-competitive culture within the education sector, the mantra being that no child should ever have to lose, for fear that it would damage their confidence. I think the results are being felt across all sports. Football again springs to mind. We started the game, and we probably have the best premier league competition in the world, but what have we achieved on a national level?

The lack of government funding and assistance has certainly not helped British tennis success. We also face a unique challenge in that we as a country have founded so many sports, and have adopted so many others. There are so many that children can try their hand at, and for each sport there will be a pack of talent scouts honing in on the same few athletic and gifted children. They do not have the same range of opportunities in other countries. Let us take the fact that football, rugby and cricket are our main sports. Cricket is played in very few countries around the world, so those that do not play are in all likelihood playing tennis instead, and devoting a lot of attention to it. Rugby again is a minority sport, played seriously by less than twenty countries. In tennis, there are now way over sixty countries playing which have male and female players of very high quality, in the top 50 in the world. There are around 130 nations taking part annually in the Davis Cup. We are facing a double hit. Tennis has grown exponentially around the world, increasing competition, while our pool of potential talent continues to be plundered by a range of competing sports. Football is played all year round and is relatively easy for everyone to play, including girls. It is a simple, easy game and that is the beauty of it. Tennis is basically a difficult game, which puts a lot of people off at an early stage. You cannot pick up a racket and hit a forehand or backhand over the net straight off, in the same way that you could run with and kick a football at the first time of asking. You need to have mastered the basic techniques. I think it is wonderful that short/mini tennis has helped to introduce youngsters to playing the game at an early age, but football will generally always have a stronger pull.

I think also a lot of kids go into tennis and enjoy it, but when they get to sixteen or seventeen, they have either had enough of it, or other interests come into play. By that stage, the problem is not so much the draw of other sports, but attractions such as the opposite sex or clubs. The junior county tournament week is a sad and graphic indictment of this. It used to be that sixty-four boys and girls would be competing at various age groups, and competition was such that you almost had to qualify to get into these events, but in many counties now, they cannot even hold the girls' tournament, as there are not enough entrants. It is not so bad at thirteen or fourteen, but at sixteen or seventeen very few are playing. We do not seem to progress our good juniors.

The problem is not confined to this country, but endemic across several of the traditional tennis playing nations. In fact, each country has its own problems. In the twenty-two years between the resumption of Wimbledon after the Second World War in 1946 and the advent of the Open era in 1968, the men's champion on nineteen occasions was either American or Australian. Yet in 2008, there were no English-speaking players in the quarter-finals of Roland Garros in either the men's or women's draw.

In the broader numbers game, with our elite players who have made it that far, we do not seem to be able to get them into the senior professional round. They do not seem up to scratch. Some say that it is because players from established tennis nations are not 'hungry' or determined enough. Cushioned with suffi-cient funding, the same incentives do not apply. Certainly, that would appear to be true when you consider the rise of the eastern bloc countries. Take Serbia's Ana Ivanovic, who had to resort to an abandoned swimming pool in which to practise. Space around the two courts that had been laid down next to each other was so cramped that collision with a wall while chasing a ball was a distinct possibility. She was trying to focus on perfecting ground strokes while her home town, Belgrade, was being bombed by Nato during the Kosovan conflict. Of conditions at the time, she says: 'We knew when the air raids would come, so I had to organise my practice schedule around them. I used to be on court at six or seven in the morning.' It does not come much tougher. Yet 2008 saw Ivanovic become the first Serb female to win a Grand Slam by taking the French Open, snatching the world No. 1 ranking on the way, while her compatriot, Novak Djokovic became the first Serb to win a Grand Slam earlier in the year by taking the Australian Open. The question is, which teenager is likely to feel more motivated to practise for hours on end, putting tennis above all else – the one facing depravation, conflict and little hope of a prosperous future, or the one with coaching and support on tap, surrounded by friends, family and the temptations facing the average western teenager?

As this debate repeats itself year on year, one of the solutions often raised is that we take away the LTA funding that finances youngsters' coaching, trips and tournaments – but if you take away the financial assistance, you are effectively calling on the parents to raise the money, which would certainly be discriminatory in some cases. When Roger Draper took over as chief executive of the LTA in 2006, he published the *Blueprint for British Tennis*. In it, he acknowledged that tennis is expensive; the LTA estimate is that it costs about £250,000 to develop a winning player from age five to age eighteen. In the early years, players rely heavily on their parents to fund transport, healthcare, lifestyle support and guidance. (It costs about £8,000 to support a ten-year-old per annum.) Beyond this, it is recognised that it takes about 10,000 hours of training spread over a ten-year period to be in with a chance of success. Many parents would baulk at this level of financial and personal commitment.

Perhaps a means test is a way around the problem. I favour the idea that we should help a child in the right manner and maybe, if they succeed as a player, he or she then gives something back in recognition of the help they have received up to that stage. I do not know what the agreement was between Andy Murray and the LTA regarding his former coach Brad Gilbert, but I would like to think that not only was Murray contracted to play representative tennis for the Davis Cup and Olympics, but that, if he were successful, over time he would be obliged to give some prize money back to the LTA for hiring Brad Gilbert on his behalf. I do not see that there is anything wrong with that arrangement. It may happen, but I have not heard that that is the case, because the terms of these contracts are rightly confidential.

There is a fine balance between giving a player a lot of incentive in terms of money and coaching time, and saying 'Off you go. Go and do it yourself.' I think the LTA are much better now in that they are prepared to take away the funding if a player is not performing – either if he or she is not getting the results or if they are misbehaving, as has been the case recently. It happens in other sports – take Danny Cipriani's exclusion from the 2008 Six Nations rugby after his nightclub jaunt.

Anyone can list the problems. The hardest part is trying to find the solutions, as the LTA well knows. Any governing body of a sport is pretty set in its ways, and like an oil tanker, is difficult to turn around. I think the current administration has made a very good start, but many of these problems are deeply entrenched and will take a lot of time and perseverance to work through. It is also difficult for the LTA as they are firing on so many fronts. So many people have views, and none of them seem to coincide. Some people say we should do more in schools, others in clubs, or that there should be more overseas coaches. Some say we do not need a national headquarters at Roehampton, we should have greater diversification. Should the money go into elite players or grass roots players? Should it go to covered courts, clubhouses, coaching, or schools? There are so many targets to aim at, and I think that the LTA has had a tendency to try and hit too many of them, which has diluted its effectiveness.

We have a lot to learn from the French, and when, in 1999, Patrice Hagelauer was brought on board by the LTA as performance director, to try to bring French ideas to play in this country, things looked as if they were set to improve. Hagelauer was France's leading coach at a time when French players won twenty-four championships and the Davis Cup twice. His view was to focus on the grass roots and get more children playing the game. There would then be more coming through junior development programmes, which would mean more chance of increasing the number of players at a higher level. He met with reasonable success, but it was an uphill task. To succeed, he also needed the buy-in at club level, and the French club culture is very different from that in the UK where tennis is perceived much more as a social pastime.

There are many problems with which the LTA has to deal and I do not envy them their task. However, I do think it is a shame when others come along willing to help, with sound ideas, and are met with a blank response. Tony Hawks the broadcaster, writer, and comedian, set up an organisation called Tennis for Free. He is a good and keen tennis player and, in an attempt to generate greater enthusiasm for the sport in the UK, wanted to get local authorities to allow their tennis courts to be used free of charge if they were not otherwise making money. He would then endeavour to get coaches in, either to coach for free or build up coaching membership. He pointed to the US, where park courts are usually free, often floodlit, and frequented by a coach affiliated to the US Tennis Association who organises ladders and competitions. He started in Surrey and it is growing slowly, but it took a huge effort to persuade the LTA that this was something that we thought was worthwhile. Our chairman, Tim Phillips, was all in favour and prominent in backing the cause. It seemed such a logical, sensible route to take to draw in kids who do not want to join tennis clubs as they perceive them as too expensive or elitist, or they think they will not get a fair game as they will be bounced off court by seniors.

The LTA has direct contact with the local authorities and the LTA's backing to do this would have been far more effective than the efforts of one man on his bike. Hawks's aim was to go in once the LTA had made the introduction, but it seemed as if the LTA thought that it was not their idea, it was not on their agenda and therefore was not a priority for them. Hawks can have quite an abrasive manner, and probably went in guns blazing, wanting action and to get things done, but no matter what the presentation, it should not have undermined the validity of the cause. I believe the LTA have now come round to helping, once Hawks had kickstarted it, but the initial reaction was very disappointing and surprising, I felt.

I do think that the LTA has changed quite rapidly and successfully over the last few years. There seems to be much more vibrancy and urgency about what they are trying to do. Stuart Smith, the immediate past president, was hugely dynamic and I was very impressed by the energy and enthusiasm that he brought to the task. In his three years, he went to every county at least twice, visiting clubs and tennis centres, which is a tremendous effort given that he was not paid for his services. He replaced chief executive John Crowther with Roger Draper, who had previously worked at the LTA as development officer but had left to join Sport England, and there has been a huge amount of restructuring since, which has come at a cost in terms of morale of existing staff. The other more obvious cost comes in terms of funding the extremely high calibre coaching team now on board. They must have spent enormous sums of money recruiting the likes of Paul Annacone, Paul Hutchins, John Lloyd, and a lot of pretty crucial people on the technical and coaching side.

It does seem to be moving in the right direction, however. During The Championships, the president of the LTA normally hosts a series of lunches, and I was there in 2006 with Stuart Smith. He gave each visitor and guest a card, to prompt them to write down what they felt he and the LTA should be concentrating on. It was a typically proactive step, wanting to make the lunches more pertinent and a worthwhile exercise. He then wrote a letter listing what the results were. The greatest number of votes went to getting more players in the top 100, followed by a demand for more players of all ages playing competitions, and then making tennis more easily accessible for everyone.

It is very interesting to note that the Blueprint for British Tennis, the result of the exhaustive consultations by Roger Draper in his first six months at the LTA, seems to mirror these opinions. All parties seem to be pulling in the same direction and there is enthusiasm and direction at leadership level. Draper's first success was in reducing the number of aims from fifty-one under the old regime to just three: to get players in the world's top 100; to put as many twelve- to eighteen-year-olds as possible on track to reach the top 100; and to have as many juniors as possible competing regularly.

The reorganisation in personnel, the expenditure on top trainers, the establishment of the excellent £40m National Tennis Centre at Roehampton; these are all huge changes, and at some stage people will be hoping and expecting to see some results coming through. I was talking to an LTA councillor who told me that they were all very supportive of these measures, which is good because I thought there might be some resistance. However, as yet, other than Andy Murray and his brother Jamie, there does not seem to be much of any significance in the pipeline from either the male or female camp. Let us hope that the great success of Laura Robson in winning the girls' singles Championship at Wimbledon in 2008 is a ray of sunshine presaging a better future. The line will be that it will not happen overnight, it will take three to five years. Whether this current management team will still be there to see it, who knows. All that is clear is that there cannot be an easy solution, otherwise the LTA would have got it right by now. They are not fools.

An area in which the LTA is currently making great inroads is its internal organisation. Over the last few years, the administration has made vast strides in cutting out bureaucracy, something that John Crowther helped orchestrate, so the management system is more streamlined than it was.

The LTA is bound to a very large council of over 100 people representing the counties and other associations. There have been gradual but persistent attempts to reduce the control of this council over the years, and it has been a very sensitive area. They are gradually getting there, but it still has quite a lot of authority. The management is still looking at ways of making it better, and has managed to reduce the number of meetings a year, but, as with many national associations, the whole area is wrapped up in history and privileges. The members of the council do a lot of good work, representing their counties in a voluntary capacity, but they do get very good rewards for their efforts. During The Championships, each council member becomes, effectively, a full member for the Fortnight. They get two Centre Court tickets per day at a discounted price and the ability to buy, if wanted, a pair of No. 1 Court tickets at face value per day. They are allowed into the members' stand in Centre and No. 1 Court, and also have access to the members' enclosure and all the other bits that go with being a member, such as members' parking. It is a nice perk to have, which no one wants to give up. As councillors would have to vote themselves out, it is a tricky thing to change, but the game has moved on, is more professional and decisions need to be taken more quickly. At present, even if everyone agrees, decisions have to go through the right procedures, which can be cumbersome.

The surplus that we have handed over to the LTA since 1994 has been consistently over £25m. Understandably, our members have from time to time said that we give all this money over, but there does not seem to be any responsibility or accountability as to what is done with it at the other end. Should we not be more involved? The simple answer is that we have enough on our plate in running the Club and Championships. For anyone on the executive, or the chairman, to get involved in running British tennis as well would be nonsensical. You either become responsible or you do not. You cannot be half and half. It is true that the Club is the principal fund-raiser for British tennis, given the government's lack of involvement, and yet it has no influence over how that money is spent, but unless you get deeply involved with something, or get to the coalface and get involved as Tony Hawks has done, it is quite difficult to put your toe in the water and then pull it out again. At our meetings with the LTA, we would always enquire and ask pertinent questions. But how do you measure success? We could not say, 'We want £5m to go into this area, or to see five people in the top 50, or we won't give you the money next year.' Neither I nor other members of the Club know whether it is right to put 25 per cent of the surplus into core facilities – or should that be 30 per cent? Or where else should it be used? Why would we have a better handle on that than anyone at the LTA? We might have a view, and we can and do express it, and they take it on board. In some ways it is not dissimilar to donating money to a political party. If you donate to the Labour party, you could suggest but you cannot decree where that money should be spent, and you certainly cannot dictate what should be in the manifesto.

As chief executive of the All England Club I sat on the council, together with one other member of the Club committee, so we did have a nominal influence, but one or two votes amongst 100 will never make a significant difference. We were really there to observe and learn, and report back to the Club on what was going on. I suppose I could have got involved at sub-committee level, but frankly I did not think I had the time. We do our bit, and we do it to the best of our ability. We try to optimise the surplus, and we are helping in a very significant manner by providing the funds in the first place. I have always been comfortable with that setup and I do not think there is any reason for guilt. I was employed by the Club, and I knew what my tasks were. I am strongly of the opinion that what has happened over my time is the right way and I would not advocate that my successor get heavily involved in LTA affairs. There are higher priorities to be dealt with inhouse.

It is also fair to point out that our involvement with the furtherance of British tennis has not been restricted to the money that is handed over to the LTA. At the Club, we have set up a number of initiatives to encourage youngsters into the sport, and we are proud of their success. They fall under the banner heading The Road to Wimbledon, which is essentially a junior tennis programme, that has as its mission getting more young people involved in the sport. The funds come out of All England Club funds, rather than money that would otherwise go to the LTA. I give credit to Tim Phillips for pushing the programme through to launch in 2001. There are various strands to it. One is the Wimbledon Junior Tennis Initiative whereby the All England Club provides a team of coaches and since 2001 has gone into 337 state schools in Merton and Wandsworth, at their invitation, to offer the opportunity of putting tennis rackets in children's hands (80,000 of them, in fact). For many, it will be the first time they have held a racket. Those who are keen and would like to continue can play on Saturday or Sunday on the All England courts, where they are coached and drilled for free, all in the shadow of No. 1 Court – quite something for a youngster. The initiative is open to children age three to fourteen and about 300 per weekend come and take up the offer. The better ones go into other squads to get more practice on the covered courts during the week, before and after school. As a result, the Club is now recognised as an official LTA Performance Centre as well as an accredited LTA Mini-Tennis Centre.

We set this up partly because we wanted to put something back into the community, and partly because we felt that we have fantastic facilities, and surely playing here, at the home of The Championships, might inspire people to play better tennis. The aim is not necessarily to look for champions as the circle, being restricted to South West London, is realistically too small, but it is wonderful to go out there and see these children enjoying themselves at the weekend. My five-year-old grandson Marcus has joined in, but modesty prevents me from talking further about the talents of the 2023 Wimbledon Champion. Dan Bloxham heads the coaching team and he is truly inspirational. The way he motivates these young players and brings the enthusiasm out is remarkable.

Around 250 children and their parents who have shown particular commitment and enthusiasm throughout the year are also invited to come to the Club the week before The Championships start to see the players practising on the Championship courts.

In 2002, we launched the national 14-and-under challenge tournament in conjunction with the LTA, run most efficiently by Paul Hutchins. At national level there are 20,000 juniors competing, from around 1,000 clubs, which makes it the biggest junior tournament in the country. The best ones go through to county finals. From that, the best sixty-four boys and sixty-four girls come forward to play on the Championship grass courts and on the courts at Aorangi Park in August. We want to make the whole thing truly memorable, so the players and their parents who escort them, are given a jolly good week. They get a boat trip down the Thames, tours round the grounds, and lots of extra-curricular events.

Our Museum Education Programme was launched in 2001, and over 4,000 children have taken part in specially developed workshops that are directly linked to the national curriculum and capitalise on the museum's facilities and artefacts. Again, this is for local children, aged fifteen to eighteen. The last element is the Playing for Success Study Support Centre (SSC), a joint initiative between the Club, Merton council and the department of education and skills. The SSC use a high-tech learning zone, set up in No. 1 Court, to run an after school programme focusing on numeracy, literacy, IT and confidence raising activities. Again, it is chiefly for primary school children in the locality. It has been operating since 2003 and is just another element of what the Club is doing in the local community.

Finally, it is worth noting that over 10,000 children attend The Championships each year through dedicated junior ticket allocations to the 650 schools affiliated to the British Schools Tennis Association and as members of parties accompanied by an LTA licensed coach.

I accept that, even when combined, the composite elements of the Road to Wimbledon are extremely small scale compared with the tasks facing the LTA, but on a limited budget, we have tried to encourage youngsters into tennis within two London boroughs, unhindered by the pressure of expectation that they may one day become champions.

I believe that the old adage 'It's easier to make money than to spend it wisely' holds true. The LTA has certainly had its critics over the years, but I have always said publicly and privately that my job was infinitely easier than being chief executive of the LTA. You should not underestimate the difficulty of running a governing body, whether it is cricket, rugby, football or whatever. If I had ever been offered the job at the LTA, I would not have accepted it. I could not do it. I could not cope with the sensitivities of dealing with councillors and the various strands of British tennis, and the haggling with politicians over funding. For the chief executives that I have known, it has been a pretty thankless task in terms of the public recognition they have received for their undoubted efforts. Maybe they would have been better off following the advice of US philosopher and writer Elbert Hubbard: 'To avoid criticism, do nothing, say nothing, and be nothing.'

Chapter 11

The Wimbledon Hall of Fame

I am often asked who, in my opinion, were the greatest stars of Wimbledon. I think the expected answer is a litany of the tennis greats, and undoubtedly there were plenty of them. As you would expect from a prodigious note-taker like myself, I have my own top ten, or, for present purposes, top seven male and top seven female players. More on them later. Some of the greatest stars of Wimbledon, however, were those who actually brought The Championships to fruition year on year, none more so than the chairmen under whom I served. Each brought their own character to bear on the Club, each being the right man for the right job at the right time.

When I joined as assistant secretary in 1973, Herman David was chairman, having been appointed in 1959. I only spent one year with him, as he died in office in 1974. I hardly knew him, but he was the chairman of my interview panel, so I owe him a huge debt of gratitude for trusting in other people's judgement of me. He had worked in the City in the diamond business until retirement and was a very influential chairman. He, probably more than anyone, brought about Open tennis in 1968, changing the face of the sport forever. Money was pervading the amateur game and it therefore made it even more essential that we did away with the barrier between professional and amateur tennis. His statement that 'Shamateurism has made international tennis a living lie,' has gone down in the annals of tennis history. He was also the chairman who had to cope with the subsequent 1973 players' boycott.

On Herman David's death, the mantle was passed to Sir Brian Burnett, who stayed until 1983. Again, I owe him a great debt in having the confidence to promote me to secretary of the Club in 1979, without even looking at external possibilities. Sir Brian was a retired Air Chief Marshal, having spent his whole working life in the RAF. He was a quiet man, almost shy, but with a strong character. You do not become an Air Chief Marshal if you are a weakling. It is a sign of his character that he was pilot/navigator of the first non-stop flight from Egypt to Australia, a distance of 7,158 miles, in 1938. He was also a good games player, representing the RAF at tennis and squash.

In his time, he made some tough decisions, one of the hardest being tackling the appointment-for-life culture within the Club. He was the first to suggest to members of the committee that they had done their bit and it was time for fresh blood. That is not easy to do with volunteers, or people who have served well previously and may not want to step down. He would take them aside and have a word, very quietly and efficiently. He practised what he preached – he was the first chairman not to die in office.

Notable points in his chairmanship included the considerable moves forward on women's prize money, and Björn Borg's early retirement. Although Sir Brian was not a players' man and was perhaps happier sitting behind his desk getting things done – and he did achieve a lot in terms of developing the estate prior to the Long Term Plan – he took it upon himself, purely out of love for the game, to fly out to Monaco to try to persuade Borg not to retire. He did not want to see an icon disappear, someone who had brought so much enjoyment to so many, particularly at Wimbledon. It was his sense of duty.

Sir Brian was incredibly thorough, diligent and conscientious. He gave everything a huge amount of thought. If there was a problem, he would write it all down and go away and think about it, in a very armed services kind of way I would imagine. He was not a quick decision-maker, but once the decision was made, he would stick to it. He had very small writing, but he always carried the smallest of pencil stubs around with him to write with, so I am not sure which came first. He had a close ally in his committee member Bimby Holt, who was vice-chairman from 1974 to 1980. They got on very well and trusted each other's judgement. Bimby, I sometimes felt, had more intellect than the rest of the committee combined. He was involved with, amongst other things, promotions and merchandising and I remember him announcing at a committee meeting, 'Next year, we'll hit a million,' talking about the surplus. The committee at that time did not believe it, as that would have meant the sum more than doubling, but he was right. Major changes were starting to occur. Slazenger and Robinson's, for example, who had been providing drinks since the thirties, were starting to pay for their exposure on Centre Court. Up to that point, I do not think the Club had ever thought it would get a facility fee out of them. They were providing a product for which Wimbledon was not paying, and it was thought that that was sufficient. Bimby was a great admirer of Mark McCormack and what he could do for The Championships and that respect was reciprocated.

No one loves the Club more than Sir Brian. He is well into his nineties, and still comes back for Club and social events, and was certainly still playing just a few years back. He was a very good chairman, a serviceman through and through, and always did the right thing for the Club. He became a life vice-president on stepping down, as have the two chairmen who followed him.

Buzzer Hadingham was a totally different character. He took over from Sir Brian in 1983, but stepped down six years later, primarily because he was relatively old when he became chairman.

His age was one of the reasons that I did not think he would be appropriate. I also did not think he was a heavyweight. I was worried about his chairmanship qualities. I wondered whether he would be strong enough, following discussions, in coming to a conclusion. However, he proved to be the right chairman for the right time, and I was happily proved wrong. He had charisma, rather similar to Tony Cooper, and real charm, which transcended all his dealings with people. It was infectious and was greatly appreciated by the players, particularly after a period when probably most of them, while they respected Sir Brian Burnett, felt they did not know him as a person. They at least appreciated Buzzer's efforts, if not his humour. Having welcomed the players to Wimbledon the day before the tournament started each year, he would end his short speech with a joke. Everybody always laughed politely, even if, given the language barrier, it was fair so say that half the room could not understand him. They felt able to relate to Buzzer very quickly, helped by the fact that he had spent his life at Slazenger working with all the top players. He had the players' respect, even from John McEnroe who, when necessary, he had no problem in admonishing. He would go down to the locker room, and very discreetly sit next to him on the bench to have a word. Having the players' confidence was fairly necessary after a period in which they may have felt they were being somewhat neglected. The players are a key ingredient for the success of The Championships. Without them, we do not have a tournament. He helped to bridge the gap between the Club and the player associations, which were getting stronger.

Buzzer, so called because when small his brother could not say 'brother', was very comfortable with anyone, royalty or the numerous celebrities he met through his work as chairman and life president of Sparks (Sport Aiding Medical Research for Kids). He was very good looking, very dapper, and well dressed. He was a huge name dropper, and a wonderful raconteur. He had stories for everything. I went to Japan with him to open a Wimbledon exhibition in a department store in Osaka. We flew out there, arrived early in the morning and had a long journey from the airport to the city. We went to the store, and to a reception in the evening, and flew back the next day. Throughout the entire time, he told me non-stop stories. For anything, any subject we talked about, he would find a story from the past to match it, or some quip to accompany it. If you were driving in a car and saw a builder carrying a scaffolding board, he would say, 'He'll be off to a board meeting then.' Or a lady walking down the street with a big hat on, and he would say, 'She looks a bit shady.' He was a great writer of innumerable letters in longhand, always by return of post. He was also a good linguist, ably demonstrated by his instigation of the 'No Spitting' signs in several different languages in the locker rooms. He founded a book club in London, and wrote a book of poems. Putting the rest of us to shame, he used to take his wife Lois a cup of tea in bed every morning, usually with a verse of a poem accompanying it, which was very romantic. Lois had a stroke in 1987 when they were in Paris attending the French Open, and that to an extent marred Buzzer's last few years as chairman. He retired in 1989 partially to look after her. Buzzer died in 2005 and there was a wonderful memorial service, reflecting the many facets of his life.

I have to admit that my lack of judgement followed through to Buzzer's successor, John Curry, who I also had my doubts about as chairman. He was a very successful businessman, running an electronics firm, and I had worries that he would not be able to spend sufficient time on Wimbledon given his existing work commitments. I also thought he would be over-commercial and would possibly neglect the Club or members' side, which I have always thought was very important. Herman David had worked while being chairman, but at that time Wimbledon was much smaller and he had lived only a stone's throw away. John also travelled on business a lot. These were my personal concerns, which I expressed to him on a flight to New York for a Grand

Slam meeting. He had just been appointed chairman and he suggested I come over with him, so we could spend some useful time getting to know each other and sharing thoughts. I was quite frank, but he did his best to allay my fears and was true to his word. I am delighted to say I was totally wrong and he gave as much time to the Club as anyone could. He put the members' interests higher than I ever thought he would and, while being a strong chairman, also had time to hear the committee's views.

John had a number of outstanding qualities. His decision-making was incredibly rapid. If you asked him a question, he would make the decision there and then, and 99 per cent of the time, it would be right, no matter how large or small. It is very helpful to have clear-cut decisions made swiftly, to enable everyone to move on. He is incredibly bright and it was a joy working with him. He always seemed to have time for you. I would sometimes ring him at home or the office and say, for example, that Mark Miles, head of the ATP was dropping in tomorrow – was there any chance he could pop in? He would say, 'Yes, no problem.' Not because he had nothing else on – he would probably have to change two or three meetings – but if he thought that I thought it was important enough for him to be at the Club, he would drop everything to be there. I have always admired people who are very efficient at managing their time. Mark McCormack was another. They were both strong, hardheaded business people, who had huge respect for each other.

John deserves great credit for the Long Term Plan, with which he continues to be involved through his chairmanship of the All England Ground Company, which manages the debenture holder income that finances the LTP. He gave it huge support and it was through his work ethic, his dynamism, that the plan was driven through – working out the finance, taking it through the Ground Company, getting the LTA to buy into it, and convincing the members that it was all worthwhile. As a result, we started the LTP in 1994. With anyone else as chairman, we would probably not have started it as early as we did. He was not a front row forward for nothing!

At the conclusion of his first year, the surplus was just under £10m. When he retired it was £30m, a 200 per cent increase. John advised that the Ground Company should purchase the Wimbledon Park Golf Club at a time when I am sure many other people would have shied away. He was adamant that we must look to the future, rather than focus just on the finances tied up with the Plan. I was very nervous of him, as he was infinitely brighter and more astute than I, but he could not have been more supportive. I suppose he would say we worked well as a team, as he would make the decisions and I would put everything into practice and clear up any mess. There was a palpable sense of change, probably because the LTP involved such an incredible amount of time, and increased everyone's workload. Buzzer would come in, and have a chat about this, that and the other: 'Did you hear the story about . . . ? and another anecdote would come out. John was much more focused, although great company. At a round table he would always be the central figure and would have people in stitches. I think the fact that he played rugby (he was an Oxford blue at rugby and tennis) and was used to rugby tours had a lot to do with it. I am not sure he liked to be the centre of attention, but it always ended up that way. The players enjoyed being in his company because he was very amusing and, like Buzzer, he could put them at ease.

During this time, the 1934 agreement with the LTA was being renegotiated. The debates went on for about seven years and John argued very strongly on behalf of the Club. There were a number of LTA presidents who greatly admired his integrity. He has helped British tennis probably more than any other Club person has ever done. It sounds a sweeping statement, but I cannot think of anyone else. Wimbledon provides 75 per cent of the LTA income, and he played a large part in delivering that sum. He certainly helped the LTA with the negotiations to get their National Tennis Centre at the Bank of England sports ground. On an international level, he was hugely respected by the other Grand Slams because of his strong leadership, fairness, and his support of Australia in particular. In 2008, he was a key person in the negotiations with the LTA culminating in the 2008 renewed deed.

He wanted to retire a year or two earlier than he did, not wanting anyone to feel he had overstayed. The committee said that to the contrary, there was no obvious immediate successor, and they would rather he stayed. In the end, John served as chairman for eleven years.

Our current chairman, Tim Phillips, has proved to be first class since his appointment in 1999. He spent all his working life at British Airways, in very senior management in many different parts of the world, and in the first few years combined the two roles, but has since retired. He was an excellent hockey, tennis, and squash player, playing for Oxford University at all three, and reaching the semi-finals of the US national tennis doubles, which is no mean feat. No one has put more time and effort into the Club than Tim. He spends longer here than any of his predecessors, and is almost like another executive in some ways. Perhaps an executive chairman is how to describe him. Some of my colleagues thought that he was a bit too hands on, but both Ian Ritchie and I have found that the experience that he has brought has been invaluable. People always remark that nothing is too much trouble for him. He does everything with an open mind and consults. In comparison with John, Tim would consult others when making a decision, but again come to the right one 99 per cent of the time, albeit in a slower, more calculated way.

It is not uncommon to see Tim at the Club at 9 a.m. and for him to stay all day. He might play a game of tennis, but it is still a lot of time dedicated to the Club. Tim is part of the Club family, getting on and mixing with everyone. He has carried on John Curry's good work, although he was part of the LTP through his committee work, so he was not wholly inheriting someone else's legacy. He kept John as chairman of the All England Ground Company.

His part in introducing the Road to Wimbledon is something of which Tim should be particularly proud. He wants to see tennis get down to the grass roots and break down any form of elitism at the Club. During the latter part of his time at BA, he switched to doing more community-based work, which enabled him to devote time to the Club as well. His wife Elizabeth is a very successful headmistress of a large London state school, and that has perhaps helped act as a driver for his beliefs. Both have fairly recently and deservedly been honoured by the Queen.

During his time, Tim has dealt with the women's prize money issue, culminating in the equal pay announcement in 2007, and successfully saw off the ATP threat for 50 per cent more prize money. The other Grand Slams look up to Wimbledon for leadership in international affairs. They certainly got that from John, and Tim has followed suit.

The Long Term Plan has been a benchmark item, and Tim has also played a large part in making the players realise they are crucial to the tournament, that they are put first, and that making money is not the be all and end all. That is the advantage of the Club having a dominant position in running The Championships. He is a very easy companion to be with at all times. He does not have Buzzer's spontaneous jokes, but has a very good turn of phrase. There are no airs and graces with Tim. He is very straightforward, good company.

Among my Wimbledon stars I also include the other executives who I have singled out earlier, and without whom, as I have said, I would have struggled terribly, and of course some very able first line managers and wonderful PAs and secretaries. The indomitable Enid Stopka was succeeded by Paula McMillan who was a great character. She had the dual role of being PA to the chairman and to me. When she started in 1979, she lived in the Lodge, at the south end of the old No. 1 Court, before moving into one of the cottages down by the hard courts. She worked incredibly long hours, and was a very forceful lady who, like a true Yorkshirewoman, spoke her mind. She had a wonderful phone manner, but could swear unbelievably. We used to have a hatch between our two offices and I could hear all of it. She was very loyal, very protective of myself and the chairman, slightly intimidating, but very well meaning. When Paula retired in 2002, Carole Hewitt took over, and is admired by everyone.

Around the spring onwards, a great deal of the PA's time is spent on royal box invitations. There are seventy-five seats to be filled for thirteen days, and to juggle that around and make sure the box is full every day, when having to deal with sensitive people, is quite tricky, but both tackled it very well. It is a chairman's invitation, which inevitably means the list will vary from chairman to chairman. That could mean a few calls from people saying, 'But I used to get one,' which had to be handled diplomatically. I was also extremely grateful to Linda Cooper, who was at the Club for fourteen years and my secretary until 2002, and to her successor Sharon Cloro, who is now Ian's secretary.

In a book like this, you cannot neglect the part that the members play and the friendships that I (and Jenny) have made. I play a lot of very enjoyable tennis with extremely tolerant fellow members, and they have been incredibly supportive over the years, with hardly a falling out with anyone. It is, without doubt, a members' Club.

On to the players. I have singled out seven men and seven women who I think have been particularly special during my time at the Club, but it has been a very hard list to devise, and is by no means exhaustive.

I will start with Billie Jean King, winner of six ladies' singles titles, and twenty titles in all. From her 'battle of the sexes' with Bobby Riggs, to her persistence in fighting for equal prize money and her undeniable ability as a player, she has probably done more for sport, and women's tennis in particular, than anyone else. It takes a lot of doing to combine being both a very successful player and an ambassador for the sport. I seemed to get to know her more in my last year or two. She has been a close friend, with interesting views. You cannot help but be a good listener with Billie Jean, because she seems to have done it all on the playing front *and* in other walks of life. She was also generous and thoughtful. She used to give the ball boys a bag of sweets at the end of the Fortnight, when many players would barely register that they were there.

Next on my list is Chris Evert. She won the title three times, but was runner-up a further seven, so was consistently around the top of her sport for a very long time. I just admired the way she played her tennis, particularly her concentration and her wonderful baseline game. She was the modern equivalent of Maureen Connolly in the fifties. She was very pleasant and friendly to us. When she retired, she did a lot of commentary for NBC and came back each year, often with her parents with whom she is very close. When Chris decided she wanted to stay at home with her family more, her parents carried on coming, renting a house in Wimbledon. I would see them and rush out for a chat, and we were sometimes able to get them the odd invite into the royal box. Her brother Drew married Fred Perry's daughter a few years ago and they had a blessing here at the Club at the Fred Perry statue. Who can tell what talent the offspring from that pairing might have!

No list would be complete without Virginia Wade, our last singles champion. I have known Virginia for a long time. I first met her when she came over from South Africa, and was playing in her first junior tournament. It was at the Westside Club, Wimbledon in 1961, and we were the two winners of the U16 singles' events. I think that was around the time that I was at my peak, while Virginia went on to slightly greater things.

Rather like a number of the British players, she is not the easiest of players to support. It is like watching West Ham. They play fantastically all match and then give away an own goal at the last minute. There have been a number of times when she has been on top and then faded away. We were all so delighted when she won in the Silver Jubilee year, which was also the centenary of Wimbledon. There could hardly have been a more fitting end to The Championships, unless it had been an all-British final, with Sue Barker there too. Virginia has gone on to be a great ambassador for the sport, acting as broadcaster and tennis pundit, and was our first female committee member. Sadly, she spends much of her time in the US where she continued playing at a high level, but has stopped now. She used to play in our senior invitation event up until a few years ago.

When Martina Navratilova was asked to comment on her feelings for Wimbledon, she said, 'It's like a love affair that grows. I loved Wimbledon from the first time I knew about it, and it's been reciprocated. It's like in a relationship where you love that person more and more. I feel this place in my bones . . . There's no place like it.' She was an exciting player, winning nine ladies' titles, and had the most fascinating battles with Chris Evert. That rivalry went on for years and did a lot in terms of raising the profile of women's tennis. It is a great benefit to have genuine rivalries in tennis, such as Borg and McEnroe, Margaret Smith/Court and Billie Jean King, Federer and Nadal. It brings out the best in players.

In my mind, Martina played in a similar manner to Billie Jean, whose record twenty Wimbledon titles she equalled. They were both very comfortable, good volleyers, who liked to come to the net. Again, she was a great personality. At her interviews, the committee member who accompanied her always had difficulty in ensuring that the time of the interview did not overrun. She was always keen to tell the press everything they wanted to know. She was certainly open about her sexual orientation, although I think took exception to the amount of press interest it generated. She was extremely focused but still had time to pop over for a cup of tea after practising on the courts backing onto the chief executive's house. She paid Wimbledon the greatest respect, and Wimbledon returned the favour. It is funny how the Wimbledon crowd takes a while to get used to people. They did not take to Martina at first, who was seen as too athletic, or to Chris, the ice-maiden, or to Billie Jean, but then it gradually and completely turned around.

The last time I saw Martina I was captain of the International Club of Great Britain in 2007. We had a quadrangular match in Prague and she was back there from the US, visiting her mother. The Czech International Club organised an exhibition match with Jan Kodeš, Martina, Helena Sukova and her brother Cyril Suk. I had to say a few words in the evening at the reception, and it was quite something to point out that between them, they had won thirty-one Wimbledon titles. That evening, we made Martina an honorary member of the International Club of Great Britain. She is a very warm character, who has mellowed hugely in the way that most players do as the years go by. The days of our spats when she tried to bring her dog into the grounds are long forgotten.

Martina's dominance in the game was only brought to an end by the arrival of another phenomenal talent, Steffi Graf. With seven singles titles to her name, she took over where Martina left off, although not without a considerable fight. It is her athleticism that stands out in my memory – the power of her forehand and her speed around the court, combined with her sheer determination. She was always pleasant and kind, and would come up to my office when she arrived each year and say, 'Hello, nice to see you.' She would also give Paula the bouquet that was handed to finalists on court, which was a nice gesture. When Steffi was in her prime, and practising the week before Wimbledon, my daughter Kim went out and watched her play. Steffi stopped and asked her if she would like a hit. Given that they have limited practice time, for a champion to spend part of it playing, with all due respect, with an 11-year old rabbit was very generous. I am not sure that many people would have put her together with Andre Agassi, but the marriage appears to have lasted well. The talent of their pairing is bound to come out somewhere.

The two final females on my list almost come as a package – the Williams sisters. So far, Venus has won Wimbledon five times, while Serena has twice been champion. The fact that two girls from the same family have achieved so much, particularly given their history, is quite phenomenal. Their father, the story goes, decided he wanted a tennis star, and set about learning how to coach by reading books. Theirs was a poor background, and all that they have achieved has been through sheer guts and determination. It was an unconventional route to the top, as Venus and Serena did not play in any junior tournaments. Their success against all the odds is amazing, though it occurs to me that they probably could have achieved a lot more to date had they not been diverted with their extra-curricular activities such as fashion design and acting.

My selection of men starts with a bit of a cheat, in that the first was not a champion during my time. However, the fact that he is the only player ever to have won two Grand Slams, that is to say four majors in a calendar year, means that many regard him as the best player of all time. On that basis, I think Rod Laver can come onto my list. He was a champion at Wimbledon four times, and perhaps would have won it more, had he not missed five years when he turned professional before the era of Open tennis. Generally, people would say the only person likely to take his place would be Roger Federer, although, as yet, Roger still has to win the French. I did not know Rod when he was playing but I have had the good fortune of meeting him since. You would not think he had been a top flight sportsman. He is a modest, really nice man, and was the quietest of all those great

Australian players – Sedgman, Hoad, Rosewall, Fraser, Emerson and Newcombe – just happy to get on with his business.

From one quiet and modest man to the next. Björn Borg won five straight singles titles, and in so doing has become a Wimbledon legend. When he lost to John McEnroe in 1981, we did not know then that it would be his last Wimbledon appearance. It is sad that his career appeared to come to a sudden halt.

It is hard to believe that in his youth he was a player who misbehaved badly and was suspended by the Swedish Federation. It is a great example of the value of coming down hard on children who misbehave because he became the epitome of good manners and coolness on court. There are parents who do nothing for fear that the child will stick two fingers up and go off and do something else, but Borg came back and had a wonderful career. He would put in infinitely more hours practising than someone like McEnroe who probably found the game easier. He won the French six times and each time, within two weeks, would come over and win at Wimbledon. That takes a lot of mental and physical power and stamina. I think, in the end, it took its toll. When the rules came in saying that players had to play a certain number of tournaments to qualify for the Grand Slams, he just did not have the same appetite to practise to stay at the top. He is certainly one of my heroes, but sadly he has not been back much until very recently. When he retired, he was invited back every year, but he never took up the invitation. Then he started to make a comeback on tour and he came to the Club to practise on the indoor courts in the spring, but he would not come during The Championships. In the end, it took the lure of the Millennium celebrations, and the persuasive power of Johan Eliasch, the CEO of Head and a close friend of his, to bring him. I always remember the rapturous reception he received, particularly when, on his way to pick up his Waterford Crystal plate, he dropped down to his knees and kissed the Centre Court grass. I always invited him to play in the senior event but he did not, though he did eventually come to Wimbledon again in 2007, to watch Federer equal his record, and also in 2008. It is almost as if he received so much attention at his peak that he is afraid of being thrown back into that limelight. It is a bit like Pete Sampras, who has always declined our invitations, saying he would find it too emotional.

'Quiet' and 'modest' are not words that should appear in the same sentence as my next great player, John McEnroe. People might be surprised that he only won three Wimbledon singles titles. Overall he won eight Grand Slam singles titles, which surprisingly is around the same as Mats Wilander who won seven, but there is perhaps some truth in Wilander's slightly doleful comment that, 'You can't be considered a great player unless you win Wimbledon. That's the way it is.' McEnroe you might have expected to have won more, because of his prodigious talent. Possibly the amount of doubles he played took its toll. His hand-eye co-ordination meant that he could take the ball as early as anyone. It seemed effortless, as if he was just nudging the ball back using the other player's pace. He was one of the greatest doubles players of modern times, with Peter Fleming once selflessly saying of him, 'The greatest doubles pair in the world is John McEnroe and anyone.' He won four times with Fleming and once with Michael Stich.

While he has undoubtedly been one of the bad boys, he has brought huge enjoyment to the crowds and is loved by many. He brought in a new generation of people to love and play tennis. Youngsters enjoyed his firebrand attitude, although I did not approve of it. I thought his on-court behaviour was dreadful at times. I am not saying that his appeals for decisions were wrong – I think there were definitely times that he was right – but it was the manner in which he then abused the officials, in a way that no player should, that I abhorred. In that respect, he was greatly at fault. It created a very bad impression for the young ones taking up the sport. We had a lot of letters from teachers and coaches saying 'If you cannot control someone like that, and let him get away with it, how can we instil discipline in the young-sters?' It was an absolutely fair comment.

More recently, people say he is one of the best commentators in the world, and I would go along with that. I think he is brilliant. He once interviewed me live on Centre Court, which was not an experience that I would say I relished. He is quite direct, and I am never quite sure whether he is trying to be serious or not.

But for one blip against Richard Krajicek in 1996, the next on my list, Pete Sampras, would hold seven straight Wimbledon singles titles, surpassing even Borg and Federer. I am sure he would also have loved to have traded one of his fourteen Grand Slams for a Roland Garros title, but he was the supreme grass court player, a huge serve and volleyer. At his best, he was untouchable. As Agassi said when he was defeated in 1999, 'I ran into a bus today.' He loved Wimbledon, which is not so surprising if you win seven times. The tennis writer Paul Hayward once described Sampras's defence of his title as 'Proprietorial, vigilant, spikily defiant. Sampras is all those things when his dominion over the most sacred patch of turf in tennis is challenged.' He was also a quiet, shy person. I never got to know him, apart from shaking his hand. It looks as though he may be coming back out of retirement, which is good. He has played the odd exhibition match against Federer, and at least two senior tour events, including at the Royal Albert Hall in 2008. We hope he will come back to Wimbledon soon, either as a spectator or a player. He said he would when his son could appreciate it. The purists loved watching him play. Some say he was just all serve and volley, but there was more to his game than that, no question. Unless he had had a fantastic return of serve, he would not have won one, let alone seven Wimbledon titles. Unfortunately, the way he wandered around the court with his head down and his tongue hanging out did not help his rapport with the crowd, although I think generally they grew to like him a bit more towards the end, and he was certainly admired for his talent.

Tim Henman is the only player on my list who never won and now never will win Wimbledon, having retired in September 2007. It was not for want of trying, and at times, during his four semi-finals and four quarter-finals matches, it seemed he was agonisingly close.

I have known Tim and his family for many years, having gone to school with his two uncles, Tim and Tony Billington. I used to play tennis with his grandfather, Henry, who would bring a tennis team down to Bradfield College. Henry was a former British Davis Cup player, and was a good age when I played against him. He wore long flannels but he was still a master at the net. Tim, since his earliest times, wanted to be a top tennis player and he dedicated his life from an early age. Most of us have no understanding or appreciation of the amount of practice, hard work and sheer determination that goes into making a top sportsman. He had so much talent. I listened to a programme soon after he retired, and they did a piece interviewing a number of the top players including Novak Djokovic, Rafael Nadal, Roger Federer, and Mario Ancic. They were asked who in the game had the best forehand, backhand, serve, mental and physical stamina etc. When it came to the volley, they practically all said, 'Now that Tim Henman has retired, I'm not sure.' They obviously felt he was the best volleyer, but he just did not have consistency I guess, or the one really big weapon to get him right to the top.

Many press writers have been disparaging about him. Now he is turning in a serious way to golf, and is putting as much dedication to practise as with tennis. It is just for fun, but it is the measure of a top sportsman.

My next player, Andy Murray, I would love to describe one day as a Wimbledon champion. He again has so much talent in all areas of his game. He is a very deceptive player and appears to have every shot in the book. At this tender age, the jury still has to be out, but he has done incredibly well already to have broken into the top four, and to have reached the quarter-finals at Wimbledon and then the finals of the US Open in 2008. The question mark is his mental and physical strength. He has a turbulent nature to him, but that may prove to be one of his assets. It was for McEnroe. He does suffer on the physical side, but seems to be working that out. If he can stay fit, he has a very exciting career ahead of him.

I have saved the best until last. Roger Federer won five Wimbledon singles titles in a row, and there may yet be more to come. He has given me more enjoyment than any other player I have ever seen. Even when he is playing badly, there are still glimpses of his majestic shots. Former players say the same. 'I'm just in awe,' said Tracy Austin. 'Roger has it all, he's just so elegant, graceful and fluid – a symphony in tennis whites. Roger can produce shots that should be declared illegal.' McEnroe agreed. 'I've won three Wimbledon titles, but I wish I could play like this guy,' was his view. I think he must be the greatest ambassador tennis has ever had. He is such a good sportsman on and off court. Off the court he gives so many interviews and so much of his time to people who ask for it, including my small grandson. Marcus and I saw him practising one day, and he came over for a quick chat. He saw that Marcus was holding a Bart Simpson toy, and started talking characters with him. Who knows how inspirational that will have been for a small boy, to be able to chew the fat about the Simpsons with the greatest tennis player in the world? He is a real gentleman, and very pleasant to talk to. The fact that he has been so successful here means that he holds Wimbledon in very high esteem. He is a close friend of Tim Phillips, a connection that was just made through Wimbledon. We are very fortunate with the people we have at the top of tennis, with both Federer and Nadal who is also a thoroughly nice chap and a great ambassador. There is nothing I would like more than for Federer to win the French, a title that he desperately wants but has so far eluded him.

I would have liked to be able to add one of the most colourful people in the game to this list, but in the interests of fairness to both sexes, I must stop at seven each and therefore not mention Andre Agassi!

The fans are an integral part of the whole Wimbledon set-up. Without them, Wimbledon would be a pretty soulless place. I think the nicest contact I have had is with people in the overnight and early morning queues. When I first started, one of my tasks was to go out at 6.30 a.m. issuing queue tickets, which then allowed people to go off and wash, get breakfast or whatever, and come back into the queue in the same place they were before. They were always so enthusiastic, even if they had been soaked to the skin. I remember John Curry having a couple of spare tickets for the following day. He wandered out that night to see if he could offer them to anyone, free of charge, as you cannot sell members' tickets. Unbelievably, he could not get rid of them. They all wanted to stay put and enjoy the camaraderie and atmosphere of queuing overnight for a ticket. There is one man, David Jacobs, who has queued for every Championships for thirty-two years. I see him every first few days of The Championships. I would walk home in the evening at about 11 p.m. and the regulars would shout across the road at me: 'Goodnight Mr Gorringe, hope you had a good day. See you tomorrow.'

For those who cannot make it to the grounds, Wimbledon is brought to life by some of the marvellous commentators we have had over the years. Before I started, I think the best commentators were Dan Maskell and Jack Kramer. Dan was a good player in his own right – for sixteen years he was the professional champion of Britain. He was such a dear man, who loved his tennis. If you got engaged in conversation with him on the subject, people used to say, you had to make sure you didn't have a train to catch, because you would end up missing it. He was the ultimate BBC TV commentator. Like John Barrett, who worked with Dan and succeeded him as the BBC's voice of tennis, he did not speak too much during play, and knew when there should be silences. It is sadly not the case now. In the US, it took them a while to understand the silences. They thought the commentator had gone off somewhere. Most are brought up working for Sky or US TV where they have commercial breaks. In the UK, the BBC can do their summarising during the changeover. In the US, they have to do it between points, and sometimes they are still talking over a point, which I think is criminal.

Dan was very quiet and mild. He started off as a ball boy, earning pence at Queen's Club. He then became a professional tennis player, in time becoming an assistant on the coaching staff. He came from an era when the players at Queen's Club were seen as gentleman, on a different social level from the professionals or staff. The latter had to respect their lower position, and accept that they were only allowed into designated staff areas. He became a great teaching professional, the first one at Wimbledon.

Max Robertson was the last one to do real ball-by-ball commentary for BBC radio. Now the pace of the game is so fast you cannot keep up with it. Another favourite of mine was Bill Threlfall, a former navy champion, and a full time coach at the Hurlingham Club. He died in 2007, and was coaching and commentating right up to the end. His style was very endearing. He was of an age that meant he did not really mind what he said, or whether he giggled or laughed or made a joke. I found that quite refreshing.

I do not think you have to have been a good player to be a good commentator, but I suppose I might take more notice of someone talking who has won a Grand Slam. My current gripe is that I cannot understand why they put three commentators in the box, as the BBC sometimes do. It is unnecessary. It makes for a confusion of voices, and in any event, you end up with one being more dominant than the others, and I cannot see that it adds anything.

Sue Barker, former French Open winner and Wimbledon semi-finalist, does a fantastic job as presenter. She is someone who converted from playing to TV work almost overnight and does it with great charm and a lot of insight. Des Lynam and Gerald Williams are also worthy of note, and together proved to be the best combination I saw for the BBC highlights progamme.

I would like to round off this tribute to the great and the good with a dash of colour. There is one man who has had more diverse roles, over a greater length of time than any other person in the tennis world. That is Ted or Teddy Tinling. Born in 1910, Ted did practically every job there was in tennis, although bizarrely will be best known for a pair of lace pants. As a teenager, he used to go to the French Riviera in the winter, for reasons of ill-health. While there, he umpired matches and soon shot to prominence as Suzanne Lenglen's favourite umpire. Although he never told me his history, he was a good tennis player himself, taking part in tournaments while in the South of France. He became a master of ceremonies at Wimbledon, escorting the players onto court for their matches. During the war, he went off to the intelligence service, and returned to find himself horrified at the state of women's tennis. Their attire, that is. So appalled was he at the functional outfits worn by the 1940s champions Louise Brough and Margaret Osborne that he set about designing prettier, more fashionable items. However, the outfit that he made for Gussie Moran, which she wore in 1949, proved a step too far. The panties had half an inch of lace trim showing, and with the 84-year-old dowager Queen Mary due to attend, the All England Club committee went into a minor panic. She did not in fact attend, but the damage had been done, and Tinling was thrown into exile. He was not seen at Wimbledon again for twenty years, which I think says more about the committee at the time than the pants. No pants can be that outrageous, although one committee member was said to have bellowed at Tinling, 'You have put sin and vulgarity into tennis!' The furore ended his career as a master of ceremonies, but began it as a dress designer. He created dresses for Maria Bueno, Billie Jean King and many other players, and was official designer to the Virginia Slims women's circuit in the seventies.

I first met him in the early eighties on the Clubhouse steps and in my naivety I had not known what to expect. To see this six-foot-five, bald headed man with a diamond stud in his left ear (which he said would pay for his funeral), dressed in outlandish clothes, was something of a shock. He spoke with a very posh English accent, but with a slight American twist. He really was quite a daunting figure and I was quite nervous of him, but he turned out to be a good friend, and I learnt a lot from him. When I met him, he was working for the Virginia Slims tour, as their chef de protocol. Given his close relationship with the female players, we asked him to be our player liaison officer, helping the Club in fostering better relations with the WTA in particular, but also players generally. He was a man who did not deserve a title like 'player liaison officer', he was too big a guy for that, but that summed up what he did. He would advise the chairman and me on how to handle certain situations. He was a diplomat and, as the term chef de protocol implies, he would show a great deal of tact between the parties. He helped us with equal prize money issues, and definitely helped calm a few ruffled feathers on both sides. The fact that we never had a WTA strike or boycott at Wimbledon was in great part down to him. He was a one-off. He died in 1990, having said that he would leave his body to medical science. With no children he said, there was no point in a grave as no one would put flowers on it. 'I'd rather someone read my book [his memoirs, *Sixty Years in Tennis*, 1983] and be nervous about my coming back in another life,' was his reported preferred alternative.

Chapter 12

Onwards And Out

When I look back over my thirty-two years at Wimbledon, the thing that strikes me most is the sheer physical size of the estate now, as opposed to the seventies. When I left, it would have taken me a good week, working hard at it all day every day, to have gone into every room on site. In 1973 it would have taken me a quarter of that time, and in truth, most of that time would have been spent looking for the keys. That was before we had master sets for Centre and No. 1 Court, and we had to walk around with a huge jailer-type key ring, as if about to detain recalcitrant players At Her Majesty's Pleasure. When the Club first bought the Church Road site in 1922, it was thirteen and a half acres. It is now about forty-two acres, excluding our own ground at Raynes Park and the Wimbledon Park Golf Club.

If you were to compose a snapshot of the Club in the year I was appointed and the year I retired, they would clearly be vastly different, yet I cannot pinpoint any one time and say, 'That is when it changed.' It was a gradual evolution. It was obvious that the business could not be run with just a secretary and assistant, and so the team was built up, but over time. When I first joined, there were forty-odd staff altogether. When I left, it was around 120.

It is also true that while so many things have changed, so many others have stayed the same. The overriding principles that define the Club and Wimbledon have barely changed at all. We did not have a mission statement back in 1973 (it originated in 1983), but if we had, I do not think it would have been any different to the one we have today – to maintain The Championships as the premier tennis tournament in the world and on grass. We still have the same committee system, with just some minor tinkerings, and our relationship with the LTA remains in place. The membership side has not changed, and many of the personnel remain the same as those appointed in the early eighties.

Most importantly, the differences that make Wimbledon special remain intact. The grass, the royal link, the Club atmosphere, the white clothing, the village location, the notion of innovation linked to tradition, combined with attention to detail, a lack of complacency, and a determination to be simply the best, all remain as relevant now as in the seventies. Traditions need to be reviewed from time to time – there is no point in keeping bad ones for the sake of it, and it is better to change before you are forced to – but so far they have stood the test of time and remain integral to Wimbledon. Some of these things we have control over ourselves, and others not. We cannot control the fact that we are in a Wimbledon village location and of course we do not have control over royalty, or the customs associated with royalty. The request to stop the bowing and curtseying to the royal box actually came from the Duke of Kent. Royal protocol had changed and the practice was ceasing in royal circles at this time. However, bowing and curtseying continue to be applicable should the Queen or Prince of Wales come to The Championships. One of the benefits had been that the players walked off the court together, which was a courtesy to each other. We do still ask players to do this when coming off Centre and No. 1 Court after a final, although it does not always happen, and I understand why when it does not. The loser wants to get off while the winner is in no hurry, soaking up the atmosphere and signing autographs.

We do have control over traditions such as grass and white clothing – both of which I would consider sacrosanct – the public ballot and on-day sales, sponsorship, and advertising rules. I would hate to see The Championships have direct sponsorship, and would not wish to see them having advertising boards around the courts. Any peripheral advertising should be done very sensitively, if at all.

Other traditions have to be modified – the queues for example. The Club now has just one on-day ticket queue, which is primarily diverted off the road, around Wimbledon Park and the golf course for safety reasons. In my opinion, the change has meant a lessening of the good PR that the queues brought. Players and spectators would see people queuing overnight in the expectation of getting in that day. They would see that Wimbledon is accessible, and that if you are prepared to queue, you can get a ticket. About a quarter of the tickets are on-day sales. At other sporting events, you cannot get a ticket for love nor money. Hiding the queues away in Wimbledon Park and the golf course is a shame, and I think they could use a little more of the pavement to get the message across. However, the important point is that the public ballot and on-day sales remain. It would save a lot of hassle to get rid of both, but it is something that a lot of us think is worth preserving. Our success and much of our strength lies in our differences. I am not saying that what they do in the US is wrong or worse than Wimbledon. It works in New York, but it would not here, and we should not try and emulate them.

What has changed far more than the running of the Club is tennis itself. The age of professionalism has inevitably brought more cash, with phenomenal leaps in prize money. That has brought about a different attitude from players, who are now more demanding, more athletic, and more aware of their market value as brand ambassadors. With so much money at stake, there have also been great advances in technology. The evolution in racket structure has created one of the biggest changes in my time, both at the highest level and down at the grass roots. It has affected dramatically the way in which the game is played. The wooden racket was substantially heavier than today's graphite one and had a standard size head. Modern heads are larger, with a bigger sweet spot, allowing for a greater margin for error. That means that players can use more energy and power in their shots with less risk of mis-hitting. With the demise of wood (1988 was the first year when no wooden rackets were used at Wimbledon) and the development of modern technology, the game changed. You do not see so many serve and volleyers these days, as players use so much more topspin, making volleys harder to control. Less volleys also means less smashes, lobs and passing shots, which all added to variety. There are exceptions, like Pete Sampras and today Mario Ancic. But in Sampras's day, the grass courts played faster than they do now, as grass technology has also evolved. The standard of return of serve has also improved enormously, giving less opportunity to volley. The rallies are now longer, in the men's game probably longer than in the women's.

It is quite remarkable to see modern players play five set matches lasting over four hours and still see them running as fast at the end. You can see the different effect it has on the courts. In the eighties and early nineties, the middle of the court was very worn, where the serve and volleyer came in, braked and volleyed. Now we hardly get any wear in the middle, but plenty behind the baseline. There is an argument that the changes have not been for the better. The game is more one-dimensional now, with everyone playing from the back, whereas before you might have had a classic encounter between a baseline player and a serve and volleyer – Sampras against Agassi for example. Those contrasts can make the game more exciting than having two people slugging it out from the baseline. However, these things go in cycles. Somewhere around the corner, there may well be a serve and volleyer who will change the trend again.

With hindsight, as secretary then chief executive, the thing that makes me most proud is the successful delivery of twenty-six Championships without any major hitch. Every year there was something different, which brought its own challenges. The analogy is preparing for an examination – you prepare for it well and then it comes and somewhere on the paper there is a trick question that you were not anticipating. Generally, they were unwelcome unexpected events, like a tube strike, or the 1973 boycott, or security risks with the IRA, or going into the third week because of bad weather – you can have no idea whether that is going to happen until Sunday afternoon. On a more pleasant note, there were surprises such as working with the *Wimbledon* film, or having a major presentation. You can plan for them, but they still create additional excitement.

I have always judged a Championships, on the one hand, by whether the public enjoyed the Fortnight, and, on the other, if the two weeks ran according to plan with no cock-ups. I have no control over the former, so the latter was more important to me. There were no Championships where we made a big blunder or where things went horribly wrong, and that gives me immense satisfaction, never more so than when I look back to 1991. If that first Middle Sunday had gone wrong, the consequences could have been appalling, but the day I dreaded most turned out to be one of the best moments – a wonderful, successful day.

Of course there were things that could have gone better. The first Monday of The Championships was always the worst day of the whole year. I would say that to staff when they joined, particularly to someone like the assistant to the Championships director, who will of necessity be very tight on logistics, making sure everything is in order. I would always make a point of seeing that person the day before and saying that when I started as assistant secretary, I went home at the end of that first Monday in tears because there were so many things that did not work. Most of the time, they were things that the public would have had no idea about, a gate not opening properly for instance.

Then there were areas where we had to bring in new measures that could have had unfortunate teething problems, like bag searching. Initially perhaps, we were not able to get people into the grounds quickly enough, but these are the sorts of things that are bound to happen when you are engaging thousands of temporary staff who do not know their way around, and are not used to working with other groups like the police, security and stewards. I used to say to our staff, 'You have done your best today, do your best tomorrow, but do not be disappointed if it is not a day of joy.'

Seeing the Long Term Plan coming to fruition also gives me great satisfaction. I suppose there is an argument for saying that there would have been more of a sense of completeness in being chief executive when the final phase is completed, but I think I can enjoy it all the more now, appreciating the finished result without enduring the pain of getting there!

There are several moments that stand out in my mind as having been particularly special. Playing on Centre Court for the first time in 1973 was an experience that money cannot buy, like seeing Virginia Wade winning in 1977. Walking out on Centre Court for the singles' presentations for the first time in 1980 was hard to beat. The opening of the new No. 1 Court in 1997 was also a moment of personal satisfaction, signalling as it did the culmination of stage 1 of the Long Term Plan.

I would also highlight the Millennium parade on Centre Court. It took an awful lot of planning to get sixty-four champions, with or without partners, flying in from all over the world. These champions have minds of their own and will not always do as you ask. To get them all lined up to go onto court in the right order was no mean feat and this was where Sir Geoffrey Cass, former president of the LTA, came into his own. Once they were on Centre Court, however, they all did as they were told, which was a relief.

The Champions' dinner at the Savoy at the end of the tournament has been either a best moment or, if we have had to come back the following day, one of the worst. Other moments that do not bring back happy memories were the first Friday in 1991, when the decision was made to play on the Middle Sunday, discovering the vandals' handiwork on Centre Court in 1976, and the four fires we have had on site, none of them, thankfully, leading to injury. There were always, also, ongoing concerns over the weather and having to make the announcements, and oversee security.

My retirement came at the right time for me. I was sixty, which seemed an appropriate age. I did not want to stay on until sixty-five; I had had enough, given the length of time that I had been in the same job. I felt it was time to go, and it was good for the Club and Championships to have someone like Ian Ritchie come in with new and fresh ideas. Also, it was good to retire before the existing chairman, so that he and Ian would have a chance to work together. It was not that there were other options tempting me elsewhere. If you want to go into tennis administration, being chief executive of the All England Club is the very best. To go to any similar job at the age of sixty was not appealing. I had thought about it for some time, and I definitely wanted to go before there was any risk of the Club asking me to leave. It was very much my decision to retire when I did. As John Major said when he announced that he would stand down at the next General Election: 'I would rather go while I am being urged to stay, rather than stay beyond the time when I should go.' This was something I felt seriously about. Also, a lot of things were neither as easy nor as pleasurable as they had been. There were more things like security, personnel and health and safety issues. There was more red tape and less freedom to act. It was not that I had lost confidence, or faith in the committee, or anything of that nature.

I just felt that I had got as much out of the job as I could and had nothing more to give of myself.

Ian and I had a reasonable handover period. He came in May 2005 and took over on the first of August, but I was there until the end of the year, so I was on hand for advice. Our CVs are chalk and cheese. For each new appointment, we seem to have gone up a notch or two. That is no disrespect to the people who have gone before. It has to be so. As the business has got bigger, so the greater the ability required. I felt I was getting out of my depth, and again, with respect, I think my predecessor Major David Mills was too. It was not so much new developments such as technology – Jeff Lucas was on hand to help there, and did (still does) a brilliant job. In any case, I was getting better, and even sent the odd email. It was more the sheer volume and complexity of things landing on my desk that did not fill me with excitement.

For my successor, I imagine that some of the more immediate concerns revolve around the economy and the surplus. During an economic downturn, there might well be less income, while expenditure will continue to grow, particularly with the size of estate that we have now. I think the Club will be less affected than most people, but I do not think anyone remains untouched.

There will be pressure on the surplus, and the LTA will be looking particularly closely at the forecasts for the next few years. The surplus in 2007 was the lowest for thirteen years, and I imagine that downward trend could continue, although I was pleased to see that the 2008 surplus went up to £25.7m. The Club may need to look for new income streams, but it has to hold firm to its principles. A concert on Centre Court might be a possibility, now that the roof is in place. If it was done soon after The Championships, there would be less risk to the grass. However, concerns over its impact would still arise, and there would also be a downside for the local community. They have put up with fifteen years of building work; concerts after Wimbledon were not part of the deal. There is the possibility of other tennis events on Centre Court, the Davis Cup for example, and there could be greater use of the new debenture holders' facilities. Another quite interesting idea is the use of the museum for corporate entertaining, although demand for hospitality of this sort may be dependent on economic conditions.

The Club will also have to look at its succession policy – no doubt they already have. There are some key people now in their sixties who will be looking at retirement timings. Richard Grier, Championships director, Rob McCowen, marketing director, Jeff Lucas, IT director and John Rowlinson, director of television are all in their early sixties. Eddie Seaward, our esteemed head groundsman has turned sixty-five. Then there is Club chairman Tim Phillips and John Curry, chairman of the Ground Company, who have both done admirable stints of duty and must soon be contemplating stepping down.

It was not ideal that Club secretary Roger Ambrose, referee Alan Mills and I retired in the same year. Ideally, I should have retired first, so that a new chief executive could have had control over the appointment of the future secretary and referee. It would be very helpful if the Club could avoid that type of clash again, but it was not their fault.

When Tim does step down, he will be sorely missed by both Ian and the Club. He is internationally respected, as was John Curry, and will be a hard act to follow. However long a person might have been on the committee, stepping up to be chairman is totally different. It is probable that the new chairman will not be able to give as much time as Tim has done, so that will put extra pressure on Ian and the executives. Tim is a hands-on chairman, present almost daily, and that has helped Ian get into position and keep each other on a parallel track going forwards.

It is important, bearing in mind that the majority of the staff work for The Championships, and their year is devoted to The Championships, for a newcomer at senior level, to remember that we are first and foremost a private members' club, and it is right and important that these members' interests are maintained and that they are not overlooked. I was lucky as I came up through the membership, so I understand that element. Perhaps I put too much emphasis on the Club side of things, but I thought it was important that the point did not get lost. If you just mention in passing that we started off as a Club and that that element is very important, and then go on to discuss The Championships at length, people tend to forget the first point. I do not think that should ever happen. Having a successful Club membership providing good quality committee members means that we will continue to run very successful Championships. The two go together in my opinion.

Whatever the challenges Ian faces, I am totally confident he has the capability to meet them. He is a very bright person and was unreservedly my choice for the job.

Whenever you retire, there will always be some unfinished business, and I have my own wishlist of things I would like to see or to have achieved at Wimbledon. One thing I always hoped for, but never managed, was to have the site ready for the Saturday before the qualifying event begins – in effect, eight or nine days before The Championships starts. I wanted the place to look much more inviting for players when they first came to the Club to practise, particularly those coming for the first time. Rather than the English garden effect, they are often met by boxes and crates and the look of unfinished business. There is a cost element to stopping the building work a week early, but I think it would be worth it in terms of retaining the aura that surrounds Wimbledon, and for the reduction of stress that builds up from taking it to the wire every year. However, it is a very hard thing to change. Most of us are deadline driven and inevitably, as people know when The Championships will start, they work right up to that date.

Attention to detail was of paramount importance to me, and I would like, for instance, to see attractive waste containers around the ground. While the wheelie bins are practical, they do not look aesthetically pleasing. However, a bin needs to be visible but not overconspicuous, must be easily movable and should not be a security threat, so it is not that easy. Similarly, I wanted to see improvements to the quality of the players' and linesmen's chairs on court, and I am pleased that they have now been updated.

I was also pleased to see that we had doubles matches being played on the first day of The Championships in 2008 for the first time ever. I think we should have more doubles on Centre and No. 1 Court. The average tennis enthusiast appreciates the variety. The difficulty is scheduling doubles games while taking into account the demands of television, where the preferred option is to show singles. We tended to put doubles on in the evening rather than first match on, but that is when people are tuning into their televisions having come home from work, and are probably expecting to see a singles match featuring a top seed on a show court. The highest viewing figures are from 6 p.m. onwards.

My wishlist also includes a plea for stricter rules regarding toilet breaks and injury timeouts for a player, both to reduce the slowness and disruption of play and to be fairer to the opponent. I think year on year, the level of gamesmanship increases. There are rules in place, and players will play to those rules, working them to their own advantage. The toilet breaks cannot be shorter – you cannot get to a loo quickly from Court 17, no matter how fast you run. However, if a player feels they have an injury, they should not be allowed treatment automatically. In the old days, if a player got cramp, too bad; they were not fit enough to carry on playing. It is true that the physical demands of today's game make injuries more likely, so it is not easy to get the right balance, but the timeouts are not an attractive feature of our game at the moment.

My final wish is for a UK singles champion. One of my

greatest joys was watching Virginia Wade win in 1977. One of my biggest frustrations was never seeing Tim Henman win – well, the nation's and mine, really. It makes me cross to see the papers writing up what he did not achieve rather than what he did. He did consistently well over fourteen years. The variety of his strokes made just sitting back and watching him play a joy – unless you were desperate for him to win, in which case it got a bit nerve-racking. His artistry around the net was wonderful. He was more than just a steady baseliner or serve and volleyer. By and large he took the press commentary in his stride, but once in a while he let rip. The lawn tennis writers have been fair, but it is usually the feature writers who get on a sportsman's back and do not appreciate the qualities. It is a lamentable tradition of ours to knock our heroes. His fellow players have already said that they miss him on the tour both as a person and for the manner of his play. He is much more fun and amusing in the locker room than would appear either on court or when he is interviewed. I think he presented a reserved front because he was a consummate professional, he did not want to be misquoted, and wanted to keep his private life private, hence wanting to keep interviews on a strictly professional level. You only have to say the wrong thing once or twice and the papers latch on to it. So instead, he was circumspect.

People were very generous on my retirement, both in words and gifts. For my part, I (and Jenny) gave the Club a barometer, which now hangs in the Clubhouse landing. It has the inscription, 'May the sun shine brightly on all our friends at the Club.' Having been the weather forecaster over the PA for so many years, it seemed an appropriate memento. Coincidentally, the Club had also given Jenny and me a barometer for our wedding. I also had retirement presents from our honorary stewards and our contractors, the latter a slightly unnerving, almost life-sized painting of myself, and at the chief executive's cocktail party Stan Smith, fairly tongue

in cheek, presented me with a copy of John McEnroe's auto-
biography *Serious*.

I had an official dinner at Cannizaro House in Wimbledon,
organised by the executive, and another, surprise, event at the
old Hyde Park Hotel, now the Mandarin Oriental, organised by
IMG. They invited Jenny and myself, and I had no idea who
else would be there. It turned out to be a very good gathering.
After dinner, they took me into another room and showed a
tribute DVD that they had put together, with contributions from
players, colleagues and friends. Prior to the film, they said that
there were two people who wanted to surprise me, and in walked
my daughters Kim and Anna. There may not have been a red
book, or Michael Aspel lurking in a cupboard, but it was the
closest I will get to *This is Your Life*. To cap it all, they invited
Jenny and me to the Masters golf the following spring at Augusta,
with business class flights thrown in. We made a three-week trip
of it, and had an excellent break.

Since retiring, I have had one non-executive job, done a little
charity work for Save the Children, and, unsurprisingly, I hold a
string of tennis-related committee positions. I have been involved
with the Rye tennis club where I am president, and I am on the
committee of the International Club of Great Britain, and the
Prentice Cup committee. The latter organises the matches that
take place every two years between Oxford and Cambridge and
Harvard and Yale. It is something that I have done since 1974,
as it came with the job: the secretary of the All England Club is
automatically honorary secretary of the Prentice Cup committee.
I am not sure why, but suspect it dates back to Colonel Duncan
Macaulay's time, after the Second World War. I am also president of the Independent Schools' Tennis Association, succeeding
John Barrett in 2007, and sit on the Club's museum committee.
The new museum opened in 2006 and is hugely impressive. It
won the Gold Visit London Best Tourism Experience Award 2007,
and received a special commendation in the 2008 European

museum of the year award. I know that, as a committee member, I would hardly say otherwise, but I really would recommend a visit. It is also being used for various education initiatives, which is all to the good.

I also do some cruise lecturing, which is really rewarding. I think it is the interest that so many people have in Wimbledon that gives me most satisfaction. The most recent cruise was a tour around the Baltic states. Passengers knew that there would be talks on the Cold War and the fall of the Berlin Wall, but they did not know that Wimbledon would be in the package. They had no reason to be interested, but they genuinely were. When I spoke on the *QE2* in 2007, it was to an international audience. It was fascinating to get other people's wider view of Wimbledon, people who had only seen it on television, and may have been more used to seeing the US Open or the Australian. It is particularly warming when members of the audience come up to me afterwards, with their own fond memories of their visit to Wimbledon, whenever it may have been.

In the near future, I would like to be involved in helping in some way with the Olympics in 2012, perhaps being a link between the Club and the IOC, but nothing has happened as yet. We want it to be the best possible Olympic tennis event. I hope the IOC will use the expertise and resources available from the Club, although it is in their power to start with a blank sheet and, say, not use our caterers or security or tap in on our ticket office expertise. If I could be of assistance in steering them in the right direction, I would be happy to do so.

Both Jenny and I have also been on hand to help out during The Championships, albeit in contrasting ways. Jenny has been doing royal box duty since Tim Phillips took over as chairman, and continues to do so on the occasions when Elizabeth Phillips is unable to escape her headmistress duties. She helps guests to their seats, and sits close to the royals, ready to help with any requests that they or the guests may have. Her duties, I believe, do not extend to retrieving esteemed guests stuck in toilets, as happened to one stewardess during a visit from King George V. The monarch having found himself detained against his will, a stewardess was sent to help. However, she had no idea who was inside, and shouted: 'Stand back. Whoever's in there, I am coming in' before unceremoniously hurtling through the door.

The first Championships of my retirement found me in the car park. The people at St Mary's church just up the road from the Club asked if I would like to help out by being an attendant during the Fortnight. On my first day of duty, one lady getting out of her car said, 'I recognise you, you have been doing this job for years, haven't you?' Slightly taken aback, I replied, 'No, actually, this is my first time.' She stared hard at me until something obviously registered in her mind, and she said, 'Ah yes, I recognise your voice now.'

I found retiring from Wimbledon very emotional at times, particularly after the 2005 Championships. I would find myself walking around the grounds, reflecting on the past. I think the fact that my retirement was a gradual process between August and the end of the year was a help. We were also able to remain in the house on site for a further three years, which was good of the Club, and meant that I still felt a part of the place, privileged to be able to see and hear what was going on. I was always keen to quiz colleagues and committee members, and I would receive the odd call for advice, particularly on historical aspects. I would have lunch and supper at the Club fairly frequently, and continued to attend social events throughout the year. Now we have moved to a house about fifteen minutes away, and the break is complete. I feel just like any other member, which is as it should be.

As for the future, I would like Wimbledon to remain in its premier position, admired and respected around the world both by players, spectators and the media, keeping it to the high quality and level that we have maintained over the years. We are all too aware that it only takes one bad Fortnight to ruin a reputation.

I hope that the Club will never sacrifice its principles on what it knows is right for The Championships in the face of commercial pressures. I also hope the Club continues to do all it can to maintain its income streams, knowing that the money made goes towards helping the development of tennis, primarily in the UK, but also around the world. That may well be through more use of Club facilities, but never to the detriment of the aura and mystique that surrounds Centre Court. Boris Becker sums it up thus: 'It's hard to compare anything with the feeling of walking out onto Centre Court, especially if it's for a final. And it's an experience where all the players agree with me – it's one of a kind.'

For myself, I inherited a contented Club membership, and a Championships that was admired around the world. I hope that I have passed on the same.

Afterword

Ian Ritchie, Chief Executive, The All England Lawn
Tennis and Croquet Club

Funnily enough, our paths had crossed years before. When
I was studying at Oxford, I ran elements of the tennis and
used to correspond with Chris about setting up fixtures,
as he was then the match secretary of the Public School Old Boys
LTA. I thought of 'that chap Gorringe' many times over the years,
during my fairly regular trips to watch Wimbledon. Then I saw
the advert for chief executive of the All England Club in the
Sunday Times appointment section, and as a sports-obsessed individual, I thought, 'There is the job of a lifetime.'

The question that the Club has had to ask itself is, 'Is this a
private members' club that has a bit of a do in the summer, or
is it the organiser of an iconic sporting event that in professional
sporting terms is a medium-sized business?' Over the years, it was
more of the former, but now the fact that they have recruited a
commercial philistine like me to replace Chris is recognition of
the gradual move to the latter. Before I took this post, I was vice-
president of global business at Associated Press, managing their
international operations outside the US. My background is very

different to Chris's. However, even with a commercial background, you still have to understand that this *is* a private members' club, and be very conscious of the fact that it is a traditional place. Any changes that are made have to be commensurate with not losing that feeling of tradition and history, or compromising cherished values. Chris to me is the epitome of decency and integrity, personally as well as professionally. You would hope that people would also feel that about Wimbledon. Even though there is a continuing transition, you hope that those values will always be there.

With the Club having had thirty-odd years with Chris and Club secretary Roger Ambrose, there was an inevitable fear of change and I was very conscious of that apprehension. However, for my first Wimbledon in charge on my own, I had a huge amount of support from a team of people who had done it for years, and could keep everything on track. That is what Chris left, together with the most thorough handover. I have arrived at jobs where the previous person has been fired: you turn up on the Monday and it is a deep breath, and, 'Here we go.' To have the luxury of being at a Championships when Chris was still here and I was able to wander about freely for two weeks, was marvellous and very helpful. He had the most selfless approach to it, and would have done anything to assist. He wanted nothing other than a completely successful handover.

The committee are focused on making this not just the best tennis event in the world, but the best sporting event in the world. That single-minded attitude has helped make Wimbledon so successful. The relative financial returns even in the eighties were fairly modest. Now, as a business, it makes somewhere in the region of £30m profit in two weeks. We are not dependent on funding from anyone else, or having to play politics to get it. What we do is entirely up to the Club and committee of management. I repeat, it is so successful because we are so single-minded. I think the Club is an important part of that. The reason that the members have put up with the building site over the past ten years is because they also and equally want The Championships to be successful. In terms of independence, our nearest comparison is probably Augusta and the Masters. My favourite story from there is that when the treasurer is called upon to give the financial report at the AGM, he stands up and says, 'The Club is solvent, gentlemen,' and sits down. At our press conferences, the press are so well schooled over the years, that they know there are certain things we will not tell them. We do not need to. We are not a publicly funded body like the FA or LTA. We are not obliged to be transparent, although we certainly do not want to be seen as a secretive society. I think the lengths we go to in fostering good relations with the press and the excellent facilities we provide to assist them are testimony to that.

The committee are hugely helpful, positive and, yes, focused on the one objective: making The Championships an enormous success – but of necessity, the committee system is one area that is under transition. I don't think there is anyone on the committee who is there but not contributing, that dreadful sort of cliché of a time-served blazer. Instead, they are a group of people with an excellent range of experience. A large proportion are in existing day jobs, or have recently retired from very serious occupations. They bring background, expertise, time and commitment. If they charged the Club at their hourly rate, it would be a very expensive situation, yet all of them give their time for nothing, which I admire hugely.

I do not see the set-up now as any different to a board of directors within which there is a group of non-exec directors who have been recruited because of their skill and expertise. That is the committee's modern day role. If you go back to the fifties, the committee drove the decisions and the secretary was sent away to implement them. Increasingly, there is a shift in professional sport. These days, it is too complicated, there is too much money, there are too many specialist skills required and it's too time-consuming to rely solely on the committee. The executive should come up with the ideas for what we should be doing and the committee should act as a supervisory group, calling them to account, checking that they are doing the right things and rightly bringing their expertise and experience to bear in terms of the decision-making process. So there is a shift in emphasis.

To take an example, someone who undoubtedly brings a lot to the committee at the moment is Debbie Jevans. She has been a professional tennis player and has worked in sports administration and management and is now director of sport for the 2012 Olympics. Fantastic in terms of experience, but she has got a bit of a job on at the moment! She can't afford to spend too much time on the committee, so de facto things have to change: you cannot say, 'We haven't got the time to get the sub-committee together, so we won't do anything.' Similarly, there are specialist skills needed for the detailed negotiation of TV deals, which is difficult for a non-specialist committee member to get involved with. Wimbledon has grown out of all proportion, so the system has to be modified, and I think the way in which the committee itself and the raft of sub-committees operate will continue to change.

The other big change has been the commercial relationship with IMG. In 1968, the Club started its association with Mark McCormack, which was right at the forefront of the invention of sports marketing, and an incredibly far-sighted thing to have done. The relationship with IMG was hugely beneficial, much of it relying on Mark McCormack personally, who did fantastic things for the Club. Sadly, he has died and IMG is now owned by a venture capitalist, Ted Forstmann, making it a different entity. I am not saying it is worse – we still have a very close relationship – just that it is different. I think it means that we need to be more commercially proactive within the management. If you look at the split of our turnover, television represents the majority, followed by sponsorship and merchandising, with actual ticket income relatively small. You don't need to be a financial analyst to work out how important the television side is.

Of course, one of the concerns with greater commercial activity is that we are here to optimise, not maximise the income. I use the chunky chicken analogy. Would you ask Chunky Chickens to be the main sponsor of Centre Court? I think not. What we do want is to be commercially astute while recognising that we are protecting the brand.

The establishment of the Wimbledon brand is fascinating. If, thirty or forty years ago you had said to the committee that The Championships was a brand, they would probably have fallen over, but that is exactly what they created, in business terms. The committee did not say stick to white clothing because it was a clever brand initiative. They did it because it was traditional – but it was one of the most astute brand recognition policies they could have invented, in the same way as not putting advertising on the court. We are one of the last tournaments to be held on grass, and the last to be in white clothing. Ask people around the world to name a tennis tournament, and they will say Wimbledon. Put it on the television and everyone immediately knows where it is, without even seeing the name.

It is a tribute to Chris and the team that the real difficulty I face is that Wimbledon was in a good state when I joined. Sitting on top of the pyramid is a fairly painful place to be and there is only one way to go. Hopefully we are still in good state. It is about providing the right setting and environment, providing a stage and hoping that someone will come along and perform, as they did with the amazing 2008 men's final. It is about making change without diluting the core values or losing the mystique of Wimbledon. The problem is that you only realise you have lost that lustre once it has gone. Chris had a clear idea of what that was, and how to keep it. He was very good at it. The challenge is to progress and bring in innovations that improve and don't diminish it. It is that interesting blend of tradition and innovation. I always wait for the letters from the Cotswolds complaining that we have changed something, but we have had nothing about Hawkeye, or changing the scoreboards. We did, however, have letters about not just changing the linesmen's outfits, but to uniforms designed by Ralph Lauren – an American. The management of change is hugely interesting.

The advantage we have is that we can afford to take the medium to long term view on things. We are not a FTSE company where everyone is chasing next year's numbers. We can focus on protecting the legacy and not chasing short term goals. We could sell our tickets through Ticketmaster and avoid the hassles and expense of running the public ballot and stewarding, policing and looking after the queues outside – but the public ballot and queuing on the day are what it is all about.

Someone once said to me that the last thing you do is call Wimbledon a tennis event. It is a social event as well. The tennis is enormously important, but it is also a day out. The thing to do is to keep it like that and keep those values and traditions. We are fortunate that commercially and economically we have been successful in the last few years, so we have not had to worry. If the surplus went down to £5m, would we then go into the Chunky Chickens situation? I don't know. We have a majority of our turnover based on TV. What would happen if the TV rights market dropped out, or we were no longer the must-have event? I am not predicting it, but if that were to happen then we would be in a very different economic environment – one that could not easily be compensated or replaced, particularly as our tickets are already sold out every year. Fortunately we have just renewed all our major TV contracts for five years, so there is no threat, and the surplus has been sufficiently high that we have been able to turn things away if we did not think they were a fit.

Whatever other changes may have been implemented during my time so far, one of the most talked about within the Club has been my *not* doing the announcements during The Championships. I always thought it was slightly odd that there Chris was, in the middle of a multi-million pound event, and when it started to rain he would lock the door to his office, take the phone off the hook and do the rain announcements. In Chris's terms, the way to make sure that it was done properly was for him to do it. Of course communicating with the public is an important thing, and we must make sure it is done properly, but it was not something that I wanted to do. I also felt that there was an opportunity to make a change. In my first year at the Club, however I almost started questioning my priorities when it was the first thing that most people asked me. Never mind, 'How's the job going?' or 'What is your strategic vision?' or 'What is your marketing strategy?' It was all 'Are you doing the announcements?' That's tradition for you.

1973 to 2005 Timeline

1973
ATP Boycott (seventy-nine players withdrew)
Twenty-two qualifiers (instead of usual sixteen)
Kodes bt Metreveli
Nastase No. 1 seed
Extended to second Sunday for final of Mixed Doubles and two other
    events
(CJG: Started at Club on 1 May. In Referee's Office before The
    Championships)

1974
Connors bt Rosewall – his fourth and last as finalist
Evert bt Morozova

1975
Players' chairs on court for first time
Ashe bt Connors
Bookmakers (William Hill) tent – for one year only

1976
14 January: Vandals on Centre Court (CC)

1977
Centenary Championships
Museum opened
CC Parade – forty-one Singles Champions
V Wade won Ladies' Singles
The Queen attended in her Silver Jubilee year
Ball girls first used
Wild Cards introduced in main draws (into Qualifying events in 1983)

1978
The film *Players* starring Dino Martin (Dean's son), Ali MacGraw,
    G Vilas and P Gonzales partly filmed at the Club

1979
CC Roof raised by one metre. Extra 1,088 seats added
Rolex clocks appear for first year
Tie-breaks changed from eight all (1971) to six all
B-Jean King won Ladies Doubles – her twentieth title and a Wimbledon
    record
(CJG: Served under arm after Borg/Tanner final
    Became Secretary after Championships
    Richard Grier – Assistant Secretary)

1980
Courts fourteen – seventeen used
Service line monitor (Cyclops) introduced for CC and No. 1 (and Courts
    2 and 3 in 1981)
Borg won fifth title in a row beating McEnroe. Final included epic
    fourth set tie-break
Twelve grass practice courts in Aorangi Park
13 July (Sunday): seventy-fifth Anniversary of the Diocese of Southwark
    on CC (with Bishop Mervyn Stockwood)

1981
No. 1 Ct rebuilt
McEnroe bt Borg

1982
Second Sunday scheduled finish. Wet weather led to third Monday finish
Aorangi Park brought into total use
Dec – V. Wade became first lady on Committee

1983
Ladies' Singles extended to 128 players
[CJG: Title of Chief Executive created]

1984
Ladies' Centenary: second Monday: seventeen past lady champions
    parade on CC
Fred Perry Statue and Gates unveiled on fiftieth anniversary of his first
    title

1985
Extension of CC and Museum on east side and 800 extra seats on CC
Second Friday: 1 ½ inches of rain in twenty mins
Becker became youngest, unseeded, first German champion

1986
100th Championship Meeting
Last 8 Club founded
Yellow balls used for first time
Drug testing introduced

1987
Pat Cash climbed to players' box after winning Men's Final

1988
No player used a wooden racket
Fifteen courts in Wimbledon Park resurfaced by the Club

1989
Raynes Park bought (twenty acres)

1990
Three new covered courts opened
Standing room replaced by seating (post Bradford and Hillsborough)
Ground capacity fixed at 28,000 (now 36,000)
Large TV Screen erected in Aorangi Park

1991
Wet! Fifty-two out of 240 matches completed by the first Thursday evening
First Friday evening – decision made to play on Middle Sunday for first
    time
Speed of serve radar gun on CC for first time – on screen in 1999 on
    CC and No. 1

1992
'Middle Saturday' introduced
New roof for CC with just four pillars instead of 26. 3061 seats bene-
    fitted from improved vision
'Radio Wimbledon' started

1993
100th Ladies' Championships
March: announced Long Term Plan
Bought freehold of Wimbledon Park Golf Club (seventy-three acres)
    from London Borough of Merton for £5.2m

1994
Bought Southlands College land (three acres including Queensmere
    House, Callard House)

July: works started on Stage One of Long Term Plan

1995
Long Term Plan
Park and Ride from Motspur Park introduced
Tim Henman disqualified for hitting ball at ball girl in a men's doubles
    match
Jeff Tarango disqualified
Murphy Jenson disqualified for non-appearance

1996
Sir Cliff Richard sang in Royal Box on CC
September: last match played on old No. 1 Court – Davis Cup v Egypt
Long Term Plan – Stage Two started

1997
Play on Middle Sunday (second time)
New No. 1 Ct Opened on first Monday – parade of Singles winners
    who had won at least three times
Broadcast Centre, Cts 18 and 19, the Tunnel, and Aorangi Park Terrace
    incorporating new large TV screen created
1 June: *Songs of Praise* on No. 1 Ct

1998
Long Term Plan continued
Fire in high-rise flats overlooking court 18 led to partial evacuation

1999
Long Term Plan continued
International Club of GB's seventy-fifth anniversary event hosted at the
    Club in July

2000
The Millennium Championships
Middle Saturday – parade on CC (Duchess of Glos). Sixty-four players
Millennium Building opened by Duke of Kent on 20 June
Coin-tossing started before both singles finals by youngsters on behalf
    of charities
BBC TV interviewed finalists on court (Sue Barker)
Pete Sampras won seventh title
Autumn: Boston Ivy removed from south end of CC

2001
Bill Clinton, immediate past President of USA, visited on second Saturday
May: Launch of 'Road to Wimbledon'
Wheelchair tennis demonstration started
Thirty-two players seeded – change in how the men were seeded to surfaced-based system
Goran Ivanisevic won on third Monday

2002
New Clubhouse and Royal Box

2003
New arrangements for Middle Saturday
New Court 11 used for first time
End of bowing and curtseying
Serena v Venus Williams – third ever sister final at Wimbledon (also in 1884 and 2002)
Martina Navratilova equalled B-Jean King's record of twenty Wimbledon titles
Practice courts fifteen and sixteen opened
July and August: *Wimbledon* filmed at the Club, starring Paul Bettany and Kirsten Dunst
Autumn: start on Museum Building

2004
Museum work continued
January: CC development plans announced
Mixed Doubles reduced from sixty-four to forty-eight pairs
27 April: five statues of GB lady singles' champions unveiled
Six new practice courts in Southlands College
Middle Saturday: Olympic Torch carried through Club prior to Athens 2004
Middle Sunday (third time)

2005
February: Olympic Evaluation Commission visit
6 July, Singapore: Olympics 2012 given to London
Federer won third title (of five in a row)
(CJG: retirement)